The Multinational Enterprise in Developing Countries

T0300048

A key distinctive feature of multinational enterprises (MNEs) as organizations resides in the fact that they span borders. This exposes them to dissimilar and often unfamiliar social and economic conditions as they venture into foreign countries. MNEs from industrialized economies that are active in developing countries and emerging markets face particularly challenging hurdles resulting from both economic and institutional discrepancies between their home and host countries.

This book focuses on the uneasy interaction between the traditional logics of developing countries and the economic logic of MNEs. The traditional logics of most developing countries are built around community-based legitimacy and an intuitive but concrete epistemology. Conversely, the economic logic of MNEs from developed economies is built around technical and economic legitimacy and an abstract intellectual epistemology. Unpacking the uneasy interactions between these two logics will help achieve MNEs' objectives of competitiveness in developing countries as well as globally.

The Montreal Local Global Research Group is a well-recognized research group that formulates and researches local and global issues in strategic management from the perspective of integrating divergent dominant logics into the strategy conceptualization process, and this is the first book to be dedicated to the study of the interaction between the traditional logic of developing country and the economic logic of MNEs. The cultural diversity of the contributing authors and the multidisciplinary approach offer a fresh perspective from which to explore beneficial corporate and local strategies that promote long-term economic growth consistent with local traditional and cultural norms. This collection will be of interest primarily to scholars of international business, international development and economics. Furthermore, this book is immediately relevant to decision makers in multinational corporations and NGOs, and political decision makers who mediate the interaction between local actors and corporate agents in developing and transitional economies.

Rick Molz is Professor of Management at Concordia University, Canada. **Cătălin Rațiu** is a researcher in the Department of Management at Concordia University, Canada. **Ali Taleb** is a researcher and lecturer in strategic management and international business at HEC Montréal, Canada.

Routledge studies in development economics

The Multinational Enterprise in Developing Countries

Local versus global logic

Edited by Rick Molz, Cătălin Raţiu and Ali Taleb

Routledge
Taylor & Francis Group

LONDON AND NEW YORK

First published 2010
by Routledge
2 Park Square, Milton Park, Abingdon, Oxon OX14 4RN

Simultaneously published in the USA and Canada
by Routledge

711 Third Avenue, New York, NY 10017

Transferred to digital print 2013

Routledge is an imprint of the Taylor & Francis Group, an informa business

First issued in paperback 2013

© 2010 Selection and editorial matter, Rick Molz, Cătălin Rațiu and
Ali Taleb; individual chapters, the contributors

Typeset in Times New Roman by Wearset Ltd, Boldon, Tyne and Wear

British Library Cataloguing in Publication Data
A catalogue record for this book is available from the British Library

Library of Congress Cataloging in Publication Data
Local versus global logic: the multinational enterprise in developing
countries/edited by Rick Molz, Cătălin Rațiu, and Ali Taleb.
p. cm.
Includes bibliographical references and index.

1. International business enterprises–Developing countries. I. Molz, Rick.
II. Rațiu, Cătălin. III. Taleb, Ali.
HD2932.L64 2010
338.8'8191724–dc22

2010002734

ISBN: 978-0-415-49252-2 (hbk)
ISBN: 978-0-203-84705-3 (ebk)
ISBN: 978-0-415-72264-3 (pbk)

Contents

Illustrations

Figures

Tables

Contributors

Marcos Bosquetti is an Associate Professor at Positivo University in Curitiba, Brazil, and a Senior Business Analyst at Copel, one of the largest state-owned electricity companies in Brazil, where he has managed corporate projects. Marcos holds a BA in management from Rolandia Business School, Brazil, and an MBA in Strategy and Change at the University of Bath, England. He completed his PhD in management at the University of São Paulo, Brazil, in 2009. Marcos attended McGill University, Canada, under the supervision of Professor Henry Mintzberg on a CREPUQ Fellowship in 2007. He also attended the University of Melbourne, Australia, under the supervision of Professor Cynthia Hardy at the International Centre of Research on Organizational Discourse, Strategy and Change on a Brazilian Council Fellowship in 2008. Marcos has done fieldwork in the Australian, Brazilian, Canadian and British electricity industries. His research focuses on strategy and change in the utilities business.

Gwyneth Edwards is a PhD candidate at the John Molson School of Business, Concordia University, Montreal. Her research deals with strategy in complex organizations and international firms. She has a specific interest in how strategic practices are identified and developed, and how these practices are understood and adopted by subsidiaries. She employs both qualitative and quantitative methods in her research, at multiple levels. Gwyneth has extensive industry experience as a global manager, giving her first-hand knowledge and experience of the phenomena that she studies.

Mehdi Farashahi is an Associate Professor of Management at John Molson School of Business, Concordia University, Montreal. His research interests combine institutional theory, organization forms and strategies, and global/local issues, with a focus on management practices of firms in the global business environment, more specifically in developing and emerging contexts. Carrying out aggregate analysis and synthesizing research through the systematic review of literature is another field of his research. His work is published in journals such as *Organization Studies*, *Management International Review*, the *Asia Pacific Journal of Management*, the *International Journal of Management Reviews* and the *International Journal of Commerce and Management*.

Bernard Gauthier is Professor of Economics at the Institute of Applied Economics at HEC Montréal in Canada. His research interests include public-sector economics, development economics and the new economics of institutions. Currently on leave from HEC Montréal, he is based at the World Bank in Washington, DC. He has been involved in micro-level research and survey work in developing countries for about sixteen years, in particular the analysis of the institutional environment in Africa. In the past few years he has been involved in governance and anticorruption studies in Africa and in the development of service delivery indicators in the education, health, and water and sanitation sectors.

Taïeb Hafsi holds an MSc in Management from the Sloan School of Management at the Massachusetts Institute of Technology, Boston, and a PhD in Business Administration from Harvard Business School. He is currently the Walter J. Somers Professor of International Strategic Management at HEC Montréal. He has written numerous articles and books dealing with strategic management and change in situations of complexity. His 2007 article in *Public Administration Review* (written with Luc Bernier) received the William E. Mosher and Frederic C. Mosher Award.

Pamela Lirio is a PhD candidate in Management at McGill University in Montreal, Canada. She holds an MBA in International Management from the Monterey Institute of International Studies, California, and a BA in Communications and French from Boston College. Pamela's dissertation investigates the global careers of Generation X managers in dual-career families and how they manage professional and personal demands while working in today's 24/7 global economy. Recent publications have appeared in *Human Resource Management Journal*, *Career Development International* and various edited books. Pamela's cultural heritage is Filipino-American. She is bilingual English–French and learning Spanish and Filipino. Pamela has worked and studied in North America, Europe and Asia.

Claude Marcotte is an Assistant Professor in the Department of Management at Concordia University, Montreal. His research interests include comparative international entrepreneurship, internationalization of small and medium-sized enterprises, international technology transfer and international management education. Claude has published in peer-reviewed journals such as the *Canadian Journal of Administrative Sciences*, the *Journal of Technology Transfer*, the *International Journal of Intercultural Relations* and the *International Small Business Journal*. He is a member of the Montreal Local Global Research Group.

Rick Molz is Professor of Management at the John Molson School of Business, Concordia University. He holds a PhD in Management from the University of Massachusetts and MBA from the University of Rochester. He is the chair of the Montreal Local Global Research Group, and his research focuses on international strategic management, corporate strategic response to public policy initiatives, and collaborative forms of global competition. He has published two previous books and more than twenty-five research articles. He has taught at graduate schools of management in Austria, Germany, India, Italy, Poland, the Czech Republic, Tunisia, Canada and the United States. He is a Canadian citizen and was born in the United States.

Rabia Naguib is Assistant Professor at the Department of Management, Marketing and Public Administration, College of Business Administration, University of Sharjah. She holds a PhD in Strategic Management from HEC Montreal. Her teaching interests range from strategic management and international business (to both undergraduate and Executive MBA students) to business ethics and leadership courses. Her primary research interests evolve around national development strategies, the behavior of MNCs in developing countries, managerial values, business ethics and corporate social responsibility, and women entrepreneurs.

Cătălin Rațiu is a researcher in the Department of Management at the John Molson School of Business and has taught strategy and international management courses at McGill University and Concordia University, both in Montreal. He has over ten years of experience in legal and management consulting positions in North America and Europe. He holds degrees in law, business administration and advanced leadership studies. Cătălin is primarily interested in understanding how organizations develop capabilities that allow them to grow sustainably. His work has been published in books, journals and conference proceedings, presented at numerous conferences worldwide, and featured in the popular press. Cătălin was born in Romania and is fluent in four languages.

Sid Ahmed Soussi holds a PhD in Sociology and is a Professor in the Sociology Department of the Université du Québec à Montréal. His research focuses on the transformation of work, employment and unionism in today's workplace. He has authored several papers on the impact of technology and management strategies on identity and modes of representation and collective action. His research on cultural diversity in workspaces and organizations (in several recent publications) has sparked his interest in the international aspect of these changes and their impact on developing countries.

Ali Taleb is a researcher and lecturer in strategic management and international business at HEC Montréal, Canada. His present research interests are related to subsidiary–parent company relationships and global strategy formation within multinationals from two perspectives. First, he explores how multinationals deal with the diversity of the institutional contexts in which their subsidiaries are embedded. Second, he investigates the means by which subsidiaries influence intentionally the global strategies of their headquarters. Prior to joining academia, Ali held various senior management positions with global responsibility and delivered consulting services to small and large organizations, mainly in Europe and North America.

Natalya Totskaya is a PhD candidate at the John Molson School of Business, Concordia University, Montreal. Her research interests are in business groups' development in emerging and transition economies, with particular focus on changes in groups' conduct and structure caused by transforming institutional environments. Prior to entering a PhD in Business Administration program, Natalya worked as a business analyst and brand manager for several large companies in Russia. She also held academic positions at the Novosibirsk State University of Economics and Management and the Novosibirsk State University of Architecture and Civil Engineering. She has a number of publications and has made conference prese ntations in Russia, Canada and the United States.

Shoaib Ul-Haq is a doctoral student in the business school at Lahore University of Management Sciences, Pakistan, and is an Assistant Professor at GIFT University, Pakistan. His research interests include the relationship between business and society, the sociology of knowledge, and workplace spirituality. He has published articles in the *Pakistan Management Review* and for the Institute of Bankers, Pakistan. He also coauthored a paper on workplace spirituality which was presented at the 2009 Academy of Human Resource Development. He received his MBA degree from Leipzig Graduate School of Management, Germany, and his Engineering degree from the National University of Science and Technology, Pakistan.

Preface

This book is the result of the efforts of the Montreal Local Global Research Group. The group was founded informally in November 2004 as an outgrowth of ongoing collaboration between Professors Taïeb Hafsi (HEC Montréal), Mehdi Farashahi and Rick Molz (both of the John Molson School of Business, Concordia University). As the three founding members began to expand their activities, graduate students became involved, followed soon by recent graduates of the Montreal Four University PhD program. Within a matter of months a nascent group was meeting bimonthly, developing new initiatives for research projects, grants and dissemination of the group's research.

Initially the mission and objectives of the group were implicitly clear to the three founding members. As new members joined and added their own unique contribution, there became a need to think through exactly what the group was trying to do. With this came some brainstorming sessions, after which the name of the group was agreed on and a mission was developed:

> The Montreal Local Global Research Group's objective is to pursue research to better understand the dynamics between corporations, both indigenous and multinational, and local pressures in developing, transitional and emerging economies. We use a multidisciplinary approach to discover beneficial corporate and local strategies to promote long term economic growth consistent with local traditional and cultural norms.

The group grew steadily, and the strength of the group is a direct result of the diversity of its members. Currently there are twenty-two active and contributing members, whose strength is in the collective. Many of our members originate from the very developing, transitional and emerging economies we study, including every populated continent of the earth. Our members represent citizenship, birth or educational background from Iran, Algeria, Brazil, Morocco, Costa Rica, Tunisia, China, Syria, the Philippines, Romania and Russia, as well as the OECD nations of France, Canada and the United States. This diversity gives us a cross-cultural research panel every time we meet, creating a laboratory for testing emerging and developing research concepts as offered by the members. The group functions as a supportive and collaborative mechanism, rather than as a formalized directive hierarchy.

This book is but one of the initiatives the Montreal Local Global Research Group has successfully carried out over the past six years. In addition to numerous conference presentations, published research articles, grant proposals and graduate student theses, the group has presented three workshops or symposiums at the Academy of Management (2006, 2007, 2009) and one at the Administrative Sciences Association of Canada (2007), and sponsored a one-day conference in Montreal in August 2009 and April 2010. These conferences included presentations from world-class scholars and executives of multinational corporations with operations in the developing, transitional and emerging economies we study. Additionally, Rick Molz and Mehdi Farashahi have served as guest editors of a double issue of the journal *International Studies of Management and Organization*, drawing world-class scholars into the discussion centered on the mission of the research group. As all of these activities were emerging, members of the group were busy working on their own research projects. It became clear that the group was developing a critical mass of research that hung together in a cohesive manner, which could be pulled together to represent the ideas and themes developed in our various endeavors. The book, as such, is also a response to calls by colleagues and students wishing to acquaint themselves with the work of the group. After initial discussions with Routledge, the potential of the book became even clearer, and what is in your hand today is the result.

An editorial team was developed, led by Rick Molz, who also acts as the chair of the Montreal Local Global Research Group's activities. He was joined by two motivated and dynamic PhD candidates, Cătă Rațiu of the John Molson School of Business and Ali Taleb of HEC Montréal. The three of us worked together as a positive "can do" team, soliciting contributions and shepherding each contribution through a rigorous process – one that compares favorably with the review process of many prestigious journals. Each chapter was blind-reviewed by two members of the Montreal Local Global Research Group and one of the volume's editors. Each chapter went through three revisions, and at each revision was reviewed by one of the volume's editors before final acceptance by all three editors.

The book could not have been developed without the support and contribution of all twenty-two members of the Montreal Local Global Research Group, three blind external reviewers of the original proposal submitted to Routledge, and our editors at Routledge, Thomas Sutton and his associate Beth Lewis. We thank each of them for their consistent support and encouragement. Of course, all content editorial decisions and errors remain with the three of us.

Rick Molz
Cătălin Rațiu
Ali Taleb

Introduction

Rick Molz, Cătălin Raţiu and Ali Taleb

The main objective of this book is to provide both initiated and non-expert readers with a fresh outlook on the strategic implications of doing business in developing markets from both foreign multinational enterprises' (MNEs) and local firms' perspectives. Accordingly, all the chapters of this volume explore, in their own way, the local–global dynamics underlying interactions between the economic and social logics that prevail in developed and developing countries. While interest in developing markets is not a new phenomenon in academia and the business world, it has gained prominence as a result of the recent surge in the economic power of emerging countries on the global stage. Their markets not only represent an instrumental source of growth for globalizing firms, but also are home to increasingly innovative and competitive firms that succeed both at home and globally. The global economic and political orders in which emerging countries play a more prominent role bring new challenges as well as opportunities to light.

Accordingly, the intent of this volume is to help unravel the intricacies underlying the tensions between the dominant economic and social logics that prevail in developed and developing markets. Understanding such local–global dynamics helps shed light on the contextual conditions that foster or hinder the global competitiveness of MNEs, especially with respect to developing countries.

This volume represents a collection of individual and joint works by authors who have been collaborating within a collegial and supportive research group for several years. We hope our readers will feel some deep connections and synergies as they read through them. The volume is structured into four parts and can be used either as a reference book for initiated readers, since the chapters are independent and self-contained, or as a progressive read, especially for non-expert readers, because the order in which these chapters are arranged allows for an incremental understanding of the phenomena.

The first part of the book sets the stage for the whole volume by clarifying some fundamental theoretical concepts such as local–global dynamics as well as by offering complementary theoretical perspectives to the analysis of such dynamics. On the one hand, Chapter 1, by Soussi, contrasts the instrumental rationality of MNEs from developed countries and the institutional rationality and local traditions that prevail in emerging countries. By deconstructing the tension underlying the two dominant logics, this chapter starts to unpack the "local–global dynamics" black box in which this book is interested. On the other hand, Marcotte *et al.* in Chapter 2 take a deeper look at these tensions and propose implementation strategies that MNEs from industrialized countries may adopt while dealing with developing markets. Essentially, both chapters conceptualize local–global dynamics as resulting from the tension between the differential dominant logics of developed and developing markets at the economic and institutional levels.

In Part II the authors explore more specifically the implications of local–global dynamics for MNEs from developed economies from particular managerial perspectives. Specifically, Lirio's chapter (Chapter 3) adopts a cultural perspective on the discussion of the key challenges expatriate managers face with reference to the motivation of local workers, as they may each operate within different cultural frameworks. The proposed model of contextualized goal setting has concrete managerial implications for global managers. Conversely, Edwards (in Chapter 4) adopts an institutional change perspective and suggests that the dominant institutional logics of MNEs evolve over time, depending on the degree of parent–subsidiary interdependence, on the one hand, and on institutional distance between home and host countries, on the other hand. Both local and global tensions have major implications for MNEs of developed economies operating in developing markets.

From an equally impactful perspective, Totskaya in Chapter 6 explores the governance mechanisms that prevail in developing economies. Specifically, she argues that business groups and their operating modes are so entrenched in developing economies that MNEs must be prepared to play by the local rules in order to ensure their survival and performance. Finally, Ul-Haq and Farashahi (in Chapter 5) suggest that in addition to adjusting their operating institutional logics and internalizing local rules, foreign MNEs might also benefit by developing proactive strategies so as to mitigate the particular political risks that are inherent in developing markets. Thus, their chapter focuses essentially on the contextual factors that shape these political strategies.

Part III includes more fine-grained empirical studies, with the objective not only of illustrating the theories presented earlier but also of proposing new theories based on actual situations in which local–global dynamics played a critical role. In this regard, Bosquetti *et al.* in Chapter 8 propose an interesting comparative case study that looks at the strategic approaches of two foreign MNEs to the acquisition of local Brazilian firms. It substantiates nicely how the tension between the predominantly economic logic of foreign MNCs and the rather traditional logic of developing countries may explain the success or failure of cross-border mergers and acquisitions. Similarity, Naguib's chapter (Chapter 9) illustrates how local subsidiaries of foreign MNEs deal with the conflicting requirements of, on the one hand, their parents and, on the other, local institutions in developing countries. The case studies show how "smart partnerships" between these subsidiaries and local governments help achieve win–win objectives. Exploring another cross-border phenomenon, Marcotte (in Chapter 7) underlines the particular importance and challenge that knowledge transfer represents in terms of interactions between foreign MNEs and developing countries. While institutional differences between home and host countries may hinder the ability of all MNEs to transfer knowledge effectively, small firms are suggested to be more effective in transferring knowledge, thanks essentially to their nimbleness and entrepreneurial capabilities. Finally, Hafsi and Gauthier (in Chapter 10) provide a compelling integrative view of the local–global challenges from both institutional and competitive environments standpoints as they investigate how multiple factors of different levels of analysis – namely, the environment, strategy and leadership characteristics – influence collectively the performance of foreign MNEs in a developing country.

In the fourth and final part of the book, emphasis is put on the emergent global role of firms from developing economies, both local subsidiaries of foreign MNEs and home-grown MNEs. On the one hand, Chapter 11, by Raţiu and Molz, is essentially concerned with the entrepreneurial behavior of local subsidiaries and how they influence corporate environmental strategies of their parents. On the other hand, Taleb's chapter (Chapter 12) completes the flow of thinking in this volume by focusing on MNEs *from* emerging markets. His key argument is that developing markets present their home-grown firms with a unique opportunity to learn how to operate in a variety of institutional settings. They may do so by developing an eclectic repertoire of strategies that can serve not only in other developing markets but also in developed and least-developed countries.

Figure I.1 presents a road map to help navigate the four parts of this book. As shown, the chief objective is to provide the reader with a coherent and complementary set of views on local–global dynamics from an MNE perspective. This overarching theme ensures the overall coherence among the constituting chapters as they all explore, in their own way, the uneasy interaction between the dominant logics in developing and developed economies as well as their implications for MNEs operating in developing and emerging markets. In addition, the arguments developed in the different chapters offer complementary

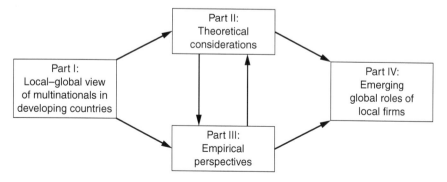

Figure I.1 Organization of the volume.

views on the nature of phenomena investigated, research methodologies used, and geographic coverage – which ranges from South Africa and Cameroon (Africa) to China, the Philippines and Malaysia (Asia) to Brazil (South America), France and Portugal (Europe), in addition to phenomena that are more global in nature. This widespread geographic coverage is consistent with our desire to infuse theory with the richness of a multitude of perspectives from all over the world.

Part I

Local–global view of multinationals in developing countries

1 Organizational and institutional rationalities and Western firms in emerging countries

Proposal for a local/global analytical model

Sid Ahmed Soussi

Introduction

This chapter discusses the dynamic produced by the local–global relationships that are created when Western firms engage in activities in so-called emerging countries. Many Western firms view emerging countries as economic, institutional and cultural spaces characterized by strong economic growth and institutional instability. Going beyond the scope of this observation, this study postulates that the dynamic created by local–global relationships is underpinned by two basic logics that, through their interactions, contribute to the construction of such relationships. Each logic is grounded in an ontological rationality that is more or less fashioned by the institutional and cultural referents in emerging countries.

Emerging countries are experiencing relatively rapid institutional changes and economic growth outstripping that of developing nations. Such growth is often accompanied by measures supporting the increased liberalization of commercial exchanges with other countries. Institutions in emerging countries, however, are still perceived as less mature than their industrialized counterparts. As a result, foreign firms feel uncertain about the future investment climate in emerging countries. Institutional changes affecting emerging markets are perceived as only slightly linear and even less predictable on political and economic levels (Peng, 2001).

In the face of such conditions, how do firms construct their strategies and adapt them to local institutional and cultural conditions? This problem is at the core of the dynamic of outsourcing activities by transnational firms, but scant attention has been focused on these two rationalities and their inescapable impacts.

Management theories have rarely been applied to explain the process used by Western firms to make their strategic choices once they enter an emerging country. To what extent do firms adapt their strategies to local conditions? This question has received far less attention than the study of the penetration strategies aimed at emerging countries. Such concern for content rather than process may be explained in part by the dominance of economic approaches in explaining the globalization phenomenon (Hench, 1997). According to London and Hart (2004), management research assumes that emerging countries are quickly and inexorably evolving toward a business environment similar to that of Western countries, and that Western firms have only a few strategic efforts to deploy while awaiting this transition. However, one cannot affirm a priori that the Westernization of emerging countries is as fast and unavoidable as some researchers appear to believe. Our general hypothesis is that the influence exerted by the globalization process on local conditions collides with endogenous conditions in emerging countries. This leads to questions about the inevitable interactions the dynamic produces locally as it combines local and global rationalities. Our critical assertion is supported by three principal observations.

First, one cannot assume that the political and historical evolution of institutions will follow the Western pattern or be systematically conducted on the basis of Western processes (Beck, 2005). In each emerging country the construction of institutional structures fits into unique historical trajectories and, in most cases, results in distinct political and institutional models, though some of these may be based on specific Western patterns. This is notably the case for countries such as India, South Africa and Algeria, which have been influenced by the United Kingdom, France, the United States, the Netherlands or another country, and which, owing to their long colonial histories, produced the above-mentioned models. Other countries, such as Malaysia, Indonesia and China, experienced a lesser degree of colonial influence, and therefore were affected in even more specific ways. Lastly, other countries, such as Thailand, never experienced colonial domination and therefore provide a significant model of distinct historical evolution.

Second, emerging countries base their strategic and long-term economic objectives on issues specific to their local realities and do not necessarily seek to align their priorities with those of Western economic models. The local rationalities of emerging countries are founded on necessarily endogenous logics, and, despite their sensitivity to the so-called universal and globalizing character of Western models, they are above all geared to local purposes (Beck, 2006).

Third, and foremost, the transition poses a problem primarily at a cultural level. The cultural impacts of economic practices on institutional environments have been at the heart of many research projects over the past several years (Hampden-Turner and Trompenaars, 2004; Hofstede, 2001; d'Iribarne *et al.*, 2002), and a widespread consensus is forming around the need to take into account the cultural context and its determinants, not only in regard to economic practices but also, and more specifically, in regard to firms' strategic behaviors, whether the firms are local[1] or, more importantly, foreign.

The role of endogenous factors is apparent in the three foregoing observations. These factors are determinant in the institutional transition of emerging countries. Their local character has a dimension at least as important as the global influences exerted by Western economic and institutional models, which, although globally dominant, are nonetheless locally exogenous. It is therefore important not to overestimate the scope of these models in view of their limited influential ability.

Whatever local conditions are in place when a Western capitalist firm ventures into an emerging country, a local–global dynamic arises at the previously described three levels as a result of a series of interactions fueled by two logics. Western firms are led by their organizational logic to act on the basis of an economic rationality (Dacin *et al.*, 2002). Their managers are guided by identity referents grounded in the cultural environment and emanating from the historical trajectories of the industrial capitalist systems in which the referents developed (Castells, 2000). This particular rationality is based on a dual technical and economic concern (Hofstede and Hofstede, 2005) and a strategic process of harnessing specialized resources (Simon, 1982). The purpose of this process is to achieve a level of efficiency defined by the historical and cultural environments. It is therefore important to consider the resulting unavoidable identity and cultural impacts on this particular logic, which demonstrate clearly the "limited" nature of the rationality attached to it.

The second interactive logic is shaped by the strategies and behaviors of decision makers in emerging countries, which are influenced not only by the cultural referents (Adler, 1994, 1997) of a nation's societies but also by institutional settings and formalized modes of operations from which the strategies take their meaning. This meaning appears to be strongly imprinted by traditional and community legitimacies in which the dominant rationality is based more on social and community relationships than on individual performance and the way individual actions affect the group.

The goal of this study is to deconstruct and analyze the local–global dynamic resulting from the interaction of the two logics. This is accomplished from an epistemological perspective, based on the general hypothesis and the three main observations presented earlier. Our perspective takes into account the local and global characteristics of the interactive dynamic, which is constructed and takes on meaning only within historically and culturally predetermined spatial boundaries. The purpose here is not to downplay the scope of the globally influential exogenous elements of the rationality of Western firms and their economic practices, but to observe that such factors do not produce the same effects everywhere (such as inevitable Westernization) because their impacts combine with the endogenous factors that are found at the three levels noted in the hypothesis.

The resulting analytical model is based on three theoretical approaches selected for their ability to explain the interactive dynamic of the local and global dimensions of the factors at play in environments as complex as those of emerging countries.

The first approach uses institutionalist theory and considers local constraints and the adaptation needs of Western firms. This approach was selected for its potential to explain the two main analytical dimensions on which it is founded. The first dimension is the set of institutional constraints created by the regulative, normative and prescriptive aspects of institutions. These constraints condition the organization's ability to act upon its own context (Doz and Prahalad, 1993; Ray, 2003) during the interaction, and to "maneuver" its strategies in a flexible way. The second dimension is the ability of organizations to take advantage of potentials that arise from institutional constraints and which, by their existence, take away much of the constraints' negative aspects. The strategic ability of organizations can therefore make all the difference and optimize institutional constraints.

The framing of institutions as the objects of a constantly evolving dynamic leads to a reexamination of structures and their effect on actors (organizations, groups or individuals). During this exercise, institutions are no longer viewed as exogenous objects that can barely propel the action of actors, but rather as a set of movable structures with no significance or intrinsic value at organizational or societal levels except through the meaning attributed to them by the agents who sustain them.

Far from opposing the traditional institutionalist approach adopted by organizational studies, this perspective sheds new light on, and leads to the reframing of, the question of the meaning and scope of action, especially when one is analyzing organizations.

The second perspective has a neo-structurationist orientation and is based on the principle of the non-exteriority of structures, thereby excluding the idea that the nature and quality of business relationships are independent from the cultural mediations that underpin institutional/organizational interactions (Giddens, 1990).

The third perspective, which draws on cultural theories (Hofstede, 1980; Adler, 1994, 1997; Hampden-Turner and Trompenaars, 2004), is based on conducting systemic comparisons of managerial and societal cultures from a standpoint of instrumental concern for organizational performance – that is, finding ways to build links between the agents that drive culture, in order to minimize negative consequences and optimize each culture's resources.

The institutionalist approach

As applied in management, the institutionalist approach has been defined in part as organizational adaptation theory (Doz and Prahalad, 1993; Dacin *et al.*, 2002; Ray, 2003). Cultural elements, along with the normative and regulative aspects of institutions that are specific to a given society, determine regulations, norms and cultural values, which, in turn, shape ways of thinking and behaving. Institutional processes set the parameters of what is agreed upon as *rational* or *logical* in a specific social setting.

Institutional logic is characterized by the idea that (institutional) structures condition the decision making of local actors, even though this occurs in combination with the influence of cultural referents (Hall, 1971). It is essential to analyze the decision-making framework (the local institutional framework) because of its influence on the rationality of actors in terms of strategy and partnership management. It is thus possible to make sense of the institutional logic and its application to emerging countries by understanding the global trend among actors to make decisions and adopt actions that are legitimized more by the institutional framework than by a rationality similar to that of Western firms.

The importance of structures and how they affect action in emerging countries is therefore apparent. In the rationalist organizational logic, managerial decision making and strategies are influenced more by their own economic rationality than by the structures that guide organizations. In this particular case, the importance of (institutional and organizational) structures is clearly less of a determining factor in the action of actors.

The structurationist approach

Structurationist theory is based on the principle of the non-exteriority of structures (Giddens, 1990) and reinforces our alternative interpretation of the institutionalist approach. In this study, our interpretation leads us to exclude the idea that the nature and quality of business relationships are independent of the cultural mediations that structure the interactions between institutions and organizations. This approach helps us understand and evaluate the structuring effects of cultural mediations on institutional–organizational interactions (Hofstede, 1980). Its distinguishing feature is that it allows us to consider that institutions should not be conceived of as rigid frameworks composed of immovable exterior structures impervious to the action of actors. The structurationist approach is based on the idea that institutions are, on the contrary, incorporated and sustained by actors who, in doing so, give the institutions their meaning, whether in an organizational framework or, in a larger sense, a societal framework. Conversely, it is in the very act of sustaining institutions that actors experience their influence as they integrate them into their actions. This positively demonstrates inter/action between structures and actors, and therefore an interactive dynamic. In this sense, institutions as structures appear to be a social production of actors as well as a framework whose boundaries have structuring effects on the action of actors. These effects have a dual nature because they are not only constraints to action but also opportunities for the action to produce, in whole or in part, the results anticipated by the actors. In turn, these principals are not so much actors, within the meaning of Crozier and Friedberg (1977), as they are agents, within Giddens's (1987b) meaning, whose action necessarily becomes a series of inter/actions with structures.

The use of a structurationist approach opens up a new perspective that leads us to restate the question of the meaning and scope of action as we analyze organizations. In doing so, we see that action is no longer understood on the sole basis of theoretical references used in the traditional institutionalist paradigm by the strategic analytic model, such as actors' goals and resources, the types of strategies they develop and the issues on which they center their actions (Crozier and Friedberg, 1977). In the strategic analysis perspective, structures (institutions or other organizational and societal frameworks for action) remain external because they are considered outside the limits of action. However, the space they form and in which the actors act cannot be presented in any way but as a framework that determines the boundaries beyond which the actors cannot act. This is the cut-off point highlighted by the structurationist project, in which actors can act upon institutions, in the sense that these are no longer considered timeless structures or frameworks that define a space of action with formally recognized and systematically respected boundaries. On the contrary, the institutions themselves become an issue of the action and, as such, allow the actors who sustain them to enlarge their potential margin of liberty and scope of action, and, to a certain extent, transform the structures by redefining boundaries. This movement gives the institutional dynamic its entire meaning and, at the same time, infuses institutions with life, because they are no longer understood as immovable, timeless frameworks, but as "fossilized traces" (Giddens, 1987a) on which the transformed structures restamp their mark in time, being modified by agents motivated by the extension of their margin of liberty.

Relationship between local actions and their global influence

Structurationist theory, as integrated in the analytical model we propose, gives us a convenient methodological tool to understand the strategies of actors – that is, managers of Western firms and their partners in emerging countries. By separating the analysis of structures from the analysis of action, it is possible to evaluate the impact of these elements on actors' local behaviors and strategies.

The purpose of using the proposed model is to assess not only the impact of structures and action on the local interaction of both of these factors, but also the potential global consequences the dynamic generates. One of the main purposes of resorting to a structurationist perspective is to assess the relationship between the local actions of actors and the effects they produce on a global scale. Indeed, the recurrence of their actions – in this case, the various activities of Western corporations in emerging countries – can produce a dynamic that the main actors are likely to reproduce, especially when the results obtained are consistent with long-term objectives. When this reproduction also occurs in other spaces, i.e. with other Western corporations in other emerging countries – that is, from the moment the same actions tend to be reproduced in the hope of attaining the same type of results elsewhere in other locations – a global scope can be assumed.[2] In this context it is safe to establish a relationship between initial local actions and the scope of their global consequences. Further on we will discuss the nature of the global scope of action, but from the outset it can be affirmed that an organic link exists between local and global effects, based on the recurrence logic. We now explain the main theoretical elements on which the proposed analytical model is based.

Institutional logic is characterized by the idea that structures (particularly economic and political institutions) condition the decision-making process of local actors, despite the fact that this influence occurs in conjunction with the local context's cultural referents. An analysis of the structural framework of the decision-making process (the local institutional framework) is highly relevant because of the way it affects the rationality of actors in terms of strategies and partnership management. It is therefore possible to better understand this logic in its application to emerging countries by analyzing the global tendency of actors to make decisions and take action that is legitimized more by the institutional framework and its cultural referents than by an economic rationality[3] similar to that of Western corporations.

The structurationist approach suggests a global explanation for the constitution of social systems and organizational dynamics. By considering actors as agents that implement social and organizational practices in time and space, it provides a clearer understanding of the action of actors in a local context. In that sense, it brings together human action, structures and institutions into one logic, making it possible to assess their dynamic within the framework of the order instituted and established by institutions. This action could generate conflict with other actors because it calls institutional order into question. From that angle, order and conflict can be understood and explained by rejecting the traditional contrasting epistemological views of rationalism/relativism, objectivity/subjectivity and structural determinism/scope of action. In other terms, the purpose is to better differentiate – and therefore better understand – the results attributable to actors' strategies from those attributable to the context's structures (institutions and so forth). During the last phase of the analysis, the principles governing the renewal of institutions (social or organizational) through local action seem to be both the conditions and the results of the activities of agents who belong to the institutions and, as such, sustain them.

Functionalism, which informs most organizational studies, has limited relevance in this context, given its tendency to focus only on the action of the actor. It therefore does not incorporate the notion of multiple interactions between agent and structures.

The structurationist perspective dismisses the functionalist premise that the behavior of agents is continuously reproduced as a result of pressure from the structures that circumscribe the agents' actions. Agents (in this case, individuals or organizations) and structures (in this case, institutions or organizational regulations) are therefore not independent phenomena. When their interactions are taken into account, *all structure provides a series of both constraints and opportunities for the action of agents*. In other words, one single institutional framework may provide genuine opportunity for agent X but present a series of constraints for agent Y that must be dealt with before action is possible.

Our analysis centers not only on specialties, strategic capacities and roles, but also on an agent's opportunity to: (1) control the system's institutional and cultural elements; (2) influence the conditions surrounding the other party's action (the other logic); and (3) interact with environmental, cultural and identity data.

Our analytical model lets us explore the agent's "competencies" and his or her ability to take action in a given context. In doing so, we conclude that, first, the activity of agents is made possible by integration practices in structures that predate the agents – or "mnesic traces," in the words of Giddens; and second, the action of agents can produce either anticipated or unintended consequences. Their decryption by the agent leads to a reflexive dynamic and the transformation of the conditions under which the action is performed.

Turning to the case of Canadian firms, we consider that as corporate organizations they sustain a logic that situates them in time and space. This logic leads them to produce and reproduce the institutional aspects of an inherent rationality in the sense that this rationality constitutes a cultural referent characteristic of their institutional environment.[4] The environment has the distinguishing trait of being subject to two types of rules, structural and conjectural. Although they are informal, the structural rules are far-reaching. The actors follow them naturally, for they are tacit; language is one example of such rules. Rules of the second type are discursive. They are formal because they are recognized by the institution, such as in the case of laws, policies and other clearly sanctioned administrative rules (Giddens, 1987a).

These elements of structurationism demonstrate that this perspective is not centered exclusively on the organization (Giordano, 1998); it is also centered on its interactions with structures and institutions. Thus, a productive operational analysis can be conducted, based on the following two considerations: (1) the temporal and spatial dimensions of the integration practices of outsourcing firms, i.e. international, global and transnational dimensions (Hampden-Turner and Trompenaars, 2004); and (2) various social organization modes (traditions and modernity in emerging countries and advanced modernity of Western corporations).

The culturalist approach: identity dynamic of both logics

Strategic analysis is traditionally considered the most dominant, productive and appropriate method to explain corporate operations and the meaning and efficiency of their actions. This model, part of the institutionalist paradigm, does not explain the impacts on actors of the cultural and identity aspects of their interactions. From this perspective, strategic dimensions are not very helpful. Many studies have been conducted over the past few years to highlight and explain cultural and identity effects on corporate operations and the behavior of members of organizations (Hall, 1984; Hofstede, 1980; Hampden-Turner and Trompenaars, 2004). The common objective of these studies is to integrate consideration of cultural referents into the analysis (Soussi and Côté, 2008).

The purpose of our analytical model is to deconstruct the interactive dynamic between the organizational and institutional logics. However, this dynamic cannot be viewed independently of the cultural context and the institutional structures sustained by the actors – in this case, corporations and the institutions of emerging countries. In contrast to the abstract notion of the institution, these actors produce concrete actions whose dynamic has been widely described by the "cultural management" body (Chevrier, 2003). We will consider this particular dynamic as we integrate the structurationist perspective into our analytical model.

This dynamic depends on a systemic comparison of the actors' values on the one hand, and the need to explain the interpretation of each cultural context (in emerging countries) through the prism of the organization's rationality on the other hand. As a structural element, the dynamic provides both opportunities and constraints for the actors who sustain the two logics we have been speaking of. To contain the constraints and optimize the opportunities, organizations must redirect the dynamic for the purpose of:

- adjusting intercultural interactions to improve the performance of organizations and their subjective experience;
- building links between those who sustain different cultures and identities to minimize the negative consequences of differences for individuals and firms, and benefiting from the resources of each culture;
- studying the technical and human aspects of international transfers of knowledge and materials.

To study the impacts of cultural referents, some theoretical models (those of Hall, Adler, d'Iribarne *et al.*, Hofstede) propose a number of conceptual tools that accurately identify identity differences (for instance, actions, reactions and feelings are dictated by culture). For example, E. T. Hall, writing about national cultural models, finds it particularly useful to study these referents through the communication methods used by different cultures. He was thus able to identify two specific dimensions: relationship to the context (rich – Japan, or poor – United States) and relationship to time. In doing so, he challenged many assumptions about the universality of formal and informal communication methods (monochromic and polychromic) and the relationship with space (distance and layout). However, one of his principal omissions is that his model does not explain diversity of individual behavior (Soussi and Côté, 2008).

A second example is societal models (Hampden-Turner and Trompenaars, 2004; d'Iribarne *et al.*, 2002), which have become increasingly dominant in recent years. Our analysis focuses on their intrinsic constraints. Despite being grounded in the institutional and intellectual structures of their original societal contexts, these constraints can change into opportunities when the actors' logics interact. Hampden-Turner and Trompenaars (2004) wrote one of the most representative studies of such models, delving even further than the seminal works of Hofstede (1980) and other European structuralists (d'Iribarne *et al.*, 2002). They presented constraints and opportunities through cultural dimensions[5] that highlight the main distinctions between the actors' (individuals and organizations) identities and behaviors. Their research is all the more relevant in the context of recent economic transformations because they try to demonstrate that the increasing obligations to adopt a certain culture and identity in the context of such transformations should be removed.[6] Societal models are at the heart of a current paradigm change because they establish a close link between national cultures, organizational structures, management styles and behavior (Chevrier, 2003).

Some dimensions highlight the cultural and identity referents that define the social and institutional contexts of emerging countries where Western corporations seek potential markets. These referents are:

- the distinction between individualist and collectivist societies;

- high power distance (emerging countries: acceptance of power differences) and low power distance (developed countries);
- high uncertainty avoidance (technical solutions, laws) and low uncertainty avoidance (lack of institutional solutions to control the future);
- male-oriented societies (traditional society, visible achievements, financial gain) and female-oriented societies (the importance of quality of life, personal relationships, solidarity, reserve): the thrust of this dimension is the division of gender roles in society;
- short-term orientation (personal steadiness and stability, the importance of saving face, respecting of social obligations, gifts, favors) or long-term orientation (perseverance, ordering relationships by status, thrift, a sense of shame).

In addition to being strongly formalized and having a necessarily relative explanatory ability, some of these indicators can contribute to an understanding of the interactive dynamic between organizational and institutional logics if appropriately integrated in our analytical model. They can provide clarity on individuals, who inevitably are the vehicles for cultural and identity dimensions, as well as organizations, which are no less supporters of the incorporation of cultural aspects in the instrumental rationality that guides their strategies, even though they prefer institutional interactions.

Conclusion

In the matter of the dynamic of the local–global relationship, the combination of the three approaches described here will lead to a better understanding of the various organizational strategies implemented by multinational firms in emerging countries, and particularly in their interactions with institutions. Where, when and how will these different strategies be operationalized? Do firms that invest in emerging countries pass through phases in which they shift strategies, or is one particular strategy dominant? It is indeed likely that their strategies will differ according to the host country's economic and political stability and the level of maturity of its institutions. For countries that have achieved greater global economic integration, global and co-learning strategies could be used to a greater extent. These issues have not been clearly dealt with in the literature. As Beamish (1993) stated, the factors that explain the success, stability and longevity of investments in emerging countries are still not well known. An empirical study based on the present conceptual research could increase understanding of these factors. A mixed qualitative and quantitative methodology would be particularly appropriate in identifying empirically the characteristics of each of the three theoretical approaches and then finding the conditions under which these approaches are deployed. Lastly, it could measure the impact of strategies on the performance of Western firms. The theoretical and empirical initiatives developed in this current research show which avenues to explore in the appropriate fields with these methods.

Notes

1 See Chapter 12 by Ali Taleb.
2 Another example of this recurrence: China's remarkable economic growth these past few years has been, in large measure, the result of its well-known controlled openness policy, instituted by the Communist Party in the early 1990s under Deng Xiaoping. The policy did not affect the political stability of China's authoritarian regime. It had indisputable local effects, to the extent that there is a current trend among several other countries with authoritarian regimes to reproduce the program now termed "the Chinese model." This is the case not only in some Southeast Asian countries but in other countries as well. Moreover, in Egypt and Tunisia, institutional decision makers – local actors – say that they are ready to "reproduce" this "first" Chinese experience on their own soil. Hence, it appears that the Chinese influence has a global aspect in view of the likelihood of its model being reproduced in each local context.
3 This rationality is often analyzed by traditional institutionalism through strategic analysis, as in the neo-institutionalist paradigm. The analysis is therefore essentially based on *bounded rationality* (Simon, 1982), and, since the seminal works of Parsons, Merton and Simon, *instrumental rationality*, which organizational theory has formalized in a wide range of still-dominant analytical models.
4 For Giddens, these institutional traits are based on organizational principles that govern capitalist societies and lead firms to adopt institutional and cultural behaviors that demonstrate a common identity such that "One of the main propositions of structuration theory is that the rules and resources drawn upon in the production and reproduction of social action are at the same time the means of system reproduction" (1987b: 19).
5 In this model, these dimensions dictate the construction of individual and group strategies, both in intra- and interorganization relationships.
6 For Adler (1994) this is nothing less than cultural blindness. She maintains, for example, that in the matter of managing international staffing, many organizations act as though nothing has changed, either in their internal structure or organization or in the economic and technological context in which they operate.

References

Adler, N. (1997) *International Dimensions of Organizational Behavior*, Cincinatti, OH: South-Western College Publishing.
—— (1994) *Mondialisation, gouvernement et compétitivité*, Ottawa: Centre canadien de gestion.
Beamish, P. (1993) "The characteristics of joint ventures in the People's Republic of China," *Journal of International Marketing*, 1: 29–49.
Beck, U. (2005) *Power in the Global Age: A New Global Political Economy*, Cambridge: Polity Press.
—— (2006) *Transnational Professionals and Their Cosmopolitan Universes*, Frankfurt am Main: Campus Verlag.
Castells, M. (2000) *The Information Age: Economy, Society and Culture*, vol. 1: *The Rise of the Network Society*, 2nd edn., Oxford: Blackwell Publishing.
Chevrier, S. (2003) *Le management interculturel*, Paris: Que-sais-je.
Crozier, M. and Friedberg, E. (1977) *L'acteur et le système*, Paris: Éditions du Seuil.
Dacin, M. T., Goodstein, J. and Scott, W. R. (2002) "Institutional theory and institutional change: Introduction to the special issue," *Academy of Management Journal*, 43: 45–57.
d'Iribarne, P., Henry, A., Segal, J.-P., Chevrier, S. and Globokar, T. (2002) *Cultures et mondialisation. Gérer par-delà les frontiers*, Paris: Éditions du Seuil.

Doz, Y. and Prahalad, C. (1993) "Managing DMNCs: A search for a new paradigm," in S. Ghoshal and D. Westney (eds.) *Organization Theory and the Multinational Corporation*, New York: St. Martin's Press.

Giddens, A. (1987a) *La constitution de la société*, Paris: Presses Universitaires de France.

—— (1987b) *Social Theory and Modern Sociology*, Stanford, CA: Stanford University Press.

—— (1990) *The Consequences of Modernity*, Stanford, CA: Stanford University Press.

Giordano, Y. (1998) "Communication et organisation. Une reconsidération par la théorie de la structuration," *Revue de gestion des RH*, 26–27 (May–June): 20–35.

Hall, E. T. (1971) *La dimension cache*, Paris: Éditions du Seuil.

—— (1984) *La danse de la vie. Temps culturel, temps vécu*, Paris: Éditions du Seuil.

Hampden-Turner, C. and Trompenaars, F. (2004) *Au-delà du choc des cultures. Dépasser les oppositions pour mieux travailler ensemble*, Paris: Éditions d'organisations.

Hench, T. (1997) "The domain of international business: Paradigms in collision," in B. Toyne and N. Douglas (eds.) *International Business: An Emerging Vision*, Columbia: University of South Carolina Press.

Hofstede, G. (1980) *Culture's Consequences: International Differences in Work-Related Values*, Newbury Park, CA: Sage.

—— (2001) *Culture's Consequences: Comparing Values, Behaviors, Institutions and Organizations across Nations*, 2nd edn., Beverly Hills, CA: Sage.

Hofstede, G. and Hofstede, G. J. (2005) *Cultures and Organizations: Software of the Mind. Intercultural Cooperation and Its Importance for Survival*, New York: McGraw-Hill.

London, T. and Hart, S. (2004) "Reinventing strategies for emerging markets: Beyond the transnational model," *Journal of International Business Studies*, 35: 350–370.

Peng, M. (2001) "How do entrepreneurs create wealth in transition economies," *Academy of Management Executive*, 15: 95–112.

Ray, S. (2003) "Strategic adaptation of firms during economic liberalization: Emerging issues and a research agenda," *International Journal of Management*, 20: 271–286.

Simon, H. S. (1982) *Models of Rationality*, Cambridge, MA: Harvard University Press.

Soussi, S. A. and Côté, A. (2008) "La diversité culturelle dans les organisations: critique du *management interculturel* et nécessité d'un nouveau regard épistémologique," *Revista Universitară de Sociologie*, no. 1/2008: 51–61.

2 Strategy implementation in emerging countries

Three theoretical approaches

Claude Marcotte, Sid Ahmed Soussi, Rick Molz, Mehdi Farashahi and Taïeb Hafsi

Introduction

Emerging countries are attracting a growing number of Western firms. This is particularly noticeable in the case of emerging Asian markets such as China, India, Indonesia and Malaysia. For example, China is now Canada's third most important trading partner. Data published by the Canadian Ministry for Foreign Affairs and International Trade indicated that more than 400 Canadian companies currently operate in China, and that, as a result of their physical presence and investments, these companies have established commercial and technological bonds with Chinese partners (MAECI, 2003). The amount of direct investment made in China by Canadian firms increased from $6 million in 1990 to $542 million in 2003 (Statistics Canada, 2004). The increase in foreign direct investments is also remarkable in the other three countries mentioned above. These direct investments can be made in wholly owned subsidiaries or in joint ventures.

This chapter aims to generate research propositions regarding the strategies implemented by Western firms in emerging countries. These are firms that are involved in foreign direct investment activities, whether through wholly owned subsidiaries or joint ventures. We are focusing here not on entry modes but on the strategic process once an emerging market has been entered.

In the first section we address the issue of institutional change and uncertainty in emerging countries, and its implications for management research. We suggest that researchers look beyond the conventional typologies based on product market positioning and make use of organizational theory in order to gain a broader perspective on strategy implementation in emerging countries. In the second section we introduce three theoretical positions on the issue of uncertainty at the international level: the institutionalist theory, the global approach and the interactive model. Each of these approaches is analyzed in the subsequent sections of the chapter, and research propositions on strategies of Western firms in emerging countries are elaborated.

Institutional change and uncertainty in emerging countries

Emerging markets are characterized by relatively rapid institutional change, as well as by higher rates of economic growth than those observed in developing countries. Economic growth in these countries is generally accompanied by a liberalization of trade policies. However, their legal, political and financial institutions are not as mature as those prevailing in the industrialized regions of the world, and this creates an ambiguous and uncertain climate for foreign investors. Institutional change frequently occurs in a non-linear, unpredictable way in many of these emerging countries (Hoskisson *et al.*, 2000; Peng, 2001, 2003). Although it may be hypothesized that emerging countries will evolve toward a business environment similar to that of the West, and that Western firms will progressively be exempted from the institutional uncertainty prevalent in these countries, it is still too early to predict that the Westernization of emerging countries will be a rapid, or even inevitable, phenomenon.

The organizational literature provides fragmented theoretical explanations as to the strategic process by which Western firms cope with these institutional differences. To what extent do these companies adapt their strategies to the local context? Are they capable of innovation and entrepreneurship, and, if so, how do these entrepreneurial abilities develop in a context that is institutionally and culturally very different? Questions such as these, dealing with the strategic process, have received less attention from researchers than the issue of choice of entry modes. This concern for content rather than process can be explained partly by the prevalence of an economically derived and functionalist approach to the internationalization of the firm (Hench, 1997). Such an approach has so far given rise to textbook typologies and continua of potential strategies for internationalizing firms, but it has failed to provide linkages between the strategies and the underlying theoretical foundations. The result has been the accumulation of descriptive or normative descriptions of potential product–process–market positioning for internationalizing firms, rather than on the evolutionary learning of new core competencies or combinative capabilities that may make such positioning possible, as was suggested by Prahalad and Hamel (1990) and Doz (1997). The understanding of the dynamic process by which such capabilities are learned requires the integration of theories emanating from different areas of organizational science.

Strategy implementation in emerging countries: three approaches

We examine three approaches to the relationships between Western firms and the environments of emerging countries. First we analyze the institutionalist approach, centered on local constraints and the need for adaptation on the part of Western firms. Then we examine the global strategy approach, together with the Schumpeterian tradition, as the two approaches share significant similarities. Finally, we examine the interactionist model (i.e. local and global), as illustrated in Giddens's structurationist theory and in the emergent paradigm of international entrepreneurship. Table 2.1 presents these three approaches. We propose a comparison of these approaches from the perspectives of economics, strategy and sociology.

Table 2.1 Strategies of Western firms in emerging countries: three approaches

Strategies	Approaches/authors	Rationality	Knowledge and learning
Adaptation of Western companies to local constraints	Institutionalist (Scott, 2001; Westney, 1993)	Multiple logic determined by the institutional and cultural context	Little knowledge sharing. Learning is done by Western firms (mimetic isomorphism)
Global strategy	Levitt (1983); Ohmae (1990); Reich (1991); Baumol (1993)	Rational actors: Western economic logic	Teacher–learner model (superiority of Western management and technology)
Local–global interaction Relations and construction of joint interpretations	Interactionist and structurationist approach in sociology (Giddens, 1990) International entrepreneurship (Etemad, 2003)	Emergent forms. No dominant form a priori	Mutual knowledge. Co-learning model. Creation of new standards, structures and strategies

The approaches differ on three key and interrelated dimensions of dynamic capability building. First, they are characterized by specific interpretations of what is rational in an international context. Then these various forms of rationality correspond with particular conceptualizations of knowledge and learning. Knowledge is a key concept in recent theories of the firm, particularly the resource-based view and the knowledge-based approach (Barney, 1991; Spender, 1996). In the former it is considered as an intangible resource that gives rise to unique, firm-specific competencies and competitive advantages. The emphasis is on the content of resources and competencies. In the knowledge-based approach the emphasis is on the processes of knowledge acquisition, use and diffusion or transfer. The research question within this approach is how knowledge is processed within the firms, not what the firm knows.

The interplay between these three dimensions of capabilities gives rise to specific types of strategy implementation. The first type is the adaptive one, the second is global and the third type is interactive. These strategies evolve and are reconfigured through time and space, although little is known as to the sequence of this evolution.

Institutional changes as sources of constraint and opportunity: the institutionalist approach

Until recently, the institutionalist view was conceptualized by international management researchers as a theory of adaptation of the firm (Doz and Prahalad, 1993; Dacin *et al.*, 2002; Ray, 2003). According to this conception, the analysis of the strategic process requires that one take into consideration the complexity inherent in the relations between organizations that have different ways of seeing the world, or that operate according to different rationalities. These rationalities are mainly determined by the institutional and cultural contexts in which the companies evolve. The cognitive and cultural elements, as well as the normative and regulating aspects of institutions, determine the rules, standards and cultural values, which in turn shape the ways of thinking and the behavior. Institutional environments thus shape multiple legitimate rationalities. The institutional processes set the parameters of what is agreed upon as being rational or logical within a given social framework. In contrast with this unidirectional view of the link between the organizations and their environment, there are very few studies that look at the capacity of organizations to act in a proactive way and to change the institutional standards (Oliver, 1991; Kondra and Hinings, 1998).

The changing economic, cultural, political and social conditions in emerging countries constitute significant constraints for Western firms. Such conditions determine a certain way of thinking and a logic very different from those of the domestic market. When they interact, actors from Western countries and those from emerging markets find themselves in a conflict of logic and rationality.

The first logic is that of Western firms. They act on the basis of economic rationality and their managers are mentally motivated and guided by the identity referents and the cultural environment specific to the Western environments where these organizations evolve. This rationality is founded on a twin legitimacy: technical and economic. It is based on a strategic process of mobilization of specialized resources guided by an orientation toward efficiency. Until the end of the 1990s the dominant strategic design of Western companies was economic and was based on a rational and analytical approach. This economic design is well described in management, through the work of Porter (1979) on competition, of Williamson (1979) on transaction costs and of Barney (1991) on resources. Managers of Western companies generally adopt strategies strongly determined by this rationality.

The second logic relates to the behavior and strategies developed by firms from emerging countries. Such behavior and strategies reflect, above all, the institutional logic implemented in each emerging country. This is due not only to the cultural referents (Adler, 1997) specific to the companies in these countries, but also to the institutional frameworks and the organizational operating modes in which these strategies are developed. This also appears to be founded on a traditional legitimacy in which the dominant rationality rests more on community-based and clan-like social bonds than on the performance of the individual and the repercussions of his or her actions for the group. This institutional logic, implemented in various forms in emerging countries, and its consequences for the adaptive capacities of Western firms, constitute particularly favorable fields for verifying the institutionalist model.

Western companies learn to adapt their management models by imitating their predecessors. This process of mimetic isomorphism makes it likely that organizations coming from the same region will tend to behave in a similar way in foreign markets. Central to the adaptive strategic approach is the transfer of adapted knowledge whose level of advancement is close to that existing in the host country.

Applying these elements of the institutionalist approach, we put forward these research propositions:

Western companies which invest in emerging markets will display the following characteristics:

- Their strategies will be more reactive and adaptive.
- Rather than innovate in the host country, they will seek to transfer that part of their managerial and technological knowledge that is closest to that existing in local organizations.
- Their main concern will be to minimize risks and transaction costs.

Institutional change as a source of opportunity and entrepreneurship: the global approach

An alternative way of understanding institutions is under development. As Dacin *et al.* (2002) noticed, it is important to examine the extent to which organizations can influence their institutional environment. Can they do so, for instance, through political lobbying in the host country, or simply by acting as models of innovation and entrepreneurship? Peng (2001, 2003) stressed that the companies from emerging countries are not all that reactive; the more entrepreneurial among them can accelerate the process of institutional change, often with the collaboration of Western partners. For example, in India, economic liberalization measures implemented by the government since 1991 seem to be mainly due to the influence of powerful groups of entrepreneurs (Pedersen, 2000). These observations seem to confirm the hypotheses put forth by Oliver (1991) and Kondra and Hinings (1998) regarding the strategic choices of organizations and their impact on the institutional environment.

This research path has been used rather infrequently. It goes back, in fact, to the concept of entrepreneurship and its role in the transformation of the economic system (Schumpeter, 1961), and to its possible impact in emerging countries (Pedersen, 2000; Peng, 2001, 2003). Entrepreneurship, in the Schumpeterian sense, is defined as a new combination of resources on the part of individuals or organizations (Schumpeter, 1961; Baumol, 1993). These new combinations, which constitute the essence of innovation, can be observed when new products are launched, when new processes, new sources of raw materials and new management methods are introduced, or even when new markets are developed. The process is the same whatever the area of the world where the entrepreneur and the enterprise are located. By dissociating the economic system from the culture, which allows us to avoid the question of cultural differences in entrepreneurship, and by showing that innovations are easily imitated and transferred, the Schumpeterian theory already contained elements of a global approach to strategy. By being the first to invest in a business sector of an emerging country, Western companies may innovate, become more competitive and contribute to the economic development of the host country. In return, this development benefits

Western investors. Economic development can be accelerated when local partners join Western companies to form strategic alliances (Baumol, 1993). These
local partners are then regarded by Western firms as invaluable means for the
attainment of their commercial objectives. The role of local firms is then strictly
instrumental: they provide their partners with unique information regarding the
local environment.

The form of rationality that underlies this approach stems from economics.
An economic, analytical and rational type of logic is characteristic of the work
of Porter (1979), Williamson (1979) and Barney (1991). When extended to the
international field, that logic has given rise to a universalistic conception of strategy, in the sense that it does not take into account the social and cultural characteristics of the areas of the world where it is established. This economic
rationality, as defined in economics textbooks, seems to have given less consideration to the social relations that occur during trade. A global strategy that
does not require a significant degree of adaptation of management practices or
the technologies or products of Western firms (Levitt, 1983; Ohmae, 1990,
Reich, 1991) allows them to be more efficient and competitive. Within this
framework, Western companies are perceived as teaching entities, whose
objective is to transmit new knowledge and skills to partners, employees or
learning parties in the host country.

More recently, some researchers have tackled this issue of global strategy
with more nuance and have suggested that a global strategy does not preclude
some degree of adaptation to local conditions (Govindarajan and Gupta, 2001).
By adapting to the needs of the local market, global firms may increase their
market share and compete more successfully with local firms.

Taking into consideration the entrepreneurial behavior of Western firms
makes it possible to go beyond the framework of the institutionalist theory and
its one-way conception of the relation between organizations and their environment. Building on this approach, we put forward the following research
propositions:

- Western firms investing in emerging markets will prefer to adopt proactive
  and global strategies.
- They will innovate in the host country in the managerial and technological
  fields.
- Their main concern will be to assume calculated risks rather than to minimize the risks and transaction costs.

Interaction and synergy between the local and the global

Some researchers have argued that global strategies are seldom used by Western
firms. Douglas and Wind (1987) offered arguments that portray globalization as
a myth, and showed why global strategies are not feasible. The conditions under
which global strategies may work are rather limited, and pertain mainly to countries where an economic logic is prevalent. An alternative perspective within the

global framework has been offered by the work of Rugman (2001), who contends that globalization, as it is generally viewed, does not exist. His work provides extensive empirical research that suggests that most business activity is carried out in regional blocks, and that global markets are not becoming homogeneous. Moreover, it is claimed that a global integration strategy is not viable in most industries, with evidence that most multinationals which dominate the global business carry out operations at the regional level rather than the global level.

The interactionist model in sociology (Mead, 1938; Blumer, 1969) proposes a micro perspective on this global–local dilemma. It also brings an interpretative dimension that does not exist in either of the two preceding approaches. This model stresses the interpretation of the various actors involved in making a decision, rather than the objective dimensions of the strategies. From the progression of their interactions, the actors build joint strategies which result from the meaning that each one places on the behavior of the other. For example, Western organizations will try to better understand the business model of their local partners or the role of the local institutions, in order not only to adapt to them but also to better cooperate with and learn from the various local actors. The implementation of their strategies rests more on progressive and mutual comprehension than on the adaptation to the local context or the establishment of their Western business model.

The structurationist approach in sociology illustrates this interpretative approach. The theory of the structuring rests on the principle of the non-exteriority of structures. This leads our research to exclude the idea that the nature and quality of the business connections are independent of the cultural interventions that structure the interactions between the organizations and their environment. This approach, developed in the 1980s, is found mainly in the work of Giddens (1987, 1990). In our work it helps to shape the interactions between two forms of institutional logic. The purpose of this inquiry is to supplement the institutionalist and globalist perspectives, in particular when considering the structuring dimensions of the organizational contexts and the cultural referents of action that characterize the institutional logic of the host countries.

This approach is applied to the case of the interaction between the institutional logic of the host countries and the corporate economic logic of Western organizations. This interaction mobilizes two actors–partners whose actions fall under different mental configurations and strategic behavior, because they are conditioned by distinct cultural referents: the Western rationalist economic logic and the institutional and cultural logic specific to emerging countries.

The structurationist theory enables us to have a convenient and efficient methodology for understanding the strategies of the actors, such as the managers of Western corporate organizations and their partners from emerging countries. By separating the analysis of the structures from the analysis of the action, it becomes possible to evaluate the impact on the behavior and strategies implemented locally by these actors. Through this model we can thus evaluate not only the impact of these two factors (structures and actions) on the procedural dynamics of the interaction which they develop on the local level, but also the potential global repercussions that this dynamic generates. Herein lies another fundamental goal which justifies the recourse to this prospect: the relationship between the local actions of the actors and the consequences that they produce on a global level. Indeed, the recurrence of these actions, through the various experiments undertaken by Western organizations in various emerging countries, can create dynamics that the principal actors tend to reproduce, especially when the results obtained are in accordance with long-term goals. In this context it would not be too hazardous to establish a relationship between the first local actions and the range of their consequences on a broader global scale. As such, local transformation may occur as a result of the global influences, but there may also be global repercussions, arising from local institutional differences. The local and the global are thus constantly in interaction.

The synergy occurring between the companies and the Western context on the one hand, and the companies and the context of the emerging countries on the other, is also detectable in the emergent paradigm of international entrepreneurship. This paradigm is founded on the relationships and the interdependence between companies which invest abroad and their subsidiaries or partners. The flow of knowledge between these companies can become bidirectional with time. Etemad (2003) provides examples of local subsidiaries that at certain times exceeded the level of managerial or technological capabilities of their Western partners. Firms can benefit from the knowledge and capabilities developed in emerging countries. Such effects of co-learning and synergy are possible only if Western companies develop close and long-term connections with companies from the host country. Moreover, their strategies must be centered on being open to the needs of the subsidiaries or partners and on planning for the latter's progressive autonomy.

The research propositions resulting from this approach are as follows:

- Western firms will implement strategies centered on the autonomy of the subsidiaries or partners.
- Their strategies will aim at developing learning capacities in the subsidiaries or partners, in order to benefit from new joint managerial and technological capacities.

Concluding remarks

The objective of this chapter was to look beyond the conventional typologies based on product market positioning and make use of organizational theory in order to obtain a broader perspective on strategy implementation in emerging countries. We have proposed a comparison between three approaches to the issue of the relationship between Western firms and the environments of these countries. First we analyzed the institutionalist approach, centered on local constraints and the need for adaptation on the part of Western firms. Then we examined the global strategy approach, together with the Schumpeterian tradition, as the two approaches share significant similarities. Finally, we synthesized the interactionist model (i.e. local and global), as illustrated in Giddens's structurationist theory and in the emergent paradigm of international entrepreneurship.

Drawing on these three approaches, we identified three types of strategies for Western firms in emerging countries: the adaptive, the global and the interactive. Each of these types of strategies is based on a distinct rationality and on a particular view of knowledge and learning in Western organizations and their counterparts in emerging countries. Moreover, each strategy may theoretically be effective, depending upon time and space factors.

To be able to examine the impact of strategy implementation in emerging countries, the issue of empirical differentiation and measurement of the various types of strategy must first be addressed. It is of course crucial that these types must be clearly distinct from one another, not only at the theoretical but also at the empirical level. Once this crucial measurement problem is addressed, two important research questions may be raised.

The first question is: What is the evolution of these strategies? Do companies that invest in emerging countries go through phases that enable them to veer from one strategy to another, or do they rely solely on one approach? It is also important to consider the cultural and institutional differences between countries and regions, as they might determine strategy implementation. It is indeed likely that the strategies differ according to the managerial and technological level of the host country. In the case of more advanced countries, the global strategies and those centered on co-learning could be used more effectively. To capture these time and space effects, a methodology that combines qualitative and quantitative tools might be particularly useful.

The second question is: What is the impact of strategic choice on longevity and on the outcomes of direct investment? These questions have not yet been tackled in a clear way in the literature. As Beamish (1993) noted, the factors that can explain the success and stability as well as the longevity of investments in emerging countries are still poorly understood. The empirical study which will be based on this conceptual work could make it possible to advance knowledge in this field.

References

Adler, N. (1997) *International Dimensions of Organizational Behavior*, Cincinatti, OH: South-Western College Publishing.

Barney, J. (1991) "Firm resources and sustained competitive advantage," *Journal of Management*, 17: 99–120.

Baumol, W. (1993) *Entrepreneurship, Management and the Structure of Payoffs*, Cambridge, MA: MIT Press.

Beamish, P. (1993) "The characteristics of joint ventures in the People's Republic of China," *Journal of International Marketing*, 1: 29–49.

Beckert, J. (2003) "Economic sociology and embeddedness: How shall we conceptualize economic action?" *Journal of Economic Issues*, 37: 769–787.

Blumer, H. (1969) *Symbolic Interactionism*, Englewood Cliffs, NJ: Prentice Hall.

28   *C. Marcotte* et al.

Dacin, M. T., Goodstein, J. and Scott, W. R. (2002) "Institutional theory and institutional change: Introduction to the special issue," *Academy of Management Journal*, 43: 45–57.

Douglas, S. P and Wind, Y. (1987) "The myth of globalization," *Columbia Journal of World Business*, 22 (4): 19–30.

Doz, Y. (1997) "Strategic management and international business research: An empirical convergence?" in B. Toyne and N. Douglas (eds.) *International Business: An Emerging Vision*, Columbia: University of South Carolina Press.

Doz, Y. and Prahalad, C. (1993) "Managing DMNCs: A search for a new paradigm," in S. Ghoshal and D. Westney (eds.) *Organization Theory and the Multinational Corporation*, New York: St. Martin's Press.

Etemad, H. (2003) "Managing relations: The essence of international entrepreneurship," in H. Etemad and R. Wright (eds.) *Globalization and Entrepreneurship*, Cheltenham, UK: Edward Elgar.

Giddens, A. (1987) *Social Theory and Modern Sociology*, Stanford, CA: Stanford University Press.

—— (1990) *The Consequences of Modernity*, Stanford, CA: Stanford University Press.

Govindarajan, V. and Gupta, A. (2001) *The Quest for Global Dominance: Transforming Global Presence into Global Competitive Advantage*, San Francisco: Jossey-Bass.

Hench, T. (1997) "The domain of international business: Paradigms in collision," in B. Toyne and N. Douglas (eds.) *International Business: An Emerging Vision*, Columbia: University of South Carolina Press.

Hoskisson, R., Eden, L., Lau, C. and Wright, M. (2000) "Strategy in emerging economies," *Academy of Management Journal*, 43: 249–267.

Kondra, A. and Hinings, C. R. (1998) "Organizational diversity and change in institutional theory," *Organization Studies*, 19 (5): 743–767.

Levitt, T. (1983) "The globalization of markets," *Harvard Business Review*, May–June: 92–102.

Mead, G. H. (1938) *The Philosophy of the Act*, Chicago: University of Chicago Press.

Ministère des Affaires étrangères et du Commerce international (MAECI) (2003) Gouvernement du Canada. Online, available at: www.dfait-maeci.gc.ca.

Ohmae, K. (1990) *The Borderless World: Power and Strategy in the Interlinked Economy*, New York: Free Press.

Oliver, C. (1991) "Strategic responses to institutional processes," *Academy of Management Review*, 16 (1): 145–179.

Pedersen, J. D. (2000) "Explaining economic liberalization in India: State and society perspectives," *World Development*, 28 (2): 265–282.

Peng, M. (2001) "How do entrepreneurs create wealth in transition economies?" *Academy of Management Executive*, 15: 95–112.

—— (2003) "Institutional transitions and strategic choices," *Academy of Management Review*, 28: 275–296.

Porter, M. (1979) "How competitive forces shape strategy," *Harvard Business Review*, March–April: 137–145.

Prahalad, C. and Hamel, G. (1990) "The core competence of the corporation," *Harvard Business Review*, May–June: 79–91.

Ray, S. (2003) "Strategic adaptation of firms during economic liberalization: Emerging issues and a research agenda," *International Journal of Management*, 20: 271–286.

Reich, R. B. (1991) *The Work of Nations*, New York: Alfred Knopf.

Rugman, A. and Hodgetts, R. (2001) "The end of global strategy," *European Management Journal*, 19 (4): 333–343.

Schumpeter, J. (1961) *The Theory of Economic Development*, New York: Oxford University Press.

Scott, R. S. (2001) *Institutions and Organizations*, 2nd edn., Thousand Oaks, CA: Sage.

Spender, J. (1996) "Making knowledge the basis of a dynamic theory of the firm," *Strategic Management Journal*, 17: 45–62.

Statistics Canada (2004) "International investment position, Canadian direct investment abroad and foreign direct investment in Canada," CANSIM Table 376-0051. Online, available at: www.statcan.gc.ca/pub.

Westney, D. (1993) "Institutionalization theory and the multinational corporation," in S. Ghoshal and D. Westney (eds.) *Organization Theory and the Multinational Corporation*, New York: St. Martin's Press.

Williamson, O. (1979) "Transaction-cost economics: The governance of contractual relations," *Journal of Law and Economics*, 22 (2): 233–261.

Part II
Theoretical considerations

3 West meets Southeast

A cultural fit of goal setting theory to the Filipino workforce

Pamela Lirio

Introduction

Walang mahirap na gawa pag dinaan sa tiyaga.[1]
No undertaking is difficult if pursued with perseverance.

The Philippines comprises over 7,000 islands in Southeast Asia and has a burgeoning population of eighty-nine million people (National Statistics Office, 2007). Filipino culture is a blend of the East and the West, with influences coming from Malay, Chinese and Arab settlers as well as periods of Spanish and American colonization (Roces and Roces, 2002). The Philippines is viewed economically as a developing country. A sizeable percentage of the Filipino workforce is highly skilled, owing to a long-standing emphasis on education and English instruction in the school system (Olchondra, 2008).

Drawing upon its educated workforce and low labor costs, the Philippines has become the second largest country of business process outsourcing (BPO) behind India (Hookway and Cuneta, 2009; Magtibay-Ramos *et al.*, 2008). In only a few short years, BPO revenue in the Philippines has tripled from approximately $2 billion in 2005 to roughly $6 billion as of 2008 (Flores, 2009; Magtibay-Ramos *et al.*, 2008). The Business Processing Association of the Philippines (BPAP) expects the industry to expand to $12 billion and roughly one million workers by 2011 (Flores, 2009; Magtibay-Ramos *et al.*, 2008). Approximately 85 percent of the BPO business in the Philippines is in banking (typically call centers) and comes mainly from US multinationals. As of August 2009 the Philippines had approximately 946 call centers within and around Metro Manila (Call Center Directory, 2009), and more expansion by Western multinationals is expected and encouraged by the Filipino government (Magtibay-Ramos *et al.*, 2008).

Despite the increasing importance of the Philippines in the global economy, there is little management scholarship focused on the Philippines. In particular, there is a paucity of research examining Filipino culture and managing and developing the Filipino workforce. One explanation for this could be the assumption that the American introduction of the English language in the society has sensitized Filipinos to adopt Western ways (Andres, 1981; Church, 1987;

Roces and Roces, 2002). As a result, it might be taken for granted that Western (largely American) management theories are simply transferable as is – what Filipino management scholar Andres critiqued as "the transplant syndrome." He cautioned that "the values and aspirations of those governing, strategized by their unique managerial processes, [could] eventually become the norms of thought and behavior of the governed" (1981: 154–155). Yet while business and governmental organizations in the Philippines may resemble American structures, the informal and unspoken behavioral conventions still remain uniquely Filipino (Gupta and Kleiner, 2001).

Another explanation for the lack of studies focusing on the Philippines could be the international management field's preoccupation with Asian management practices in Japan and China over the past twenty years. While these two countries have represented global economic opportunities, they may have also seemed to present more of a cultural challenge to Americans and other Westerners than the Philippines. In a recent study on East–West differences in employee motivation examining China (Hong Kong) and the United States, Canada and Finland, Chiang and Birtch (2007) found the Western respondents attributing internal factors to successful performance, in contrast with the Chinese mix of internal and external factors. However, the authors point out that while Hong Kong has been widely used as a representative sample for Asia, the inclusion of other cultures is needed to truly represent the Asian context.

Increasingly, scholars are questioning the implementation of Western management theories in developing countries (Earley, 1997; Galang, 2004; Hafsi and Farashahi, 2005; Kiggundu *et al.*, 1983), and conceptualizing culturally fit or local models (Andres, 1981; Mendonça, and Kanungo, 1993). In their review of 170 management articles, Hafsi and Farashahi discovered "widespread applicability of western-based general management concepts and organizational theories to developing countries" (2005: 505). Yet Hafsi and Farashahi (2005) support broadening the scope of theoretical frameworks past Western boundaries, pointing out that today's organizational scholarship is evolving from all locales, including developing country contexts.

Galang (2004) found that many of the human resource management practices in US and Canadian corporations in her study were also being implemented in the Philippines. However, the outcomes varied somewhat among the Western (US and Canadian) organizations as compared with the Filipino organizations. Andres (1981) has asserted from early on that Western management models can be effective in the Philippines but ought to be modified for Filipino culture. In particular, he viewed a process-based approach, such as a management by objectives model, as potentially successful there.

So, how might a Western manager in a multinational enterprise effectively motivate his or her workforce in the Philippines? Incorporating local norms into management theory respects the developing economy's natural work rhythms; yet juxtaposing them with Western dimensions might further inform non-Filipino managers through an accessible blend of the local and global. In taking this approach, I will first present salient themes in the literature on Filipino values and behavior, closely followed by an overview of Hofstede's (1980, 2001) oft-cited cultural dimensions. As the Filipino norms are less widely known, I present them first and draw attention to them throughout the remainder of the chapter. Then I review goal setting theory and propose a culturally fit model for the Filipino context based on Locke and Latham's (1984) and Kanungo's (1986) models of goal setting theory.

Shared meanings among Filipinos

Andres says, "Filipino values ... can be a help or hindrance to productivity depending on how they are understood and practiced" (1981: 63). For non-Filipinos in MNEs to manage effectively, it is important for them to understand that Filipinos act from a personalized stance. The essence of a Filipino is based on relationships, feelings and personal honor or dignity (Gupta and Kleiner, 2001). Within Filipino culture there are specific values known as *barangay, hiya, amor proprio* and *utang na loob*.[2] These terms are inherently understood and recognized as concepts that guide Filipinos toward the establishing of productive working relationships in the workplace.

Filipino cultural values

Barangay

The term *barangay* encompasses the esteemed value of affiliation through family and kinship among Filipinos. Filipinos demonstrate the greatest loyalty and trust to their own immediate family; however, expressions of loyalty and debt can extend to other kin farther outside of one's immediate circle. For example, one's identity is often informed by one's *barangay* affiliation. Therefore, those outside of the *barangay* are treated on the basis of a different set of values according to the situation (Roces and Roces, 2002). However, bonds of ritual kinship can be formed with acquaintances through the system of *compadrazco*, or godparent-hood, where the idea is to extend one's network in the hope of securing future favors, employment or small gifts for the person sponsored (Roces and Roces, 2002).

Hiya *and* amor proprio

The combination of the two concepts of *hiya* and *amor proprio* in Filipino culture is crucial to respecting others and safeguarding against personal affront (Andres, 1981). *Hiya* and *amor proprio* represent the notion of "saving face," often described as characteristic of other Asian cultures (Moran *et al.*, 2007; Roces and Roces, 2002). Social propriety is maintained among Filipinos through the expression of *hiya*, meaning a sense of shame. It controls and motivates an individual's behavior so as to avoid a "universal social sanction" or a failure to live up to society's standards (Roces and Roces, 2002). Reinforcing this concept is the notion in Filipino society of *amor proprio*, or self-esteem (literally, "love of oneself"). Building of one's self-esteem is essential in Filipino society, such that personally affronting someone, or damaging his *amor proprio*, invites intense conflict. Filipinos often seek to avoid conflict, which is possible through the interaction of *hiya*. Roces and Roces say, "[when] a Filipino hesitates to bring up a problem,... *hiya* is in operation. Filipinos feel uneasy if they are instrumental in making waves, rocking the boat, and exposing someone's volatile *amor proprio* to injury" (2002: 36–37).

Utang na loob

Another salient characteristic of the Filipino personality involves reciprocity – the expression of *utang na loob*, or a debt of gratitude. The word *utang* translates as "debt" in English, with *loob* literally meaning "interior" and connoting a sense of affecting one's being (Mataragnon, 1988). Therefore, the concept of *utang na loob* encompasses the idea of feeling indebted to someone for a favor rendered, which one should endeavor to repay or for which one displays extreme respect and acknowledgment. Moreover, it can also manifest itself as something that can never really be repaid, such as a debt of gratitude to one's parents for providing opportunities in life. The *utang na loob* fosters a sense of loyalty among one's social circle or group, as it is implicitly understood among Filipinos that they may "remain indebted for a favor for a long period of time, perhaps several generations" (Moran *et al.*, 2007: 464).

These values can in turn manifest themselves in the following behaviors: *pakikiramdam, pakikisama*, using euphemisms and go-betweens, *bahala na*, the *mañana* habit and *ningas kugon*. As will be shown in what follows, the first four terms relate to Filipino interpersonal behavior, whereas the remaining two can be said to express Filipino behavior relative to locus of control and task completion.

Filipino cultural behavior

Pakikiramdam

The term *pakikiramdam* in Filipino literally means "politely requesting the act of feeling." It can be described as considering another's feelings in social interactions (Mataragnon, 1988). Respecting the delicate balance between one's *hiya* (shame) and *amor proprio* (self-esteem) guides Filipinos to display sensitivity when dealing with another person. It serves as a coping mechanism in Filipino society. Similar to the Western view of etiquette, *pakikiramdam* is not written down, but rather is an intuitive code of ethics (or etiquette). Someone who demonstrates *pakikiramdam* well is said to be thoughtful and caring (Mataragnon, 1988). For example, a paternalistic managerial style is seen as a positive demonstration of *pakikiramdam*. *Pakikiramdam* is believed to be essential to achieving the following behavior of *pakikisama*.

Pakikisama

Pakikisama is defined as giving in or following the lead of others, and as such is the main element of the theory described by Lynch as smooth interpersonal relations (SIR), or "a facility of getting along with others in such a way as to avoid outward signs of conflict" (1973: 10). When Filipinos yield their own desires to the will of the group, they avoid challenging the *hiya–amor proprio* of others and help maintain group harmony. *Pakikisama* is a behavior that is taught from an early age in one's family or *barangay* and can be very useful when carried over to the Filipino workplace. For example, similar to the notion of "emotional intelligence," employees who demonstrate a facility with *pakikisama* are seen as bringing more to their work than purely job-related skills and are often valued over employees with no understanding of *pakikisama* (Roces and Roces, 2002).

Euphemisms and go-betweens

The use of euphemisms and go-betweens complements Lynch's (1973) idea of SIR. Because Filipinos value *hiya–amor proprio* (saving face) and *pakikisama* (reticence toward direct confrontation), they will prefer to communicate in a more indirect style, using euphemisms to cloak a potentially negative message. Even constructive criticism is best prefaced with disclaimers such as "This is just my personal opinion, but it seems to me that…" (Roces and Roces, 2002). Another form of euphemistic expression occurs when Filipinos use light-hearted teasing to criticize.

A go-between, or intermediary, is often used to maintain smooth interpersonal relations among Filipinos. Because of their reluctance to say "no" upfront, Filipinos will often use a go-between to settle a potentially embarrassing or adversarial situation. Moreover, the use of a go-between has been said to be particularly beneficial to a non-Filipino manager when dealing with Filipino employees in order to avoid misunderstandings (Andres, 1981; Roces and Roces, 2002).

Bahala na

The expression *bahala na* in Filipino literally means "leave it to God." Figuratively, it is the Filipino version of fatalism (Roces and Roces, 2002). Andres (1981) is critical of this expression of behavior in saying that

> it harnesses one's behavior to a submissiveness that eats up one's sense of responsibility and personal independence … [and] provides one with a false sense of self-confidence to proceed with an unsound action in the belief that somehow one will manage to get by

(1981: 132)

However, it could also be interpreted more neutrally to embody flexibility in the face of adverse, uncontrollable events in the environment (Andres, 1981; Church, 1987).

Mañana *habit and* ningas kugon

A *mañana* habit, or tendency toward procrastination, can pervade Filipino society. Filipinos may have a tendency to put things off as much as possible, seldom completing things on time despite deadlines (Andres, 1981; Moran *et al.*, 2007). Related to this is the concept known as "Filipino time." "Filipino time" typically means delays vis-à-vis "American time," because time to a Filipino is a fluid concept rather than a fixed one with clear beginning and ending points (Andres, 1981; Church, 1987; Moran *et al.*, 2007; Roces and Roces, 2002). In cases where Filipinos can no longer delay an endeavor and are faced with beginning a project, there is a tendency to stop what they are doing mid-way. This is described as *ningas kugon*. It manifests itself as an expression of enthusiasm at the start of a project, which steadily progresses to a loss of interest, such that matters may never really come to fruition (Andres, 1981; Church, 1987).

Hofstede on Philippine national culture

Hofstede's (1980, 2001) *Culture's Consequences* lays out findings from an extensive study of organizational work values among 116,000 IBM employees within forty countries. Initially he presented four dimensions of culture[3] in his 1980 book; a fifth appears in the revised 2001 edition. As this work is a widely accepted body of empirical research in the international management field, his five major cultural dimensions – power distance, individualism versus collectivism, uncertainty avoidance, masculinity versus femininity and long- versus short-term orientation – are presented in this section in relation to the Philippines. A discussion of the Filipino norms will be presented in each section in contrast to the Hofstede (1980, 2001) dimensions.

Power distance

The dimension power distance depicts the inequality found among members in a society and the degree to which status and authority are respected and maintained. Hofstede (1980, 2001) measured the relationship between managers and employees – particularly, whether employees would likely question or defer to their managers. The Power Distance Index (PDI) for the Philippines was found to be the highest of all forty countries in the study (94 versus a mean of 51). Hofstede (1980, 2001) suggests that the Philippines' status as a former colony is a salient explanation for this appearance of a large power distance. The PDI is particularly high because the Philippines was a Spanish (Latin-based) colony for over three hundred years, and the influence of authoritative Roman rule was passed on through figureheads. This notion is corroborated in many visible aspects of Filipino society. There is a strong respect for authority, which is learned initially within the family or *barangay*. Filipinos often look to superiors for support and decision making, and accept their orders or advice with less hesitation than Americans (Andres, 1981; Roces and Roces, 2002).

Individualism versus collectivism

The second dimension, individualism versus collectivism, reflects the way an individual situates him- or herself relative to the collective in a society – that is, placing importance on family, kinship ties and other group affiliations versus valuing independence and inner-directed efforts. The Individualism Index[4] (IDV) presents a composite of workplace cultural values such as the employee's emotional relationship with the company, importance of job security, and outlook on personal time and life goals. In the Philippines there is a relatively low IDV (32 versus a mean of 51), indicative of a typically collectivistic society. As reflected in the discussion on the value of the *barangay* and the importance placed on *pakikisama*, this dimension appears supported by the Filipino literature.

Uncertainty avoidance

The Uncertainty Avoidance Index (UAI) in the study measures the amount of uncertainty about the future certain cultures can handle. In organizations this dimension manifests in the presence or absence of decision making and strategic planning in light of uncertainty. The Philippines shows a relatively low UAI (44 versus a mean of 64), similar to the United States (which has a UAI of 46). Hofstede (1980, 2001) points out that religion typically interacts with this dimension, such that predominantly Catholic countries (such as the Philippines) generally show higher UAIs. However, the Philippines does not follow this pattern; therefore, he says, other forces must be in play. The concept of *bahala na*, if perceived as fatalistic, may also seem to lead to a higher UAI, or it could be synonymous with one of Hofstede's (1980, 2001) expressions of low UAI: "the uncertainty inherent in life is more easily accepted and each day is taken as it comes" (1980: 140). Hofstede (1980, 2001) also describes low UAIs as appearing typically among highly educated people and those from a higher social stratum, a category into which the majority of his sample in the Philippines office might fit. Furthermore, the similar scoring to the US respondents could be indicative of the strong influence of American culture in the Philippines.

Masculinity versus femininity

Unlike most other, collectivistic, Asian nations, the Philippines is more similar to individualistic cultures on the fourth dimension, masculinity versus femininity. Hofstede (1980, 2001) describes this dimension as reflective of the distribution of sex roles in a society. High on Hofstede's Masculinity Index (MAS) are countries such as the United States, where both men and women in the society are encouraged to achieve outside of the home, and money and possessions are valued. In a low-MAS environment, personal relationships are most important, and caring and nurturing are highly regarded. Along this dimension the Philippines ranks very close to the United States (which has a MAS of 62), with a moderately high MAS (64 versus a mean of 51). Like the Uncertainty Avoidance dimension, this scoring may mirror that of the United States as a result of the long-standing American presence in the country. Moreover, as *amor proprio* (self-esteem) shows, Filipinos may use career achievement as a measure of self-worth. However, some descriptions of this dimension do not seem to reflect the Filipino experience. The expression of *pakikiramdam* and *pakikisama* seem more demonstrative of low-MAS cultures. Also, the deep loyalty of *utang na loob* behavior seems more characteristic of Hofstede's (1980, 2001) definition of less "masculine" cultures.

Long- versus short-term orientation

This final dimension, long- versus short-term orientation (LTO), relates to a society's time horizon (i.e. future versus past/present orientation) and deferment of gratification. Hofstede (2001) adapted this dimension from Bond and colleagues' work (1987) examining East–West value differences in the Chinese Value Survey. In long-term-oriented countries, such as Eastern Asian nations, persistence, thrift and having a sense of shame are characteristic (future orientation), while in short-term-oriented countries, values include protecting one's face, respecting tradition and the reciprocation of favors and gifts (past/present orientation). Along this dimension the Philippines ranks as one of the lowest of the twenty-three countries in the study, with an LTO of 19. The United States scores higher, with an LTO of 29. Hofstede (2001) stated that less economically developed countries in the study ranked the lowest, so the Philippines, despite being an Asian nation, presented as an outlier on this dimension. The Filipino cultural framing, however, may better elucidate the unexpected scoring on this dimension. Filipino values of *hiya–amor proprio* (saving face) and *utang na loob* (repaying debts) both mirror Hofstede's (2001) short-term orientation characteristics, as do the Filipino behaviors of *pakikiramdam* (social sensitivity) and *pakikisama* (smooth interpersonal relations). The particular *ningas kugon* (lack of follow-through) stance speaks more to a short-term orientation than to a long-term one where activities are pursued with future rewards in mind.

While Hofstede's (1980, 2001) study has provided the international management field with a parsimonious framing for interpreting culture and representing culture as a variable in cross-national studies, it has also received its share of criticism in recent years (Ailon, 2008; Earley, 2006; Javidan *et al.*, 2006; McSweeney, 2002). Interestingly, Ailon (2008) reexamines Hofstede's (1980, 2001) dimensions, essentially culturally fitting his framework to expose intrinsic Western country biases (those of Hofstede and the international management field as a whole) in forcing responses from non-Westerners into West-dominant framing. She highlights the need for more examination of the methodology executed in international research and for it to be reflective of other cultural mindsets beyond predominantly Western ones. Nonetheless, because of the scope of the countries covered and the widespread familiarity with the dimensions, the Hofstede (1980, 2001) framework continues to be widely used by researchers.[5]

Taking stock of both these local and global cultural frameworks, how does a non-Filipino manager in a multinational enterprise motivate the Filipino work-force effectively? To begin addressing this question, in the following section I present an overview of the motivational approach known as "goal setting".

An overview of goal setting theory

Goal setting theory and well-known management practices such as management by objectives (MBO) are approaches to motivating a workforce. Research on the theory and application of goal setting has proliferated over the years, resulting in the widespread adoption of its practice in Western organizational settings. How best to implement goal setting theory in the workplace is discussed in what follows.

Aims of goal setting theory

Goals provide direction to an organization, enabling it to accomplish its business mission. The employees are the means to accomplishing these goals. Locke (1968) formulated and tested goal setting theory as a motivational technique. He believed that the needs and values of an individual, along with his or her know-ledge, determine a goal. The goal in turn represents the individual's intention for choosing to satisfy needs. The basic tenets of goal setting theory are presented in Figure 3.1.

In order for goals to lead to improved performance, Locke (1968) found that they must be both difficult and specific. Yet while a goal must be difficult, the employee should not perceive it as beyond his or capability.[6] Specific goals should be quantified in terms of the performance outcome.

Setting goals initially

Before employees begin goal-directed efforts, several aspects of goal determina-tion should take place first, such as choosing the type and content of the goal, setting the goal, and choosing the means of measuring it (Erez, 1986; Erez and Earley, 1987; Kanungo and Mendonça, 1997; Locke and Latham, 1984). Types of goals are either performance based or end result based; the former should be chosen in cases where environmental constraints may interfere with goal achievement, whereas the latter should be chosen for completing simple tasks within the employee's control. Choosing correctly will assist in goal acceptance and commitment (as discussed in what follows). As for the content of the goals, they should include behaviors critical to achieving the job objectives if perform-ance based, or be based on the employee's past experience if end result based. Overall, if the potential for several environmental constraints exists, performance-based goals are better than end-based goals.

Erez (1986) and Erez and Earley (1987) introduced the importance of employee participation in goal setting and performance. These studies showed that participative goal setting could promote ownership of the goals, particularly

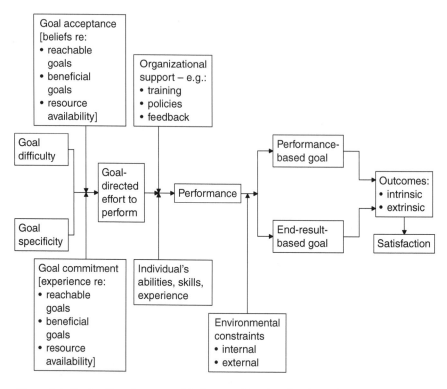

Figure 3.1 Goal setting theory model: (source: Based on Locke and Latham (1964) and Kanungo (1986)).

when employees value participation and the goals set are reasonably difficult. The effectiveness of assigned goals will depend on employees' trust in a manager to set fair and reasonable goals (Kanungo and Mendonça, 1997). Measurement of goals is based on either individual or group performance. In the case of work teams, goals could be set on the basis of both individual and overall team contributions (ibid.).

Toward goal attainment

Once goals are determined, goal acceptance and goal commitment moderate the goal-directed effort (Kanungo and Mendonça, 1997; Locke and Latham, 1984). Goal acceptance is highly contingent upon the employee's perception that goals are *reachable* (the employee has the ability) and *beneficial* (the goals will lead to valued outcomes), and that his or her manager will provide the necessary *resources* to achieve the goal (Kanungo and Mendonça, 1997). Goal commitment is similarly composed; however, it depends on the employee's actual experiences during the goal-directed effort. It is imperative that a manager regularly monitors an employee's goal commitment, as it can change readily (ibid.).

When employees begin their goal-directed efforts, it is only useful if they have the appropriate knowledge, skills and experience to perform well. If they do not possess this ability, they will need to acquire it first. In addition, proper organizational support consisting of employee training and skill development, policies regarding resource allocation, and regular and accurate feedback mechanisms are important (Locke and Latham, 1984). If employees do not have any or all of these factors, particularly feedback, their efforts will most likely wane. While the employees are performing the goal-directed behavior, environmental constraints – internal and external – can affect final goal attainment (Kanungo and Mendonça, 1997). Internal constraints are concerned with material, technological and human resources, whereas external constraints consist of market conditions, technological changes and legal and fiscal regulations. The greater the constraints in the environment, the less likely employees are to perform satisfactorily.

Outcomes of goal setting

Regarding outcomes, the intrinsic rewards can take the form of feedback from accomplishment while performing, and experience of having finished or achieved the goal. Extrinsic rewards can be such things as money or a promotion (Kanungo and Mendonça, 1997). Depending on whether employees have performance-based goals or end-result-based goals, outcomes will vary when a goal is achieved, partially achieved or not achieved at all. For performance-based goals, employees can achieve both types of intrinsic rewards only if the goal is achieved. If it is partially achieved, only feedback through the process is obtained. Extrinsic rewards would be received upon goal attainment, but rewards might also be given for partial achievement. The case of end-result-based goals is similar to that of performance-based results; however, when the productivity goal is not entirely achieved, some intrinsic rewards can still be obtained (e.g. feedback as one performs behaviors).

Finally, satisfaction depends upon employee perception of the equity of the outcomes (Kanungo and Mendonça, 1997: 87). If employees feel that they should have received a reward for partial achievement because there were factors hindering completion, they may perceive inequity and will not be satisfied.

Goal setting theory in the Philippine context: proposing a culturally fit model

The following interpretation of implementing goal setting theory in the Philippines aims to be inclusive – that is, addressing how best to bridge Western and Filipino cultural norms in order for managers and employees to smoothly achieve organizational goals together. I continue the discussion of goal setting theory from the previous section, proposing a culturally fit model with an understanding of Filipino culture.

Goal determination: assigned versus participative goals

Because of the high respect for authority, as demonstrated through Hofstede's (1980, 2001) high PDI score for the Philippines, assigned goals will be readily accepted by Filipino employees. Also, because of their high regard for family and *barangay* (i.e. their collectivist nature), Filipinos will be more comfortable with following a leader's guidance (Andres, 1981; Earley, 1997; Hofstede, 1980, 2001). Filipinos look to managers as people in positions of expertise; they regard their managers, particularly Western managers, as possessing a more advanced knowledge base. However, they also expect benevolence in their leaders, as evidenced in their appreciation for a paternalistic leadership style (Adler, 2008; Andres, 1981; Church, 1987). Trust in one's manager is key among Filipinos. If employees observe genuine *pakikiramdam* from their manager's actions, they will trust the manager to set goals for them. Participation in goal setting could follow later, as the manager–employee relationship strengthens and the employee gains confidence in the process.

Effectively measuring and evaluating goals for a Filipino workforce presents more challenge. Although Filipinos are collectivistic, they also value pride in accomplishments, as evidenced by the delicate *hiya–amor proprio* balance. To address both of these somewhat contradictory traits, organizing employees and their respective tasks into management-directed work groups might prove useful. As was shown by Kanungo and Mendonça (1997), the subsequent measurement of the goals could be based on group performance, with individual contribution readily taken into account. This would promote SIR or *pakikisama* in the workforce without neglecting the Filipino *amor proprio*.

Goal determination: performance versus end-result goals

In order to motivate a Filipino workforce effectively, goals should be perceived as possible to attain. As previously pointed out, it is best to set performance-based goals when elements beyond the employee's control can interfere with goal achievement. Behaviors such as *ningas kugon* and the associated *mañana* habit could make it difficult for Filipino employees to reach goals based only on productivity results. Moreover, they could perceive the pursuit of the set outcomes to be futile and potentially lapse into a *bahala na* (fatalistic) stance as a coping mechanism. Performance-based goals might appear more within employee control, particularly if set with an awareness of the local performance standard.

Goal determination: difficulty and specificity

As Locke (1968) determined, goals should be both difficult and specific to be effective in motivating employees. Hofstede's (1980, 2001) low UAI rating suggests that Filipinos would appreciate a degree of difficulty or challenge in their work. Andres (1981) corroborates this as well, saying that "in the Philippine industries, a good managerial leader will ... structure work assignments so that the employee will find them at least interesting – and if possible, challenging" (p. 81). It is critical that the manager demonstrates *pakikiramdam* in determining the difficulty of a goal, so that employees do not risk extreme failure, thereby losing face and triggering their *hiya–amor proprio*.

When determining the specificity of goals, time factors and deadlines are critical issues. Environmental constraints such as traffic jams, inclement weather in the rainy season and "brown-outs" (power shortages) are common occurrences in the Philippines. In addition, planning should allow for the expressions of *bahala na*, the *mañana* habit and *ningas kugon*, and then clearly define whether deadlines are based on an informal understanding of Filipino or American time (Andres, 1981; Church, 1987; Roces and Roces, 2002).

Moderator of goal-directed effort: goal acceptance

Both goal acceptance and goal commitment affect goal-directed effort, as shown in Figure 3.1. Filipino culture presents the non-Filipino manager with several means of garnering and retaining both acceptance and commitment throughout a project. As was illustrated previously, in the discussion on setting performance-based goals, Filipino employees will be inclined to accept a goal if they perceive it as within their reach to perform. Moreover, if they believe it will lead to valued outcomes such as monetary rewards, status and/or social acceptance, again the goal will tend to be accepted. Possibly the most important factor in goal acceptance for Filipino employees, however, will be the manager's role in making available the resources necessary for them to succeed (Andres, 1981). When a manager provides for employees, it is perceived as showing paternalism and *pakikiramdam* toward the workforce. The trust fostered within the employees for their manager will likely facilitate goal acceptance. Another means is also available to the manager in the form of a trusted go-between; however, this is mainly used in situations of conflict mediation rather than positive persuasion (Andres, 1981; Roces and Roces, 2002).

Moderator of goal-directed effort: goal commitment

In order to move beyond goal acceptance to goal commitment in a Filipino work environment, it is best to appeal to a Filipino's sense of loyalty and debt in the form of *utang na loob*. For example, if the employees actually experience the manager providing the necessary resources for them to achieve the goal, they may feel a need to reciprocate the manager's *pakikiramdam* (perceived generosity and thoughtfulness). If the outcome of the goal is extremely salient to the employees or their families, this may trigger the feeling of *utang na loob*. When a manager taps into this level of loyalty, it can almost on its own serve to motivate employees toward the goal, as they attempt to respond to the manager's generosity (Andres, 1981). Moreover, social belonging is another significant outcome that can serve to influence goal commitment among Filipinos. This is evidenced by the value of the *barangay*, *pakikisama* and SIR (Andres, 1981; Lynch, 1973; Roces and Roces, 2002).

Moderators of performance

Performance is affected by both the individual abilities of employees and the organizational support received. As previously seen, employees should have the appropriate knowledge, skills and experience to achieve a goal. The manager in a Filipino work environment will have a good deal of influence in assessing which employees could handle which tasks. However, as Andres points out, "the work of the bottom level employee is dependent on the organizational setup but generally, it involves the utilization of his physical skills and abilities. He is mainly responsible for his own contribution" (1981: 45). If Filipino employees feel inferior in performing a task, this may trigger feelings of inferiority and their *hiya–amor proprio*.

If we take this into account, we can suggest that Filipino employees will be willing to acquire any skills they do not possess, through training if necessary. Filipinos place a high value on education and learning, as demonstrated by their high MAS score and influence from the American education system introduced in the country (Andres, 1981; Church, 1988; Hofstede, 1980, 2001). Because of the acceptance and expectation of a paternalistic leadership style, Filipino employees will expect that organizational support in the form of adequate training and skill development will be provided. Also, they will come to expect regular feedback presented in a considerate manner. What might seem "micromanaging" to an American employee is more likely to be perceived by Filipinos as caring and attentive management (Adler, 2008; Andres, 1981). Therefore, despite the delicate balance of one's *hiya–amor proprio*, "positive criticism is definitely acceptable to Filipino employees as long as it is done in a euphemistic and indirect way" (Andres, 1981: 49).

Moderators of goal attainment

Actually attaining the goal is dependent largely on environmental constraints, which can take the form of either internal or external factors. As we have seen, such factors as Filipino perceptions of time and locus of control can affect the composition of the goal. More importantly, however, it can affect the actual performance leading to successful goal attainment. Filipino employees will trust that the manager will plan for these factors, as well as be flexible in adjusting the goal or determining whether the goal is properly attained. This is corroborated by Andres when he says that "perhaps the major motivational factor of these employees is not monetary; perhaps it is related to their work environment or to the way they are treated by their superiors" (1981: 60).

Outcomes and satisfaction of goal setting

Filipino employees will be responsive to both intrinsic and extrinsic rewards. As their *amor proprio* is highly valued, the attainment of intrinsic rewards from performance-based goals will be a welcome outcome. Moreover, extrinsic rewards such as money and promotion can satisfy the *amor proprio* value as well as the Filipino's desire for social mobility (Andres, 1981). However, it is suggested that at least some rewards be given for partial goal attainment. Filipino employees will be able to save face and perhaps find this motivating. As seen, sustained motivation in a task or project can sometimes be a challenge because of the *mañana* habit and *ningas kugon*, therefore the assurance of some form of reward may prove motivating.

In order for Filipino employees to be satisfied with their outcomes, they will need to perceive a sense of equity (Andres, 1981; Earley, 1997). Because of their need for achievement, Filipinos will want to feel properly compensated for their performance. This is typical of countries displaying high masculinity (achievement orientation) and either a high or a low power differential (Earley, 1997; Hofstede, 1980, 2001). In order to avoid negative interpersonal relations in the workplace, it is suggested that objective reward systems be established and the rewards discussed with each employee personally, one on one. This will help maintain the SIR between employees – not stirring up a negative *hiya–amor proprio* – while still playing to the esteem needs of each individual employee.

Conclusion

With several desirable cultural characteristics and structural systems in place, the Philippines attracts global business from Western multinationals, and in particular the business process outsourcing industry (Magtibay-Ramos *et al.*, 2008; Olchondra, 2008). We see that the Filipino culture presents a unique blend of Western and Southeast Asian norms. Overall, research has only just begun to scratch the surface in exploring this increasingly important pool of talent in global business today. While business processes may be becoming more global, the human element of business remains deeply rooted in culture. In this chapter I have suggested a culturally appropriate model of goal setting theory in relation to the Filipino workforce as one way to bridge the differences between Southeast and West.

With global business expanding and talent shifting worldwide, more awareness of other models and management styles should naturally emerge. The widespread use of technologies not only is expanding business opportunities globally but also can bridge management scholarship and learning across distant locales. Theoretical approaches can and should be drawn out from developing economies and contribute to management scholarship generally (Ailon, 2008; Hafsi and Farashahi, 2005). To move the international management field farther calls for opening access to management ideas from developing countries and encouraging collaboration between scholars from developing and developed countries. However, it is possible, going forward, that management theories may no longer be strictly bound by geographical or organizational boundaries (Hafsi and Farashahi, 2005), or by existing notions of cultural relativism (Ailon, 2008).

It would be insightful to test management models using Filipino constructs; it is not known to what extent Filipino constructs have been tested in a management setting in multinational corporations. Further, it might be useful to survey in Filipino rather than English. For example, Watkins and Gerong (1997) felt that the Filipino college students in their study of self-concept may have "culturally accommodated" their answers to reflect American values when responding in English. In fact, their responses revealed more identification with a global identity category than with traditional Filipino roles. As the younger generations in other countries are displaying work-related and personal values divergent from those of previous generations (Egri and Ralston, 2004; Lirio, 2008), it would be interesting to see whether similar patterns are developing in the Philippines and how they may be affecting the workplace there. Much of the current population is young, and employees typically working in call centers in the Philippines are from the younger generations (Comerford, 2005; Hookway and Cuneta, 2009).

The Philippines seeks to continue to prosper economically, largely by increasing its revenue from BPO services (Olchondra, 2008) and expanding into KPO (knowledge process outsourcing) in the future (Magtibay-Ramos *et al.*, 2008). As we have seen, Western cultural dimensions do not neatly map onto the Filipino culture, and knowledge of local values and behaviors has largely remained contained in the Philippines (Andres, 1981; Gupta and Kleiner, 2001). Examining the culture through both local and global lenses would allow non-Filipino managers and scholars to better examine management theory for the Filipino context. As global business continues to grow in the Philippines, perhaps new management research will emerge in this setting as well.

Notes

An earlier version of this work was presented at a joint conference of the International Federation of Scholarly Associations of Management and the Administrative Sciences Association of Canada (ASAC-IFSAM), Montréal, Québec, August 2000.

1 A traditional Filipino *salawikain* (proverb): www.fact-archive.com/quotes/Filipino_proverbs#W.
2 Filipino and English are official languages of the Philippines. Filipino terms are presented in italics.
3 Hofstede (1980, 2001) uses the nation-state to represent culture.
4 The indices related to the dimensions of *individualism versus collectivism*, *masculinity versus femininity* and *long- versus short-term orientation* are represented by only the first term in the dimension title (e.g. IDV).
5 No similar large-scale studies on culture had existed until House and colleagues (2004) conducted the "Global Leadership and Organizational Behavior Effectiveness" project. See Lirio (2009) for an overview of the GLOBE project and results.
6 An exception was found with those employees who are high on need for achievement. They can set much more challenging goals for themselves (Kanungo and Mendonça, 1997: 82).

References

Adler, N. J. (2008) *International Dimensions of Organizational Behavior*, 5th edn., Cincinatti, OH: South-Western College Publishing.

Ailon, G. (2008) "Mirror, mirror on the wall: Culture's consequences in a value test of its own design," *Academy of Management Review*, 33 (4): 885–904.

Andres, T. D. (1981) *Understanding Filipino Values*, Quezon City, Philippines: New Day.

Bond, M. C. *et al.* (1987) "Chinese values and the search for culture-free dimensions of culture," *Journal of Cross-cultural Psychology*, 18 (2): 143–164.

Call Center Directory (2009) "Philippines call center locations." Online, available at: www.callcenterdirectory.net/call-center-location/Philippines/directory-2-page-1.html (accessed 2 August 2009).

Chiang, F. F. T. and Birtch, T. A. (2007) "Examining the perceived causes of successful employee performance: An East–West comparison," *International Journal of Human Resource Management*, 18: 232–248.

Church, A. T. (1987) "Personality research in a non-Western culture: The Philippines," *Psychological Bulletin*, 102 (2): 272–292.

Comerford, M. (2005) "Manila call centers may surpass India: Young Filipinos work the phones at night," *Daily Herald*, 17 April, Manila, Philippines. Online, available at: www.dailyherald.com/special/philippines/part2c.asp (accessed 15 August 2009).

Earley, P. C. (1997) *The Transplanted Executive*, New York: Oxford University Press.

—— (2006) "Leading cultural research in the future: A matter of paradigms and taste," *Journal of International Business Studies*, 37: 922–931.

Egri, C. P. and Ralston, D. A. (2004) "Generation cohorts and personal values: A comparison of China and the United States," *Organization Science*, 15: 210–220.

Erez, M. (1986) "The congruence of goal-setting strategies with socio-cultural values and its effect on performance," *Journal of Management*, 12 (4): 585–592.

Erez, M. and Earley, P. C. (1987) "Comparative analysis of goal-setting strategies across cultures," *Journal of Applied Psychology*, 72 (4): 658–665.

Flores, K. (2009) "BPO industry lowers revenue goal, delays target to 2011," *abs-cbnNEWS.com*, 16 June, Manila, Philippines. Online, available at: www.abs-cbnnews.com/business/06/16/09/bpap-lowers-revenue-goal-delays-target-2011 (accessed 15 August 2009).

Galang, M. C. (2004) "The transferability question: Comparing HRM practices in the Philippines with the US and Canada," *International Journal of Human Resource Management*, 15: 1207–1233.

Gupta, A. and Kleiner, B. H. (2001) "Effective personnel management practices in the Philippines," *Management Research News*, 24: 149–152.

Hafsi, T. and Farashahi, M. (2005) "Applicability of management theories to developing countries: A synthesis," *Management International Review*, 45: 483–511.

Hofstede, G. (1980) *Culture's Consequences: International Differences in Work-Related Values*, Newbury Park, CA: Sage.

—— (2001) *Culture's Consequences: Comparing Values, Behaviors, Institutions, and Organizations*, 2nd edn., Thousand Oaks, CA: Sage.

Hookway, J. and Cuneta, J. (2009) "Philippine call centers ring up business," *Wall Street Journal*, 30 May, Manila, Philippines. Online, available at: http://online.wsj.com/article/SB124365325744868859.html (accessed 21 August 2009).

House, R. J., Hanges, P. J., Javidan, M., Dorfman, P. W. and Gupta, V. (2004) *Culture, Leadership, and Organizations: The GLOBE Study of 62 Societies*, Thousand Oaks, CA: Sage.

Javidan, M., House, R. J., Dorfman, P., Hanges, P. J. and de Luque, M. S. (2006) "Conceptualizing and measuring cultures and their consequences: a comparative review of GLOBE's and Hofstede's approaches," *Journal of International Business Studies*, 37 (6): 897–914.

Kanungo, R. N. (1986) "Productivity, satisfaction and involvement: A brief note on conceptual issues," *International Journal of Manpower*, 7: 8–12.

Kanungo, R. N. and Mendonça, M. (1997) "Goal setting theory," in *Fundamentals of Organizational Behavior*, Dubuque, IA: Kendall/Hunt.

Kiggundu, M. N., Jorgensen, J. J. and Hafsi, T. (1983) "Administrative theory and practice in developing countries: A synthesis," *Administrative Science Quarterly*, 28 (1): 66–84.

Lirio, P. (2008) "Generation X women professionals in the global workforce," paper presented at the Academy of International Business conference, 30 June–3 July, Milan. (Runner-up for the IIB/WAIB Best Paper Award for Increased Gender Awareness in International Business Research.)

—— (2009) "Global Leadership and Organizational Behavior Effectiveness project," in C. Wankel (ed.) *Encyclopedia of Business in Today's World*, Thousand Oaks, CA: Sage.

Locke, E. A. (1968) "Toward a theory of task motivation and incentives," *Organizational Behavior and Human Performance*, 3: 157–189.

Locke, E. A. and Latham, G. P. (1984) *Goal Setting: A Motivational Technique That Works!*, Englewood Cliffs, NJ: Prentice Hall.

Lynch, F. (1973) "Social acceptance reconsidered," in F. Lynch and A. de Guzman II (eds.) *Four Readings on Philippine Values*, Quezon City, Philippines: Ateneo de Manila University.

McSweeney, B. (2002) "Hofstede's model of national cultural differences and their consequences: A triumph of faith – a failure of analysis," *Human Relations*, 55: 89–118.

Magtibay-Ramos, N., Estrada, G. and Felipe, J. (2008) "An input–output analysis of the Philippine BPO industry," *Asian-Pacific Economic Literature*, 22: 41–56.

Mataragnon, R. H. (1988) "Pakikiramdam in Filipino social interaction: A study of subtlety and sensitivity," in A. C. Paranjpe and D. Y. F. Ho (eds.) *Asian Contributions to Psychology*, Troy, NY: Rensselaer Polytechnic Institute.

Mendonça, M. and Kanungo, R. N. (1994) "Managing human resources: The issue of cultural fit," *Journal of Management Inquiry*, 3 (2): 189–205.

Moran, R. T., Harris, P. R. and Moran, S. V. (2007) *Managing Cultural Differences: Global Leadership Strategies for the 21st Century*, 7th edn., New York: Elsevier.

National Statistics Office, Republic of the Philippines (2007) *2007 Census of Population.* Online, available at: www.census.gov.ph/ (accessed 15 August 2009).

Olchondra, R. T. (2008) "BPO: Bright light in sea of global gloom," *Philippine Daily Inquirer*, 14 November, Manila, Philippines. Online, available at: www.outsourceit-2philippines.com/news-outsource/BPO-Bright-light-in-sea-of-global-gloom.htm (accessed 2 August 2009).

Roces, A. and Roces, G. (2002) *Culture Shock! Philippines*, Portland, OR: Graphic Arts Center.

Watkins, D. and Gerong, A. (1997) "Culture and spontaneous self-concept among Filipino college students," *Journal of Social Psychology*, 137 (4): 480–488.

4 Emergent global institutional logic in the multinational corporation

Gwyneth Edwards

Introduction

In a research note for the *Journal of International Business Studies*, Buckley (2002) challenges the research community with a thought-provoking question: Is the international business research agenda running out of steam? Concerned that the community may be out of big ideas, Buckley reaches into the past to predict the future. Starting from the post-World War II period, he outlines three major sequential areas of international business focus: flows of foreign direct investment; the existence, strategy, and organization of the multinational corporation; and new forms of international business (internationalization to globalization). Buckley (ibid.) points out that in all three areas there is an absence of both theory and empirical studies that integrate the construct of culture, specifically as it relates to the impact of different national cultures on the firm. "The interplay of national cultures and organizational cultures, including the organizational culture of multinational organizations which might augment, transcend or conflict with particular national cultural traits, represents a research agenda with much life left in it" (ibid.: 369).

Although Buckley's (2002) main aim is to further the research agenda in international business, notably he argues that the interplay between cultures is an important area of study. Tsui *et al.* (2007) also support this notion. In their review of the moderating role of culture in organizational behavior research, they note that of the ninety-three studies in their analysis, only 8 percent were conducted at the national level, while 84 percent were conducted at the individual level. In their recommendations, Tsui *et al.* (ibid.) suggest that a group approach to the measurement of culture is needed, through either global (e.g. population, GDP), shared (common perceptions, cognitions, behaviors) or configurational (e.g. variance within groups) approaches. They also argue for the need to go beyond commonly used culture measures to incorporate other country-level indicators, such as social institutions. In combination, the works of Buckley (2002) and Tsui *et al.* (2007) suggest that the role of culture in the study of organizations is an area of research that is worth pursuing, specifically as it relates to the interplay between organizational and national cultures.

Farashahi *et al.* (2005) also discuss the need to study the effect of culture and, more elaborately, the effect of institutions, not only within the MNC at the organizational level but also between the MNC and local institutions. They suggest that institutions exist at various levels and model this hierarchy of institutions as a nested system, where endogenous changes at one level act as exogenous forces at another. Farashahi *et al.* (ibid.) broaden Buckley's (2002) argument to include not only the influence of culture but also the influence of regulative, normative and cognitive institutions, the latter two of which they consider to be more prevalent into today's international business research. Like Tsui *et al.* (2007), they call for research that recognizes the influence of normative and cognitive institutions.

Although these scholars call for further research on global organizations in terms of culture and the extended institutional environment, it is Buckley and Ghauri (2004) who highlight why research in international business should pursue research on the interplay of national culture and institutions. Their argument is that although there are serious consequences of globalization, there are also many myths. For example, critiques at the 1999 World Trade Organization meeting in Seattle raised concern that globalization would lead to the destruction of local communities and a reduction of cultural diversity (due to standardizing on modern Western values), along with the potential demise of national sovereignty and the power of independent states. Buckley and Ghauri (ibid.) do not pretend to have all the answers; conversely, they acknowledge that the impact of globalization is a complex issue, especially since the various economies of the world are changing at different rates. As a result, the role of multinational corporations and the behavior of managers within multinational corporations are of particular interest given the influence of these firms on the ongoing evolution of global institutions.

Geppert *et al.* (2006) extend the discussion on the role of multinationals in the ongoing process of globalization, arguing that research needs to focus not only on how MNCs respond and react to global institutional pressures, but also on how they influence and shape institutions around the world. The challenge in this avenue of research, however, lies in the decoupling of the MNC from its environment (Nelson and Gopoalan, 2003). Earlier research (Kostova, 1999) argues that the MNC parent adopts the country institutional profile (which includes culture) of the MNC's home country, while subsidiaries adopt the profile of the host country in which they are embedded. Subsidiaries are faced with issues of institutional duality whereby they continually seek legitimacy from both the parent and the local external environment in potentially conflicting ways (Kostova and Roth, 2002). This implies that the MNC is a collection of institutions whereby actors within the MNC seek legitimacy in unique ways (Kostova *et al.* 2008), and isomorphism does not occur.

Within the MNC however, the degree of interdependence between the subsidiaries and the parent varies (Bartlett and Ghoshal, 1989; Harzing, 2000; Vora and Kostova, 2007). If a subsidiary is highly dependent on the parent, actors within the MNC might seek legitimacy primarily with the parent, and do so through isomorphic behavior. When the institutional distance between the subsidiary's host country and the parent's home country is large – that is, the country institutional profiles (see Kostova, 1999) are vastly different – the process of seeking legitimacy could be complex, especially if the dependence of the subsidiary moves toward an interdependent relationship.

Although it is likely that in the internationalization process the parent will indeed adopt the country institutional profile of its home country, MNCs also have a dominant logic that prevails (Prahalad and Bettis, 1986). The dominant logic is created by the dominant coalition (Cyert and March, 1963) through operant conditioning, paradigms, pattern-recognition processes and cognitive biases (Prahalad and Bettis, 1986). From an institutional perspective this dominant logic can be expressed through rules, norms and cognitive beliefs, defined here as the dominant institutional logic. Within the subsidiaries, especially those that are institutionally distant from the parent, a local institutional logic may prevail. In the case of MNCs based in developed nations, these institutional logics may be economic (parent) or traditional (subsidiary) in nature (Molz, 2007). Over time, as the parent and subsidiary move through various levels of dependence, and the subsidiaries seek legitimacy between the parent and the local external environment, how will this dominant institutional logic change? Bettis and Prahalad (1995) suggest that, as the external environment changes, the dominant logic must also change. The question thus becomes, will the dominant institutional logic of Western-based MNCs change over time?

Drawing on previous research, it is argued that although isomorphism within MNCs may occur under certain circumstances, the dominant institutional logic of the MNC will change over time given the institutional duality created by the local institutional environments of the MNC subsidiaries. Through a process of deinstitutionalization (Oliver, 1992) and effective discourse (Maguire and Hardy, 2006), a new global institutional logic of the firm will emerge, reflecting both the old dominant institutional logic of the MNC and the local institutional logics of the subsidiaries.

The chapter is laid out as follows. First, institutional theory and its role in MNCs are discussed, with a specific focus on institutional distance and the process of institutional change. The conceptual argument is then developed, followed by a model and a series of propositions. A discussion on the implications and limitations of the model closes the chapter, to include empirical research considerations and further avenues of research.

Culture and institutional theory

Since Buckley (2002) pointed out the importance of the interplay of national cultures and the need for comparative research, international management researchers have broadened their focus beyond culture, to the influence of institutions, arguing that institutional theory provides greater explanatory power (Kostova *et al.*, 2008; Peng, 2006; Peng and Pleggenkuhle-Miles, 2009; Shenkar, 2001; Singh, 2007). Singh (2007) specifically argued that culture is typically a micro-level construct (supported by Tsui *et al.*, 2007) and lacks the ability to predict macro-level concepts. Institutional theory, on the other hand, is able to describe to describe both formal (e.g. rules and regulations) and informal institutions (e.g.

cognitive and normative beliefs) at a macro level, all of which both constrict and encourage different types of business behaviors (Peng and Pleggenkuhle-Miles, 2009). Institutional theory, as a broad, descriptive approach, incorporates aspects of culture and therefore does not neglect culture's effect; rather, it broadens the analysis (Peng, 2006; Peng and Pleggenkuhle-Miles, 2009; Shenkar, 2001; Singh, 2007). Culture, as an example, can be and has been incorporated into research on country institutional profiles, both conceptually and empirically (Kostova and Roth, 2002; Parboteeah *et al.*, 2008, 2009; Xu *et al.*, 2004). In support of this line of research, this chapter use institutional theory as a means to study the interplay that exists between both cultures and broader societal institutions.

To institutionalize is to "infuse with value beyond the technical requirements of the task at hand" (Selznick, 1957: 17). Over time, an organization evolves from being an expendable tool to becoming an institution, a natural product of social needs and pressures. This process of institutionalization occurs as a result of adaptive change and evolution of organizational forms and practices – through the decline of old patterns and the emergence of new ones (Selznick, 1957).

DiMaggio and Powell (1983) describe institutionalization as something that occurs owing to coercive, mimetic and normative processes, which lead organizations to become homogeneous in nature. The more central the resources and the more dependent on those resources, the greater the degree of homogeneity of the changing unit. DiMaggio and Powell (ibid.) suggest that this process occurs over time and is beyond the control of the organizations in question, implying that some final homogeneous state exists.

Oliver (1991), however, argues that the firm does in fact have a choice in how it responds to external pressures. Depending on willingness and ability to conform, the firm will choose to acquiesce, compromise, avoid, defy or manipulate in response to pressures. These choices will be influenced by institutional antecedents of cause, constituents, content, control and context. This allowance for choice may lead to the strengthening of internal organizational cultures in resistance to external expectations and beliefs, which suggests that conflict between diverse institutional logics may occur (ibid.).

Organizations are constrained by environmental pressures (Suchman, 1995) and the underlying motivations of these pressures must be carefully understood. However, organizations can choose how they will respond to institutional pressures through a pragmatic understanding of legitimacy. Suchman (ibid.: 574) defines legitimacy as a "generalized perception or assumption that the actions of an entity are desirable, proper, or appropriate within some socially constructed system of norms, values, beliefs, and definitions." The management of legitimacy is played out through the strategies that organizations undertake to gain, maintain and repair legitimacy in respect of the institutions that affect them. These legitimacy strategies – pragmatic, moral and cognitive – can be used by firms to achieve corporate objectives.

Organizations go through an adaptive process toward institutionalization and organizations dependent on another for resources are at risk of isomorphism (DiMaggio and Powell, 1983). However, firms do have the option of resisting such pressures (Oliver, 1991). With careful consideration of the impact of such strategic decisions, firms can gain, maintain and repair legitimacy, and do so to their advantage (Suchman, 1995). Legitimacy can therefore be considered an important strategic tool that can be leveraged to achieve organizational goals.

The process of institutionalization through the decline of old and emergence of new patterns suggests that institutionalization is not, in fact, a means to an end but rather an ongoing process (Selznick, 1957: 12). Research on institutional change, however, has only recently taken flight (Farashahi *et al.*, 2005), and research in the area of deinstitutionalization is still thin (Dacin *et al.*, 2002). Oliver (1992) provided a conceptual theory on the antecedents of institutional change, but it was not until recently that empirical research on deinstitutionalization and institutional change was given significant attention (Dacin *et al.*, 2002).

Deinstitutionalization can be defined as "the erosion or discontinuity of an institutional organization activity or practice" (Oliver, 1992: 563). The political, functional and social pressures both within the organization and in the organization's environment will lead to the possible dissipation, rejection or replacement of institutional behavior. Intra-organizational factors (changes in political distributions, functional necessity and social consensus) and organization–environment relations (competitive environment pressures, social environment pressures, random external occurrences, and changes in constituent relations) will empirically predict deinstitutionalization (Oliver, 1992). The pressures most likely to lead to deinstitutionalization are changing government regulations, performance problems and organizational crises, the last-named of which is often joined by conflicts of interest, power reallocations, executive succession and weakening socialization mechanisms (ibid.).

The deinstitutionalization process will lead to the emergence of a new institution. This can occur through either convergent or radical change (Greenwood and Hinings, 1996) as dictated by the function of the organization's internal dynamics. The depth of radical change is influenced by the organization's pattern of value commitments, which reflect the degree of commitment toward the institutional template-in-use. These value commitments are on a continuum: status quo (all groups committed), indifferent (neither committed nor opposed, acquiescence), competitive (some support, others do not) and reformative (all opposed). Change will occur when value commitments are either competitive or reformative, both of which are more likely to occur in peripheral organizations, complex environments or loosely structured institutions (for example, the template-in-use is normatively weak). Reformative commitment has the greater likelihood of leading to radical change, while competitive commitment will be associated with evolutionary change (Greenwood and Hinings, 1996).

Radical or evolutionary change, however, will occur only with the existence of two enabling dynamics: capacity for action and supportive power dependencies (Greenwood and Hinings, 1996). Given that changes in organizational dependencies threaten some coalitions and make new ones possible (Thompson, 1967), all coalitions must not only be capable of managing the institutional change but also perceive a shift in power due to the shift in resource dependence.

Capacity of action can be assessed in terms of the availability of requisite skills and motivation to use those skills (Greenwood and Hinings, 1996). Although leadership skills within both the dominant and the emerging coalitions are significant, the importance of discourse throughout this process cannot go unmentioned. Discourses are defined by Maguire and Hardy (2006: 9) as "structured collections of meaningful texts – along with the related practices of producing, disseminating and consuming these texts – that 'systematically form the object of which they speak' (Foucault 1979: 49)." Within organizations, when legacy beliefs are challenged, discourse of the old and discourse of the new are positioned in relation to each other. As each set of actors use each other's discourse to support their respective positions, reconciliation takes place. The discourses overlap and, through the struggle, the meanings of both are changed. As a result, a new institution emerges (Maguire and Hardy, 2006). Other researchers, such as Hargrave and Van de Ven (2006) and Seo and Creed (2002), espouse similar arguments based on the assumption that institutional change is a dialectical process.

Institutional theory and the MNC

Toward the end of the twentieth century, although some research on MNCs began to acknowledge the influence of institutional theory (Ghoshal and Bartlett, 1990) and resource dependency (Gupta and Govindarajan, 1991), international business research focused on network theory to explain the behavior and performance of the firm (Andersson *et al.*, 2002; Ghoshal and Bartlett, 1990; Malnight, 1996; Rugman and Verbeke, 2001). More recently, however, concepts such as legitimacy, institutional distance and institutional duality have been used to describe the impact of local institutions on MNC subsidiaries (Hillman and Wan, 2005; Kostova and Roth, 2002; Kostova and Zaheer, 1999). Recent work continues to develop these theories and to test them empirically (Ahlstrom and Bruton, 2001; Bianchi and Ostale, 2006; Li *et al.*, 2007; Treviño and Mixon, 2004; Xu *et al.*, 2004; Xu and Shenkar, 2002; Yiu and Makino, 2002). Institutional theory is an important method used to describe the behavior of the firm. Multinational corporations, like all other organizational forms, can be effectively studied by understanding how institutions are created and change over time.

The wholly owned foreign subsidiary (hereafter referred to as "subsidiary") of the MNC is faced with institutional pressures both from within the organization (by the parent) and external to the organization, by the local environment (Kostova and Zaheer, 1999). Because of the subsidiary's dependence on both environments, the unit is challenged to gain, maintain and repair legitimacy both internally and externally (Oliver, 1991). This process of legitimacy is complex, in that actors of the subsidiary must carefully select their legitimacy strategies and consider the implications of resisting pressures applied from various perspectives. If the subsidiary resists internal institutional pressures too strongly, the subsidiary is at risk of losing resource support for local initiatives. Conversely, if the subsidiary ignores local pressures, resources available within the external environment (e.g. customers, employees, societal support) will be jeopardized. Empirical examples of successful local legitimacy attempts (Ahlstrom and Bruton, 2001; Treviño and Mixon 2004) and failed attempts (Bianchi and Ostale, 2006) contribute toward this conceptual argument.

Given that every country has its own set of regulatory, cognitive and normative institutions, each country can be considered to have its own institutional profile (Kostova, 1999). Country institutional profile is defined as "the set of all relevant institutions that have been established over time, operate in that country, and get transmitted into organizations through individuals" (Kostova, 1997: 180). Regulatory institutions include both the formal and the informal rules and laws by which the society lives, established through various types of national institutions (Scott, 1995). Normative elements are represented by values and norms, and often referred to by North's (1990) conceptualization as the "rules of the game." Cultural-cognitive elements "such as schemas, frames, inferential sets, and representations affect the way people notice, categorize, and interpret stimuli from the environment" (Kostova, 1999: 314). It is through these three institutional pillars – regulative, normative, and cultural-cognitive – that the institutional profile of a country is enacted.

The country institutional profile effectively describes how countries are similar and different across their respective institutions. Developed countries will have more similar institutional profiles vis-à-vis their counterparts in emerging and development economies. For example, Xu *et al.* (2004) found the normative profiles of Sweden, Canada and the United States to be considerably different from those of India, Poland and Venezuela.

Both the subsidiary and the parent are affected by a country's institutional profile. As was noted earlier, the subsidiary must seek legitimacy within its external environment – the country in which it operates. This external environment can be characterized by the country's institutional profile. When the demands of the local environment are immediate, the subsidiary will give priority to local pressures. Owing to these local pressures that are exerted through the country's institutional pillars (regulative, normative and cognitive), the subsidiary will establish a local institutional logic.

The parent is similarly affected by the institutional profile of the country in which it is based. Regardless of whether an MNC evolves from a national enterprise or immediately joins the international stage, the parent will be pressured by the home country's institutional profile. Thus, the parent's institutional logic will tend to be similar to its home country's institutional profile.

The parent's institutional logic can also be considered the dominant institutional logic of the MNC. When businesses are strategically similar, the dominant coalition of the organization influences the way in which decisions are made and resources are allocated. Their decisions are based on their own personal experiences, which are consummated in a system of beliefs, theories and propositions that are represented by a set of schemas (Prahalad and Bettis, 1986). Within the organization the dominant coalition creates a mental structure within which the dominant management logic is stored. This structure contains both knowledge and management processes, and represents the worldview of the coalition. This worldview can either be reinforced through market success or challenged by other logics that demand the attention of the coalition (ibid.). When conditions within a complex organization change – that is, when the firm moves away from equilibrium – a new dominant logic must be developed quickly through a process of unlearning and creation of new dominant logics, in order to ensure the firm's survival (Bettis and Prahalad, 1995).

In the MNC the dominant coalition will reside (in most cases) within the parent. The dominant coalition will therefore be influenced by local institutional pressures of the home country, represented through the country's institutional profile. This chapter therefore proposes that the parent institutional logic is also representative of the MNC's dominant institutional logic. The dominant institutional logic of the parent directs knowledge and resources within the MNC, overriding the local institutional logics of the subsidiaries.

The subsidiary, however, is required to seek legitimacy both externally, in the local environment, and internally, with the parent. If the distance between the parent's dominant institutional logic and the subsidiary local institutional logic is wide, gaining both internal and external legitimacy will be difficult. The contrasting institutional pressures will create an institutional duality (Kostova and Roth, 2002). Subsidiary managers will be faced with operating in this dual institutional environment on a day-to-day basis, forced to balance the demands of each set of agents. For subsidiary managers this will result in dual organizational identification whereby they may identify with both the MNC parent and the subsidiary (Vora and Kostova, 2007). When the institutional distance between the home and host countries is high, subsidiary managers may identify distinctly with the subsidiary or with the parent (e.g. in the case of expatriates) (ibid.). When subsidiary managers identify strongly with both, they perform boundary-spanning functions that can be enacted through the roles of front-line implementer, knowledge provider, advocate and defender, and bicultural interpreter (ibid.). The subsidiary manager as boundary spanner may also spur the roles of change agent and entrepreneur (Birkinshaw, 1997). The group of subsidiary managers will represent the dominant coalition within the subsidiary and, by extension, the local institutional logic. The question thus becomes, "How does this local institutional logic influence the dominant institutional logic of the MNC?"

As indicated by DiMaggio and Powell (1983), institutionalization is mediated by the extent to which an organization is dependent on another's resources for survival. In the case of the subsidiary, dependency is on both the local external environment and the internal organization, which leads to the condition of institutional duality in cases where institutional distance is great. As the balance of resource dependency fluctuates between the local environment and the parent, so too will the attention toward legitimacy. However, when a resource is equally sourced and shared by both the subsidiary and the parent, the relationship evolves to one of resource interdependence. Knowledge is one such resource.

"The creation, diffusion, and absorption of knowledge by organizations in general and, by MNCs in particular, constitutes one of the most important subjects for research in the fields of organization theory, strategic management, evolutionary economics, and international business" (Gupta and Govindarajan, 2000: 491); recent empirical findings suggest why. Ambos *et al.* demonstrate that MNC parents are not only providers of knowledge to their subsidiaries but also receivers of knowledge, and "seem to benefit most from the type of knowledge they get least" (2006: 303). Adenfelt and Lagerstrom's (2006) case study on two methods of learning within the same MNC supports the view that knowledge is developed and shared both locally and globally. Although the effectiveness of such sharing is moderated by structure, knowledge contributions can be made by the subsidiaries.

The flow of knowledge creation and sharing between subsidiaries and the parent suggests that resource dependency changes when the subsidiary creates and shares knowledge beyond its borders. Resource interdependency replaces the subsidiary's dependent relationship, and power shifts away from the parent. With less dependency and more power, the subsidiary has less reason to seek organizational legitimacy. Conversely, the parent and other subsidiaries may start seeking legitimacy in an effort to obtain the knowledge. It is therefore proposed that the interdependent relationship between the parent and the subsidiaries, along with the institutional distances between these entities, will influence the emergence of a new global institutional logic within the MNC, as shown in Figure 4.1.

When the interdependence between the parent and its subsidiaries is low, the collective power of the individual subsidiary coalitions will be low. In this case, the subsidiary is naturally dependent on the parent for knowledge, but the converse is not true. In the case of high institutional distance, the value commitment from the subsidiaries will be competitive and conflicts may arise, but the dominant parent will have little reason to enter into discourse with these units. Over time, the survival of the subsidiaries may actually be threatened, as it will become impossible for the subsidiary coalition to achieve both external and internal legitimacy concurrently. The subsidiaries will seek legitimacy either with the internal organization or with the local external environment. The former condition will result in subsidiary failure and lead to the disintegration of the unit. The latter may extend the life of the subsidiary but eventually it will fail, owing to lack of organizational resources, or the subsidiary may leave the MNC in favor of local ownership. This gives rise to the first proposition:

Proposition 1: When the institutional distance between the parent and subsidiaries is high and parent–subsidiary interdependence is low, the MNC's dominant institutional logic will be sustained and the subsidiaries' survival threatened (Figure 4.1, quadrant A).

When there is low institutional distance between the subsidiaries and the parent, and the interdependence is also low, the subsidiaries behave as an extension of the parent. As an example, an MNC operating out of the United States with subsidiaries in Canada and the United Kingdom will experience a degree of

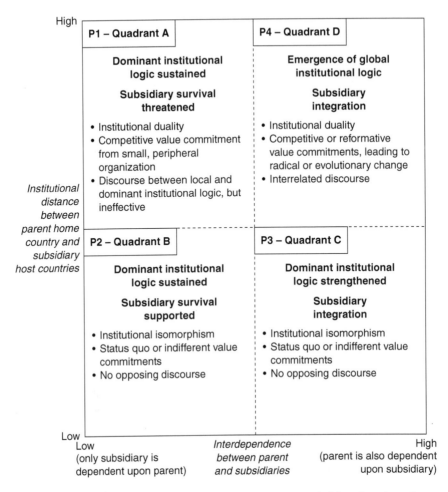

Figure 4.1 The influence of institutional distance and parent–subsidiary interdependence on multinational corporations' dominant institutional logic.

isomorphism within the internal environment, given that the country institutional profiles of these countries are similar. Value commitments will either be status quo or indifferent, and separate institutional discourse will be minimal to non-existent. The subsidiaries will be supported by the parent and the dominant institutional logic sustained. The second proposition is therefore as follows:

Proposition 2: When the institutional distance between the parent and subsidiaries is low and parent–subsidiary interdependence is low, the MNC's dominant institutional logic will be sustained and the subsidiaries' survival supported (Figure 4.1, quadrant B).

When institutional distance between the subsidiaries and the parent is low and parent–subsidiary interdependence is high, institutional isomorphism will prevail. As with proposition 2, status quo or indifferent value commitments will exist. The high interdependency between the parent and subsidiaries, however, will raise the power of the subsidiaries within the corporation, which will fuel their integration into the corporate structure, offering them a role extending beyond their respective geographical boundaries.

Proposition 3: When the institutional distance between the parent and sub-sidiaries is low and parent–subsidiary interdependence is high, the MNC's dominant institutional logic will be strengthened and the subsidiaries will be integrated (Figure 4.1, quadrant C).

When the institutional distance between the subsidiaries and the parent is high, and the parent–subsidiary interdependence is high, two-way knowledge transfer will occur between the parent and its subsidiaries, and among the sub-sidiaries themselves. As the resource interdependence between the subsidiaries and the parent increases, so will the power of the subsidiaries. As they are no longer entirely dependent on the parent, their need for organizational legitimacy will decrease. The parent will seek legitimacy among the subsidiaries, owing to its dependence on subsidiary knowledge. The institutional duality experienced by the subsidiaries will create competitive or reformative value commitments. Although the subsidiaries are on the periphery of the organization, the depend-ency of the parent and shift in power toward the subsidiaries will enhance their bargaining position. The parent, now strategically dependent on the subsidiaries, will acknowledge the institutional duality and respond through discourse. The subsidiaries and the parent will then enter the discursive process, arguing for their respective positions. This process will lead to the emergence of a new global institutional logic within the MNC that reflects a combination of regula-tive, cognitive and normative beliefs of both the subsidiaries' local institutional logics and the parent's dominant institutional logic. Whether this process occurs radically or through convergent means will depend on the value commitments held by the dual institutions. Reformative commitment, which has the greater likelihood of leading radical change, will occur when both the parent and the subsidiaries are dissatisfied with the template-in-use and are driven to move to a new institutional logic. Competitive commitment, which is more likely the case, will be associated with evolutionary change.

Proposition 4: When the institutional distance between the parent and sub-sidiaries is high and parent–subsidiary interdependence is high, a new global institutional logic will emerge (Figure 4.1, quadrant D).

An interesting application of this model is offered, using Vora and Kostova's (2007) elaboration of Bartlett and Ghoshal's (1989) MNC typology. Vora and

Kostova (2007) link organizational design parameters to the four types of MNCs: multinational, international, global and transnational. According to their analysis, multinational firms are decentralized, independent from headquarters and highly differentiated. Global and international MNCs, on the other hand, have concentrated power at the headquarters and have low differentiation, with subsidiaries that are dependent upon the parent. Transnational MNCs lie in the middle of two extremes where differentiation is moderate and power is distributed equally throughout the firm (ibid.).

When institutional distance between the parent and subsidiaries is low, the multinational, international and global MNCs will retain their dominant institutional logic (as in proposition 2), given that competitive value commitments will not exist. In the case of the transnational firm, not only will the dominant logic be sustained but indeed it will be strengthened, given the interdependent relationship between the parent and its subsidiaries, all of which are operating in similar institutional environments (as in proposition 3).

When institutional distance between the parent and subsidiaries is high, dominant institutional logic in the multinational firm will be sustained. The subsidiaries, however, may leave the firm, owing to competitive value commitments and their independence from the parent (as in proposition 1). In the global or international MNC, where subsidiaries are dependent on the parent and power is centralized, the survival of the subsidiaries will be threatened. Once again the subsidiaries will be unable to resolve the competitive value commitments, but the unwillingness of the parent to engage in discourse, along with the subsidiaries' reliance on the parent, may result in an inability to continue operations within the subsidiary (also as in proposition 1).

In the transnational MNC, where interdependent relationships exist and power is equally distributed among the parent and the subsidiaries, institutional distance will encourage the emergence of a new global institutional logic. Competitive value commitments within the subsidiaries will exist and the dominant coalitions within these subsidiaries will instigate discourse with the parent. The dominant coalition of the parent will engage in this discursive process because of its reliance on the subsidiaries, resulting in a new dominant institutional logic that is particular to the transnational firm (proposition 4).

This application of the model demonstrates that MNC type can predict the emergence of a new dominant institutional logic over time. The challenge in such an application, which stems from the model itself, is the ability to perform an empirical test. Not only does an empirical test require a longitudinal study but also it begs for comparative analysis – that is, analyzing a number of MNCs within the same industry or operating in the same set of foreign countries. The intent of this approach would be not only to examine what initiates institutional change and whether new institutional logics do emerge, but also to determine how this process takes place from one MNC to another. Is it in fact unique? It is possible that within the same industry, certain institutional behaviors are more common across the MNC than they are in other industries. For example, global or international firms operating in internationally regulated industries such as aviation may be more homogeneous than multinational firms that operate in more locally regulated industries, such as legal firms. If variance does exist between firms and between industries, what are the variables that lead to this variance?

Although these questions reflect the need for further study in this area, the immediate challenge is the measurement of such a model. Institutional distance, as noted earlier, is the difference between two countries' institutional profiles along three dimensions: normative, regulative and cognitive profiles. To determine the distance between two countries, each of these three dimensions must be measured for the countries involved in the study. Although the measurement of country institutional profile, and the subsequent institutional distance between profiles, continues to be a challenge (Liu *et al.*, 2008), some success has been obtained by scholars (Kostova and Roth, 2002; Jensen and Szulanski, 2004; Pattnaik and Choe, 2007). Xu *et al.* (2004), for example, created an independent measure using data provided by the *Global Competitiveness Report* (published annually by the World Economic Forum). The report contained eight factors of over 170 different items – openness, government, finance, infrastructure, technology, management, labor and institutions – two of which (management and institutions) were used to measure regulative and normative profiles. This same report could also provide measures for the cognitive pillar, using factors drawn from the institutions pillar (and possibly others).

Parent–subsidiary interdependence can be measured by MNC type, as demonstrated earlier, but could also be measured through in-house surveys of the dominant coalition. Coalition members could either rank the strategic importance of each subsidiary and/or classify subsidiaries by their strategic roles, as defined by Bartlett and Ghoshal (1989) (i.e. black holes, implementers, contributors and strategic leaders).

Measuring the dominant institutional logic of the MNC provides a greater challenge. Although the parent's country institutional profile could be used as the starting point, it would be insufficient as a means to measure changes over time, assuming that a new logic may emerge. In order to measure the institutional logic within the firm, a new scale would have to be developed using MNC employees as respondents. Survey items from the *Global Competitiveness Report* could be reformulated for organizational level measurements. Additionally, qualitative data could be gathered through parent and subsidiary interviews. The key indicator would be the change of the institutional logic over time and the reflection of the subsidiaries' local institutional logics in the newly emerged environment.

Conclusion

The conceptual model proposed in this chapter suggests that it is possible for Western-based MNCs to operate successfully in foreign countries where the institutional profile is vastly different from the parent, as in the case of emerging and developing economies. The dominant coalition of the MNC, if aware of the conflicting logics that may exist over time and from one subsidiary to another, has a choice in redefining the dominant institutional logic as the needs of the subsidiaries change (Prahalad and Bettis, 1986). Even if the businesses themselves are strategically similar, institutional distance between the countries may dictate a need to change the way knowledge is created and transferred, and how management processes are defined and carried out. Together, the MNC parent and its subsidiaries can abandon institutionalized rules, norms and beliefs through deinstitutionalization, and together, through discursive processes, create a new global institutional logic that more accurately reflects the diversity of the firm. This new logic will allow subsidiaries to more effectively gain legitimacy with both the parent and the local external environment, in a concurrent manner. The new global institutional logic can balance traditional institutions of the developing and emerging economies with the economic values of the developed countries.

Further research in this area could move beyond the empirical testing by also looking at the moderating effects of the institutional change process. Institutional change within the MNC is complex, as the firm must deal with institutional pressures at the individual, organizational, national and transnational level (Aguilera *et al.*, 2007). When MNCs, through either competitive or reformative value commitments, go through the process of establishing new institutional logics, how do external pressures at each of these levels moderate the process? The firm is not a closed system (Thompson, 1967); although the parent and the subsidiaries engage in a discursive process that addresses the institutional duality within the firm, collectively they are affected by external pressures at all levels.

Given that the subsidiaries each have their own local institutional profiles, does this institutional change process stem beyond dyadic analysis? Can the subsidiaries justifiably be analyzed in aggregate vis-à-vis the firm or does the change process involve a more complex, integrated system?

The international business research agenda

Recently, Barner-Rasmussen *et al.* (2007) reviewed a collection of six books that focused on the multinational corporation and globalization. They categorized the works into three research perspectives: classical (dominant approach emphasizing economic efficiency), network (MNC as a network of units) and critical (effect of global, institutional and social forces on firm success). Although these three diverse perspectives demonstrate that the debate initiated by Buckley (2002) is still very much alive, a common thread among the perspectives was that local legitimacy is critical to subsidiary survival. Authors of the collection also agree that MNC parents continue to seek ways in which to achieve their economic goals. The model proposed in this chapter is critical to moving ahead within this research agenda; instead of staying within the market economy paradigm, the model suggests that MNCs need to reinvent themselves to more accurately reflect the diverse nature of the global environment.

The collective power and influence held by the global MNC population, over both economic markets and societies, is increasing. Institutions in and of themselves, MNCs not only are affected by institutional pressures but also pressure other institutions (regulatory, cognitive and normative) the world over. Given that the majority of Western-based MNCs are dominated by economic logics, how will their power and influence manifest? Is the successful expansion of developing nations at stake?

The conceptual model of this chapter suggests that MNCs can choose to move beyond the constraints of their current institutional environments and seek out new global institutional logics that more appropriately reflect the institutional profiles of all countries. Peng (2004) suggests that the big international business research question should be and always has been, "What determines the international success and failure of firms?" Maybe it is now time to ask an additional question: "How should we define the success and failure of the MNC?" By reconsidering the way in which MNCs are evaluated, it is possible that further support for the new global institutional logic will be provided.

References

Adenfelt, M. and Lagerstrom, K. (2006) "Knowledge development and sharing in multinational corporations: The case of a centre of excellence and a transnational team," *International Business Review*, 15: 381–400.

Aguilera, R., Rupp, D., Williams, C. and Ganapathi, J. (2007) "Putting the S back in corporate social responsibility: A multilevel theory of social change in organizations," *Academy of Management Review*, 32: 836–863.

Ahlstrom, D. and Bruton, G. D. (2001) "Learning from successful local private firms in china: Establishing legitimacy," *Academy of Management Executive*, 15: 72–83.

Ambos, T. C., Ambos, B. and Schlegelmilch, B. B. (2006) "Learning from foreign subsidiaries: An empirical investigation of headquarters' benefits from reverse knowledge transfers," *International Business Review*, 15: 294–312.

Andersson, U., Forsgren, M. and Holm, U. (2002) "The strategic impact of external networks: Subsidiary performance and competence development in the multinational corporation," *Strategic Management Journal*, 23: 979–996.

Barner-Rasmussen, W., Piekkari, R., Scott-Kennel, J. and Welch, C. (2007) "New perspectives on the multinational corporation," *Academy of Management Perspectives*, 21: 93–101.

Bartlett, C. A. and Ghoshal, S. (eds.) (1989) *Managing across Borders: The Transnational Solution*, Boston: Harvard Business School Press.

Bettis, R. A. and Prahalad, C. K. (1995) "The dominant logic: Retrospective and extension," *Strategic Management Journal*, 16: 5–14.

Bianchi, C. C. and Ostale, E. (2006) "Lessons learned from unsuccessful internationalization attempts: Examples of multinational retailers in Chile," *Journal of Business Research*, 59: 140–147.

Birkinshaw, J. (1997) "Entrepreneurship in multinational corporations: The characteristics of subsidiary initiatives," *Strategic Management Journal*, 18: 207–229.

Buckley, P. J. (2002) "Is the international business research agenda running out of steam?" *Journal of International Business Studies*, 33: 365–373.

Buckley, P. J. and Ghauri, P. N. (2004) "Globalisation, economic geography and the strategy of multinational enterprises," *Journal of International Business Studies*, 35: 81–98.

Cyert, R. M. and March, J. G. (eds.) (1963) *A Behavioral Theory of the Firm*, Englewood Cliffs, NJ: Prentice-Hall.

Dacin, M. T., Goodstein, J. and Scott, W. R. (2002) "Institutional theory and institutional change: Introduction to the special research forum," *Academy of Management Journal*, 45: 45–56.

DiMaggio, P. J. and Powell, W. W. (1983) "The iron cage revisited: Institutional isomorphism and collective rationality in organizational fields," *American Sociological Review*, 48: 147–160.

Farashahi, M., Hafsi, T. and Molz, R. (2005) "Institutionalized norms of conducting research and social realities: A research synthesis of empirical works from 1983 to 2002," *International Journal of Management Reviews*, 7: 1–24.

Geppert, M., Matten, D. and Walgenbach, P. (2006) "Transnational institution building and the multinational corporation: An emerging field of research," *Human Relations*, 59: 1451–1465.

Ghoshal, S. and Bartlett, C. A. (1990) "The multinational corporation as an interorganizational network," *Academy of Management Review*, 15: 603–625.

Greenwood, R. and Hinings, C. R. (1996) "Understanding radical organizational change: Bringing together the old and the new institutionalism," *Academy of Management Review*, 21: 1022–1054.

Gupta, A. K. and Govindarajan, V. (1991) "Knowledge flows and the structure of control within multinational corporations," *Academy of Management Review*, 16: 768–792.

—— (2000) "Knowledge flows within multinational corporations," *Strategic Management Journal*, 21: 473–496.

Hargrave, T. J. and Van de Ven, A. H. (2006) "A collective action model of institutional innovation," *Academy of Management Review*, 31: 864–888.

Harzing, A.-W. (2000) "An empirical analysis and extension of the Bartlett and Ghoshal typology of multinational companies," *Journal of International Business Studies*, 31: 101–120.

Hillman, A. J. and Wan, W. P. (2005) "The determinants of MNE subsidiaries' political strategies: Evidence of institutional duality," *Journal of International Business Studies*, 36: 322–340.

Jensen, R. and Szulanski, G. (2004) "Stickiness and the adaptation of organizational practices in cross-border knowledge transfers," *Journal of International Business Studies*, 35: 508–523.

Kostova, T. (1997) "Country institutional profiles: Concept and measurement," *Academy of Management Proceedings*, August: 180–189.

—— (1999) "Transnational transfer of strategic organizational practices: A contextual perspective," *Academy of Management Review*, 24: 308–324.

Kostova, T. and Roth, K. (2002) "Adoption of an organizational practice by subsidiaries of multinational corporations: Institutional and relational effects," *Academy of Management Journal*, 45: 215–233.

Kostova, T. and Zaheer, S. (1999) "Organizational legitimacy under conditions of complexity: The case of the multinational enterprise," *Academy of Management Review*, 24: 64–81.

Kostova, T., Roth, K. and Dacin, M. T. (2008) "Institutional theory in the study of multinational corporations: A critique and new directions," *Academy of Management Review*, 33: 994–1006.

Li, J. T., Yang, J. Y. and Yue, D. R. (2007) "Identity community, and audience: How wholly owned foreign subsidiaries gain legitimacy in China," *Academy of Management Journal*, 50: 175–190.

Liu, B., Tang, N. and Zhu, X. (2008) "Transferring technology across borders: Institutional effects in Chinese context," *Journal of Technology Transfer*, 33: 619–630.

Maguire, S. and Hardy, C. (2006) "The emergence of new global institutions: A discursive perspective," *Organization Studies*, 27: 7–29.

Malnight, T. W. (1996) "The transition from decentralized to network-based MNC structures: An evolutionary perspective," *Journal of International Business Studies*, 27: 43–65.

Molz, R. (2007) "Doing business in developing countries: The uneasy interaction between local traditional and global economic dynamics," paper presented at the Academy of Management Meeting, Philadelphia, August.

Nelson, R. E. and Gopalan, S. (2003) "Do organizational cultures replicate national cultures? Isomorphism, rejection and reciprocal opposition in the corporate values of three countries," *Organization Studies*, 24: 1115–1151.

North, D. (1990) *Institutions, Institutional Change and Economic Performance*, Cambridge: Cambridge University Press.

Oliver, C. (1991) "Strategic responses to institutional processes," *Academy of Management Review*, 16: 145–179.

—— (1992) "The antecedents of deinstitutionalization," *Organization Studies*, 13: 563–588.

Parboteeah, K. P., Hoegl, M. and Cullen, J. B. (2008) "Managers' gender role attitudes: A country institutional profile approach," *Journal of International Business Studies*, 39: 795–813.

—— (2009) "Religious dimensions and work obligation: A country institutional profile model," *Human Relations*, 62: 119–148.

Pattnaik, C. and Choe, S. (2007) "Do institutional quality and institutional distance impact subsidiary performance," *Academy of Management Proceedings*, August: 1–6.

Peng, M. W. (2004) "Identifying the big question in international business research," *Journal of International Business Studies*, 35: 99–108.

—— (2006) *Global Strategy*, Cincinnati, OH: South-Western Thomson.

Peng, M. W. and Pleggenkuhle-Miles, E. G. (2009) "Current debates in global strategy," *International Journal of Management Reviews*, 11: 51–68.

Prahalad, C. K. and Bettis, R. A. (1986) "The dominant logic: A new linkage between diversity and performance," *Strategic Management Journal*, 7: 485–501.

Rugman, A. M. and Verbeke, A. (2001) "Subsidiary-specific advantages in multinational enterprises," *Strategic Management Journal*, 22: 237–250.

Scott, W. R. (1995) *Institutions and Organizations*, Thousand Oaks, CA: Sage.

Selznick, P. (1957) *Leadership in Administration: A Sociological Interpretation*, Evanston, IL: Row Peterson.

Seo, M.-G. and Creed, W. E. D. (2002) "Institutional contradictions, praxis, and institutional change: A dialectical perspective," *Academy of Management Review*, 27: 222–247.

Shenkar, O (2001) "Cultural distance revisited: Towards a more rigorous conceptualization and measurement of cultural differences," *Journal of International Business Studies*, 32: 519–535.

Singh, K. (2007) "The limited relevance of culture to strategy," *Asia Pacific Journal of Management*, 24: 421.

Suchman, M. C. (1995) "Managing legitimacy: Strategic and institutional approaches," *Academy of Management Review*, 20: 571–610.

Thompson, J. D. (1967) *Organizations in Action: Social Science Bases of Administrative Theory*, New York: McGraw-Hill.

Treviño, L. J. and Mixon, F. G., Jr. (2004) "Strategic factors affecting foreign direct investment decisions by multi-national enterprises in Latin America," *Journal of World Business*, 39: 233–243.

Tsui, A. S., Nifadkar, S. S. and Ou, A. Y. (2007) "Cross-national, cross-cultural organizational behavior research: Advances, gaps, and recommendations," *Journal of Management*, 33: 426–478.

Vora, D. and Kostova, T. (2007) "A model of dual organizational identification in the context of the multinational enterprise," *Journal of Organizational Behavior*, 28: 327–350.

Xu, D. and Shenkar, O. (2002) "Institutional distance and the multinational enterprise," *Academy of Management Review*, 27: 608–618.

Xu, D., Pan, Y. and Beamish, P. W. (2004) "The effect of regulative and normative distances on MNE ownership and expatriate strategies," *Management International Review*, 44: 285–307.

Yiu, D. and Makino, S. (2002) "The choice between joint venture and wholly owned subsidiary: An institutional perspective," *Organization Science*, 13: 667–683.

5 Political strategies of multinational enterprises in emerging economies

A theoretical model

Shoaib Ul-Haq and Mehdi Farashahi

Introduction

During the latter part of the twentieth century the global business environment changed significantly, owing to drastic economic reforms in China in the late 1970s, the neoliberal wave that swept Latin America in the 1980s, and the decade of reform that followed the opening up of Central and Eastern European countries, along with India, in the 1990s. This trend of economic liberalization in the emerging economies gathered further momentum in the 2000s as more countries have opened up their markets to the majority of the world's multinational enterprises (MNEs). For example, in 2006, emerging economies received approximately $448.40 billion in foreign direct investment (FDI) inflows, registering a growth rate of 26.13 percent over the 2005 figure (UNCTAD, 2007). This change was brought about by the government policies of these countries favoring pro-market reforms ranging from international policy (international trade, exchange regime and foreign investment) to the macroeconomic environment (price liberalization, labor markets and fiscal policy), and finally to privatization in specific sectors. For conceptual clarity an emerging economy is defined as a low-income country that satisfies two criteria: a rapid pace of economic development, and government policies favoring economic liberalization and the adoption of a free-market system (Arnold and Quelch, 1998). A list of sixty-four such emerging economies was identified by Hoskisson *et al.* (2000).[1] Moreover, Dunning has defined an MNE as a firm that "engages in foreign direct investment and owns or controls value-adding activities in more than one country" (1992: 1).

The growing importance of FDI inflows in these emerging economies is reflected in an upsurge of international business (IB) research on this topic. However, most of the published scholarship addresses the interdependencies between the MNEs and the economic environment of the emerging economies and pays relatively less attention to theories that can explain interdependencies between MNEs and the political environment of emerging economies. Nevertheless, a well-managed MNE must deal effectively with the political and legal dynamics of its environment as well as the more traditional product- and market-focused variables (Baron, 1995). Vernon (1971) suggests that MNEs have strong incentives to influence host-country government policies on an ongoing basis to safeguard their often substantial investments, particularly given the threat of repatriation of earnings, immigration laws, trade laws and investment laws. Similarly, Dunning asserts that "any theory of MNE activity which does not explicitly seek to understand and explain the role of governments, not just another variable, but, like the market, as an organizational entity is, in its own right, bound to be deficient" (1993: 49). Failure to understand this political angle might lead to over-simplistic models of MNEs. Therefore, there is a need to conduct research on the factors that determine the choice of political strategies by MNEs operating in an emerging economy context. Note that these political strategies are not an end in themselves, but rather a means for an MNE to achieve public policy outcomes that are favorable for its economic success.

This theoretical study aims to fill this gap in the literature by first discussing the existing work on the political strategies of MNEs and then presenting a theoretical framework with specific propositions that predict the effect of different variables on the choice of these political strategies. Institutional theory is the focused theoretical framework in constructing the propositions because it emphasizes the relationship between the MNE and its "institutional environment," including government actions and the way through which this relationship shapes the MNE's internal structures and processes (Westney, 1993). Institutional theory is also appropriate for the emerging economies' contexts since it emphasizes contextual factors influencing both market and non-market forces (Peng *et al.*, 2008; Oliver, 1991). Since the environment faced by an MNE is characterized by high uncertainty and multiple demands, institutional theory provides a suitable theoretical framework with which to study MNEs' strategies, especially when one seeks to understand how MNEs attempt to reshape institutional environments (Xu and Shenkar, 2002). Given that the government is a major source of uncertainty for MNEs (Brewer, 1992), and political strategies by definition (Baysinger, 1984) are attempts to reshape a firm's opportunity set, or that of its rivals, institutional theory is particularly considered as relevant to the study of MNEs' political strategies.

Moreover, in line with calls for research using multiple levels of theoretical explanation (Klein *et al.*, 1994), factors at firm, industry and institutional level are considered in the theoretical framework. This has enabled us to develop a holistic model for political strategy formulation. Some of the practical implications of this model, along with suggestions for future research, are explored in the concluding remarks.

Literature on political strategy

The importance of host government public policy

It is well established in the existing literature that firm performance is affected by host government policies (Shaffer, 1995). Host governments set the "rules of the game" that make up the fundamental reward structure of an economy and thereby shape the behavior of business activities. The host government of an emerging economy controls critical resources through such means as the authorization for trade and investment, protection against sovereign risk, and permission of competitive advantages against rivals (e.g. subsidies, monopolies), which shape the environment that MNEs face in that country. Firms in a wide range of industries of an emerging economy are regulated by government agencies that control different policy dimensions, including, for example, market structure, product standard and testing, environmental factors, labor standards, and subsidies. These agencies are responsible for interpreting, implementing and enforcing laws of the host government.

Whereas most of the literature classifies political environments as risks to factor into planning, Boddewyn and Brewer (1994) argue that governments also represent opportunities for MNEs. Firms can take advantage of political strategies by increasing overall market size, gaining advantages related to their competitors and increasing their bargaining power relative to suppliers and customers (Hillman and Hitt, 1999). This perspective assumes that governments are not simple and efficient systems for interpreting public needs and incorporating them into national policies without any external intervention. Instead, governments are the targets of political activities designed to generate firm-specific advantages.

MNE political strategy

We define political strategy as an integrated set of activities by the MNE that are directed toward the political, social and legal institutions of the host country and intended to influence the public policy process of the host government in its favor. These strategies might seek to maintain the firms' economic survival or growth, to hinder their competitors' progress and ability to compete, or to exercise a voice in government affairs. A well-documented example of MNEs influencing the public policies of a government is the automobile industry of Mexico (Bennett and Sharpe, 1985). The intention of the López Mateos government in the 1960s was to create an auto manufacturing industry with majority Mexican equity to replace the foreign-owned firms that were then assembling vehicles from imported kits. This, along with a number of other issues raised by the state planners, gave rise to sharp conflicts with MNEs, especially Ford and General Motors. These MNEs began their efforts to win themselves a place in the Mexican market and to shape the market structure to fit their global strategy. While the state planners were conducting their study on the auto industry, Ford submitted a two-volume study of its own to outline the possible shape of the industry. Ford managers met frequently with the Mexican Minister of Industry and Commerce to make sure that the plan contained policies in favor of Ford. Both MNEs pointed to the disruption and the damage to national interests that their exclusion would cause, particularly in view of the fact that between them they held half the current market. They also mobilized support in the Mexican private sector, urging their distributors to make separate representations on their behalf. However, when the strong intention of the state to Mexicanize the industry became clear to them, they turned for support to the US government. Its explicit backing of the MNEs meant that Mexican policy toward its automobile industry would be linked with and affect what was happening in other spheres of US–Mexican relations. This prompted the Mexican government to relax its policies, and consequently both Ford and GM were approved as wholly foreign-owned subsidiaries in the decree of 1962 (ibid.).

Let us now turn to the theoretical understanding of why firms formulate political strategies. This literature draws mainly from political science, economics and organization science. The major theories used are interest group theory, public choice theory, resource dependency theory and institutional theory (Getz, 1997). Although all of these theories offer unique and highly insightful explanations of the political strategies used in the developed economies, it is important to question whether the choice of these political strategies is uniformly applicable in an emerging economy. In other words, emerging economies provide a new context that can further illustrate the relative strengths and weaknesses of these theories.

Interest group theory suggests that public policy is the result of interest group competition and represents a compromise between competing interests of many interest groups, including civil servants, businesses, consumers and politicians (Dahl, 1961; Lowi, 1969). From this viewpoint, business works collectively to secure its own interests, often to the exclusion of competing interest groups that are not a part of its social class (Epstein, 1980; Francis, 1993). Therefore, the policies and regulations governing inward FDI in emerging economies are not developed in a vacuum but are usually the result of power plays by interest groups.

Public choice theory explains the political process as a form of market-like exchange between public officials and private actors as self-interested agents (Buchanan and Tullock, 1962). Public officials supply government intervention to meet the demands of private actors. This market for political influence (or political market) is an arena in which demanders of policies (e.g. firms and consumers) interact with providers of policies (e.g. politicians and bureaucrats) to shape policies that favor the demanders' interests (Bonardi *et al.*, 2005). Firms and policy makers exchange resources, such as votes and campaign contributions, for favorable public policies, including direct subsidies, and control over entry and prices and the rules that determine substitutes. Like public interest theory, this perspective has also tended to treat business as a single coalition (Oster, 1982).

Pfeffer and Salancik (1978), in their resource dependency theory, argue that an organization can be viewed as dependent on another to the extent that (1) the latter controls a resource that is important to the survival of the former, (2) the latter holds discretion over the use of that resource, and (3) there are no other sources for that resource. The dependence of multinationals on government for favorable regulations, lower tariffs and higher levels of privatization can be used to explain why MNEs are more likely to formulate a political strategy to shape public policies. However, the resource dependency perspective focuses more on predicting the conditions under which firms will be motivated to formulate a political strategy rather than on the conditions under which political strategies will be effective in improving firms' performance (Oliver and Holzinger, 2008).

Institutional theory emphasizes the role of political, social and economic systems surrounding firms in shaping their behavior (North, 1990). Institutions are defined here as "the humanly devised constraints that structure human interaction" (ibid.: 3), which include formal rules (laws, regulations) and informal constraints (customs, norms, cultures). Institutions potentially dominate other organizations through the enforcement of these formal and informal constraints (Powell and DiMaggio, 1991). Examples of institutions are government, religion, education systems and any other systems of power. Institutional theory suggests that firms make political strategies to obtain formal and informal institutional resources, among which are laws, favorable public opinion and legitimacy (Getz, 1997).

Typology of political strategies

At the broadest level, Hillman and Hitt (1999) differentiate between proactive and reactive political strategies. The former include actions such as redefining constituents' norms or establishing standards that redefine current legislation. These proactive strategies are more useful for an MNE because they help to define what constitutes successful public policy in the first place, and thus they are able to shape public policy of the government of an emerging economy to fit the MNE's unique advantages and interests. The latter include activities such as developing efficient pollution control processes to meet environmental standards. In these reactive political strategies, firms make no attempt to play a role in policy formulation but react only *post hoc* to new legislation. The proactive strategy closely resembles "bargaining" (Boddewyn and Brewer, 1994) and "buffering" (Blumentritt, 2003) strategies. By contrast, the reactive strategy resembles "non-bargaining" (Boddewyn and Brewer, 1994) and "bridging" (Blumentritt, 2003) strategies.

After an MNE has decided to be proactive or reactive, its next decision relates to the specific strategies it should employ. Hillman and Hitt (1999) suggest three political strategies that MNEs may use to compete in the public policy process, based on the fundamental resources exchanged: (1) information, (2) financial incentive, and (3) constituency building. An information strategy centers on providing public policy makers with the information they need to expound their plans for the industry's future. These include tactics such as lobbying, reporting research and survey results, provision of expert witnesses and providing decision makers with technical papers. A financial incentive strategy targets political decision makers by providing them with a financial stimulus. This strategy includes such tactics as providing financial support directly to a political candidate or to a political party, or hiring personnel with direct political experience as managers and directors (Getz, 1993; Hillman *et al.*, 1999). This financial support is most common in government procurement, provision of infrastructure services and in business licensing, all of which heavily influence MNEs. A constituency-building strategy seeks to create awareness among interested groups, such as individual voters and citizens, and stimulate their support for given causes. This strategy includes tactics such as press conferences, public relations and advertising campaigns.

Getz (1993) noted that different combinations of political strategies may be used to solve various agency problems that arise between firms and their agents, public policy makers. It has also been argued that the opportunities for a firm to manipulate a public policy issue decrease as an issue moves through its life cycle (Baron, 2000). "This means that after a certain point, a firm may lose its opportunity to have an effective impact on a particular public policy" (Bonardi *et al.*, 2005: 406).

Factors affecting political strategies

Recent reviews of the political strategies of firms (Getz, 1997; Hillman *et al.*, 2004; Shaffer, 1995) reveal a developing consensus around some of the factors that influence these strategies. For example, at the firm level, firm size and the importance of the issue (i.e. issue salience) have been shown to increase the likelihood of a firm's participating in political strategy (Epstein, 1980; Meznar and Nigh, 1995; Schuler and Rehbein, 1997; Yoffie, 1987; Vogel, 1996). At the industry level, the scope or severity of political pressures imposed on the industry tends to establish whether firms engage in political strategies (Oliver and Holzinger, 2008). Industry structural variables such as concentration have been shown to increase the likelihood of political actions (Zardkoohi, 1985) because the costs of coordinating concentrated industries are lower than for fragmented industries (Lenway and Rehbein, 1991), and opportunities to free-ride are more limited (Schuler *et al.*, 2002).

The context of emerging economies

The literature is biased toward the political strategies of MNEs in developed economies (Windsor, 2007), which makes it difficult to apply the same constructs and/or variables to emerging economies. Even if some of the factors are theoretically common among developed and emerging economies, it is likely that they will be different in function and magnitude.

Many emerging markets have distinctive commercial practices and business cultures that are people oriented and socially embedded. For that reason, interpersonal networking with the authorities is often necessary in order to nourish business activities. Moreover, the challenge of explaining political strategies of MNEs is magnified by the heterogeneity of emerging economies. Among the sixty-four emerging economies referred to earlier (Hoskisson *et al.*, 2000) there is considerable variation in their progress in economic, political and institutional developments. Furthermore, most of the emerging economies are undergoing unparalleled transitions in their social, legal and economic institutions, transitions that raise serious acclimatization problems for MNEs (Boisot and Child, 1996; Peng and Heath, 1996). Nevertheless, the majority of the existing models of political strategies are static in their application since their main concern is to identify the antecedents (Lamberg *et al.*, 2004). Consequently, they might not be suitable for emerging economy contexts where political strategies must be explained as sequences of events unfolding across time and space.

In addition, government influence is more personal as well as secretive in emerging economies (Pearce, 2001). The host governments are dominated by personalities instead of political parties, and personal social capital often supersedes formal laws. That being so, the choice of a political strategy becomes extremely important for managers of an MNE.

We now turn to the discussion of various factors suggested as affecting MNEs' choice of which type of political strategies to adopt. Owing to the multi-level nature of the main construct, we have decided to consider some of the major factors at firm, industry and institutional level of analysis in the suggested theoretical framework. These factors do not represent an exhaustive list of determinants but in our opinion they are the most relevant.

Factors affecting MNEs' choice of political strategy

Firm-level factors

Firm size

As already described, firm size has been considered as one of the most important factors for engaging in political strategies. Schuler *et al.* (2002) suggest that size is often a proxy for resources, political clout and visibility, and that it often determines the benefits from pursuing political strategies. Larger firms are politically active because they feel more susceptible to the power of government, owing to their visibility (Getz, 1997). However, this argument assumes a relationship of equality between MNEs and host governments that might be valid only in developed economies.

In an emerging economy context the government is resource constrained and more receptive to MNEs that can contribute positively to the country's economic development by providing much-needed technologies or export markets. In order to promote industrial development, the host governments of emerging economies often provide economic inducements through grants, tax holidays and special zones to attract larger foreign firms to invest in their manufacturing sectors. For example, Mexico was forced to take a drastic turn in its economic policy in the late 1980s from import-substitution industrialization to export-led industrialization. Faced with high international interest rates, massive capital flight, a debt of US$82 billion, almost no foreign exchange reserves and an inward-looking economy, Mexico enticed large MNEs by removing all restrictions on capital flows while letting in foreign banks, securities firms and insurance companies, as well as selling state assets to large US as well as Spanish MNEs (Schatan, 1993; Toral, 2008).

These waves of neoliberalization in the emerging economies have washed away protective barriers, and as these countries integrate themselves into the world economy, MNEs from North America, Western Europe and Japan are being attracted by them. Therefore, in emerging economies, governments are at a disadvantageous position relative to MNEs from the beginning. Larger MNEs, especially, can significantly impact the employment level and investment in a particular industry. Governments are more cautious of entering into conflict with firms that can provide the economy with advanced technology and valuable resources, and they are more likely to accommodate those firms' interests. Therefore, the size of MNEs provides them with power relative to the government officials, and engaging in a political strategy is a means to exploit that power.

Proposition 1: Larger MNEs are more likely to formulate a proactive political strategy in emerging economies.

Past experience

Academics have recognized the importance of organizational learning in prior studies (e.g. Levitt and March, 1988; Zollo and Winter, 2002). In a seminal paper, Levitt and March (1988) claimed that organizational actions "involve matching procedures to situations" and are "history dependent," implying that "routines are based on interpretations of the past more than anticipations of the future." This phenomenon is also explained by institutional theory, which suggests that institutions circumscribe behaviors to assure submission to and consistency among value patterns (Scott, 1994). In an MNE, internal institutions limit the range of acceptable behaviors to those that have been used previously and thus are institutionalized within the organization. When problems arise or events occur for which multiple routes are possible, managers' attention is likely to be directed toward institutional patterns of response. Indeed, conformity to institutionalized rules may generate "path dependence" leading to specific ways of thinking and doing.

Therefore, an MNE may use political strategies because it is part of its solution set. MNEs that have used these strategies successfully in other emerging economies and those MNEs that have established formal business–government relationships in similar institutional environments are likely to possess an analogue to refer to when they are confronted with a problem in their host countries.

Proposition 2: The choice of an MNE's political strategy depends on its past experience in the political market of emerging economies.

Industry-level factors

Concentration level

An industry's concentration level implies the degree of competition that an MNE will face. If an MNE is able to invest and function in a highly concentrated industry of the emerging economy, it will be more likely to achieve abnormal profits because it is likely to become one of the few oligopolist or monopolist players in that industry, as characterized by holding a dominant market share and market power. Since high concentration prevents free competition, many host-country governments of the emerging economies are cautious of entry by MNEs into already concentrated local industries. Therefore, MNEs in these industries are likely to encounter a high level of governmental intervention. In order to avoid or manage such interference, MNEs should gain governmental support during entry and maintain a good relationship with governmental authorities during their operations. This demands that MNEs engage in a proactive political strategy while managing their relationships with the host government.

According to the collective action theory (Olson, 1965), in a fragmented industry a firm does not have enough economic incentive to incur the costs of political strategies. A firm pursuing a proactive political strategy would have to share the potential benefits of winning favorable public policies with other firms in the industry that did not participate in the political process (Esty and Caves, 1983; Grier *et al.*, 1991; Zardkoohi, 1988). Under these conditions it is more probable that a firm will look forward to free-riding instead of engaging in political activities.

On the other hand, in a concentrated industry the potential of economic gain for the oligopolistic or monopolistic firms through political strategies counteracts the propensity to free-ride. Consequently, in these industries it is easier to organize political cooperation, which results in larger overall collective benefits and larger gains for individual firms (Schuler *et al.*, 2002).

Proposition 3: MNEs are more likely to be engaged in a proactive political strategy when they are in concentrated industries of an emerging economy.

Regulatory environments

Governments of many emerging economies have sought to trim down their scope of activity within national economies and industries, for example through privatization of state-owned organizations or by forming joint public–private partnerships. However, while it is true that governments are shifting their focus from state ownership to private ownership, they are still retaining a degree of regulatory control over significant policy dimensions for different industries. This implies that liberalization does not constitute the withdrawal of government from the economy. Therefore, firms in diverse industries are subject to regulatory supervision for some aspects of their business, such as product pricing, input sourcing or process techniques (Holburn and Vanden Bergh, 2008). These regulatory tasks are performed by different agencies that establish, scrutinize and implement administrative regulations on an array of policy dimensions (Buchholz, 1990; Hillman and Keim, 1995).

In establishing these regulatory procedures, regulators take on policy positions that vary on a continuum of being friendly or hostile toward regulated firms' interests (Holburn and Vanden Bergh, 2008; Armstrong and Sappington, 2006; Stigler, 1971). As described by Holburn and Vanden Bergh,

> Friendly actions are those that establish policies close to the firm's desired outcome. Hostile regulatory decisions, however, establish policies far from the firm's preferred position. They include, inter alia, delays or refusals to issue operating permits, reductions in regulated rates, or the imposition of costly new production standards.
>
> (2008: 521)

The ability of MNEs to manage their interactions with these regulatory agencies and to secure more advantageous policy rulings is an important means of improving overall firm performance. For example, MNEs can formulate a proactive strategy by providing new information on policy alternatives and consequences (i.e. lobbying) or by making monetary contributions to the regulators. The objective of such a strategy is to gain the collaboration of that regulatory body in pressing for a policy different from the policy that would have been espoused in the absence of the MNE's political activities.

Proposition 4: As an industry in an emerging economy becomes more regulated, MNEs are more likely to involve themselves in proactive political strategies.

Institutional-level factors

Institutional void

The institutional milieu of an emerging economy includes political institutions such as the type of government, the national structure of policy making and the judicial system as well as economic institutions such as the structure of the national factor markets and the terms of access to international factors of production. The institutional environment also contains sociocultural factors such as informal norms, customs and religions, but the focus of this study is on the political and economic institutions.

Many host governments in the emerging economies have revoked many direct and indirect state intrusions in the market and have introduced different new autonomous and market-supporting institutions, including regulatory systems. However, these reforms are only the beginning steps of building new institutions. Therefore, the new institutions have yet to become embedded in society and are hardly able to perform their functions (Khanna and Palepu, 1999). The economic liberalization of a country does not guarantee a strong judicial system, without the help of which it is hard to prevent the state or its bureaucratic institutions from bending their own rules. For example, South Korea clearly liberalized its financial services sector in the 1990s, but there was no court to stop the executive branch from bending the rules on the implementation of banking regulation (Haggard, 2000). Apart from these regulatory institutions, the emerging economies also lack specialized intermediaries that make the markets work, such as consumer protection organizations, agencies that define property rights, and capital market analysts.

Moreover, in most emerging economies both the factor market and the institutional support needed for economic take-off and expansion of business activities are relatively ineffectual. Factor markets such as a capital market, a labor market, a production materials market, a foreign exchange market and an information market are generally underdeveloped and thus still prone to intervention by governmental institutions and departments. Institutional supports such as services provided by central and commercial banks, efficient customs offices, transparent government policies, and services offered by commercial and administrative agencies are generally incomplete. This institutional incompleteness has the potential to deter MNE strategies for growth.

An important means by which MNEs can bridge this institutional void is to form network ties with large local firms with political links. A number of scholars have found that firms gain advantage by developing interfirm network ties in emerging economies (e.g. Peng and Heath, 1996; Luo and Chung, 2005). Scholars have noted how membership in these networks provided a channel to overcome missing or weak market institutions. For example, Luo and Chung (2005) found that network ties within business groups were associated with superior financial performance following Taiwan's political and economic transition. Peng and Luo (2000) also reported that political connections in China were related to a greater market share and greater profitability.

These connections, usually in the form of joint ventures, are also important for the local firms of the emerging economy (Gereffi, 2005). These firms are usually looking to enter high-tech manufacturing industries that require robust knowledge bases. Since that knowledge is often tacit and spatially contained (Romer, 1994), it can be acquired quickly only by forming a joint venture or alliance with a foreign MNE. For example, Westphal (1990) noted that after liberalization, South Korean firms wanted to enter the chemicals, electronics, automobile and heavy electrical equipment industries. However, MNEs from the North Atlantic area and Japan had already developed technological and market know-how in these industries over a series of decades (Amsden, 2001). Moreover, these capabilities often existed in the form of tacit knowledge that could not simply be purchased. Therefore, the South Korean firms had to enter into joint ventures with these MNEs. One way to induce the MNEs to share benefits is to provide them upfront with shared access to the benefits provided by political allies in the government (Siegel, 2007). For example, consider the alliance between LG and the Dutch electronics manufacturer Philips in 2003. LG's political acquaintances helped it to acquire low-priced land just outside Seoul, and beneficial tax treatment with government support, and the company used those resources to attract joint investment from Philips in a multibillion-dollar joint venture producing liquid crystal display (LCD) screens (Park *et al.*, 2008).

In conclusion, partnering with MNEs helps these elite local firms to secure technology and finance. On the other hand, by forming a joint venture with large business conglomerates – the chaebols and grupos of the emerging economies – MNEs fill the institutional void by ensuring property rights and political support. Moreover, an MNE that has reservations over government expropriation or negative future changes in government policy will find collaboration with local partners to be one of the best ways to guard its interests (Aharoni, 1966; Evans, 1979). If a government unexpectedly changes its economic policies and chooses to tax or otherwise confiscate assets from certain foreign firms, it is the foreign firms without a local network connection that are the most exposed (Moon and Lado, 2000; Moran, 1974). Therefore, forming a joint venture with a local firm is not only a market maneuver but also a significant tactic in a proactive political strategy.

Moreover, once an MNE enters into a joint venture with a local firm, it will be more likely to intervene in political markets to shape policy pertaining to its economic environment in its favor, since it is now able to carry out a political strategy at a lower cost.

Proposition 5: With increasing levels of institutional void in an emerging economy, MNEs are more likely to engage in a proactive political strategy by formulating joint ventures with members of elite local political networks.

Institutional transitions

Since institutions are typically conceptualized as "the rules of the game in a society" (North, 1990: 3), institutional transitions are defined as "fundamental and comprehensive changes introduced to the formal and informal rules of the game that affect organizations as players" (Peng, 2003: 275). The institutional transitions in emerging economies are qualitatively of a different genre when compared with industry-specific changes in the developed economies (Newman, 2000). There are two major normative views on these transitions, namely the Washington consensus and the evolutionary-institutionalist perspective. The former, associated with the views of the international lending agencies such as the IMF and the World Bank, can be conceptualized as big bang or shock therapy (Williamson, 1990). The latter can be viewed as gradualism or incrementalism (Roland, 2001).

Some emerging economies, such as Poland and Russia, following the advice of Western economists (like Jeffrey Sachs) and under pressure from the IMF, chose to jump from a command-and-control system into a free market by engaging in sweeping macroeconomic reforms, whereas other countries (e.g. China) believed that sequencing and pacing reforms are key determinants of successful transition to market systems. They adopted a gradualist policy of restructuring their economy on a sector-by-sector basis. Therefore, market-oriented institutional transitions can be conceptualized as being either incremental or discontinuous. The latter entail rapid and all-encompassing change in the economic system and fiscal infrastructure of an economy and are usually the result of the shock therapy. The changes undertaken in most countries of Central and Eastern Europe after the demise of communism are clear examples of this discontinuous transition. Communism was discarded almost instantaneously but only slowly replaced with contemporary norms, values and assumptions more consistent with democracy and a market-based system (Newman, 2000).

Recent research on economic liberalization and privatization has suggested that policy shocks also create strategic opportunities (Ghemawat and Kennedy, 1999). During discontinuous transitions, governments of emerging economies are more receptive toward proactive political strategies such as lobbying or financial inducements by MNEs. For example, consider the cases of assignment of licenses for monopolies over new technology, quotas for import of certain products and lucrative public-sector contracts, as well as purchase of strategic state-owned enterprises. Profitability during discontinuous transitions, therefore, depends not only on the economic control held by the MNE but also on the MNE's political skill in securing favorable exceptions from, or changes to, existing public policy.

On the other hand, it is harder to sway the public policy process in a more established and structured institutional environment where norms are recognized and interests of competitors are entrenched.

Proposition 6a: During the discontinuous phase of institutional transition in emerging economies, MNEs are more likely to engage in proactive political strategies.

Proposition 6b: During the incremental phase of institutional transition in emerging economies, MNEs are more likely to engage in reactive political strategies.

Theoretical framework

Our theoretical framework seeks to explain the political strategies of MNEs in emerging economies not only by firm-level factors but also by higher-level industry and country institutional factors. Hence, the use of multilevel analysis allows us to construct a holistic theoretical model (Figure 5.1).

Managerial implications

As more and more MNEs spread out in the emerging economies, it is of utmost importance that their managers be cognizant of the opportunities for, and limitations on, business involvement in the political processes of their host

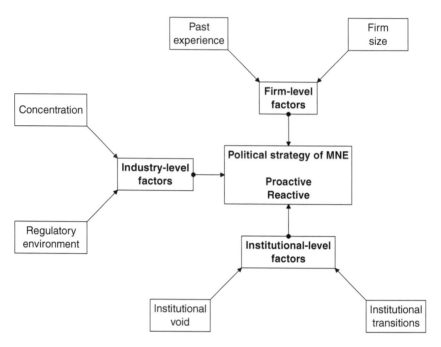

Figure 5.1 Political strategy of multinational enterprises: theoretical framework.

governments. This framework will help managers to become aware of the contingencies present in emerging economies and also about the fit between the host institutional environment and the choice of political strategies. The most potent proactive strategy will be one in which managers change institutional structures so that the government is led to act differently without there beingany visible conflict. The interests and powers of the state and the MNE are shaped by the structures in which they operate, and altering these structures might lead them to behave differently. Furthermore, better knowledge regarding the factors that play a pivotal role in the formulation of political strategies by MNEs can enhance our understanding of MNEs' successes and failures in the emerging economies.

Finally, this study can also guide government policy makers in forestalling the kind of political strategies they are likely to have to deal with in their given specific institutional environment. Acquaintance with these political strategies would help them to anticipate the limits and possibilities for using state power to compel MNEs to act in ways perceived to be more beneficial for the host country. For example, if the proactive political strategies of MNEs are leading toward oligopolistic behavior in a sector, then public policy should address the contested issues of the number of firms engaged in the industry as well as the extent of domestic ownership. On the other hand, if the strategies are reactive, then the government might be interested in antitrust legislation in order to ensure effective competition. Therefore, the exercise of power by the state should change, given knowledge of the political strategies available to MNEs.

Future research

We hope to motivate additional research into the nature of the political strategies of MNEs. We believe that much progress needs to be made to understand the complexity of the political markets in the emerging economies and how MNEs contrive their way through these markets. In the course of outlining our theoretical framework, we have offered a number of testable propositions. Researchers from IB and strategy fields can test these propositions in an emerging economy context, especially in economies that have readily embraced the free-market capitalistic system after independence such as Pakistan, Latin American and Central Asian states. Among the empirical challenges is the usage of multilevel modeling to ascertain the effects of factors at firm, industry and institutional level on the usage and choice of the political strategies.

Another important research question concerns the boundaries of rational political action in the emerging economies, since the political strategies executed by MNEs might generate ethical dilemmas. If these strategies are viewed by managers from a short-term profit-maximization perspective, then the strategies may negatively affect the overall development of the host society. Therefore, the managers must be sensitized to the moral questions and the ethical underpinnings of their political strategies.

In future work, scholars could also examine the interrelationships between actions in the economic and political markets. A work covering the integration of strategies in these two domains in a single framework would indeed be a seminal one, since some factors, such as firm size and industry concentration, drive both strategies. This integration has also been called for by Bonardi *et al.* (2005), but a comprehensive framework is still to emerge.

Although we have developed a multilevel conceptual model to analyze political strategies of MNEs, our study does not seek to theorize the effects of all levels. Moreover, we have not systematically scrutinized the interrelationships between different independent variables, which would be worth undertaking in a future research study. However, these limitations are common in most research settings and also offer starting points for future research.

In conclusion, formulation of political strategies by MNEs in emerging economies is an understudied topic in political science, strategy and IB literature. Nonetheless, as long as the state is in charge of the access to markets, the relationship between MNEs and governments will continue to be important. We hope that our work will encourage debate and empirical examination of how MNEs formulate their political strategies to intervene in the political market to shape the public policies of host governments.

Note

1 These sixty-four countries are, in alphabetical order, Albania, Argentina, Armenia, Azerbaijan, Bangladesh, Belarus, Bosnia, Botswana, Brazil, Bulgaria, Chile, China, Colombia, Côte d'Ivoire, Croatia, the Czech Republic, Ecuador, Egypt, Estonia, Georgia, Ghana, Greece, Hungary, India, Indonesia, Israel, Jamaica, Jordan, Kazakhstan, Kenya, Korea, Kyrgyzstan, Latvia, Lithuania, Macedonia, Malaysia, Mauritius, Mexico, Moldova, Morocco, Nigeria, Pakistan, Peru, the Philippines, Poland, Portugal, Romania, Russia, Saudi Arabia, Slovakia, Slovenia, South Africa, Sri Lanka, Taiwan, Tajikistan, Thailand, Trinidad and Tobago, Tunisia, Turkey, Turkmenistan, Ukraine, Uzbekistan, Venezuela and Zimbabwe.

References

Aharoni, Y. (1966) *The Foreign Investment Decision Process*, Boston: Harvard Business School Press.

Amsden, A. H. (2001) *The Rise of "the Rest": Challenges to the West from Late-Industrializing Economies*, Oxford: Oxford University Press.

Armstrong, M. and Sappington, D. E. M. (2006) "Regulation, competition, and liberalization," *Journal of Economic Literature*, 44 (2): 325–366.

Arnold, D. J. and Quelch, J. A. (1998) "New strategies in emerging economies," *Sloan Management Review*, 40: 7–20.

Baron, D. P. (1995) "Integrated strategy: Market and nonmarket components," *California Management Review*, 37: 47–65.

—— (2000) *Business and Its Environment*, 3rd ed., Upper Saddle River, NJ: Prentice Hall.

Baysinger, B. D. (1984) "Domain maintenance as an objective of business political activity: An expanded typology," *Academy of Management Review*, 9: 248–258.

Bennett, D. C. and Sharpe, K. (1985) *Transnational Corporations versus the State: The Political Economy of the Mexican Auto Industry*, Princeton, NJ: Princeton University Press.

Blumentritt, T. P. (2003) "Foreign subsidiaries' government affairs activities: The influence of managers and resources," *Business and Society*, 42: 202–233.

Boddewyn, J. J. and Brewer, T. L. (1994) "International-business political behavior: New theoretical directions," *Academy of Management Review*, 19: 119–143.

Boisot, M. and Child, J. (1996) "From fiefs to clans and network capitalism: Explaining China's emerging economic order," *Administrative Science Quarterly*, 41: 600–628.

Bonardi, J. P., Hillman, A. J. and Keim, G. D. (2005) "The attractiveness of political markets: Implications for firm strategy," *Academy of Management Review*, 30: 397–413.

Brewer, T. L. (1992) "An issue-area approach to the analysis of MNE–government relations," *Journal of International Business Studies*, 23: 295–309.

Buchanan, J. M. and Tullock, G. (1962) *The Calculus of Consent: Logical Foundations of Constitutional Democracy*, Ann Arbor: University of Michigan Press.

Buchholz, R. A. (1990) *Essentials of Public Policy for Management*, Upper Saddle River, NJ: Prentice Hall.

Dahl, R. A. (1961) *Who Governs?* New Haven, CT: Yale University Press.

Dunning, J. H. (1992) *Multinational Enterprises and the Global Economy*, Wokingham, UK: Addison-Wesley.

—— (1993) *The Globalization of Business: The Challenge of the 1990s*, London: Routledge.

Epstein, E. M. (1980) "Business political activity: Research approaches and analytical issues," in L. E. Preston (ed.) *Research in Corporate Social Performance and Policy*, Greenwich, CT: JAI Press.

Esty, D. C. and Caves, R. E. (1983) "Market structure and political influence: New data on political expenditures, activity, and success," *Economic Inquiry*, 21: 24–38.

Evans, P. B. (1979) *Dependent Development: The Alliance of Multinational, State, and Local Capital in Brazil*, Princeton, NJ: Princeton University Press.

Francis, J. G. (1993) *The Politics of Regulation: A Comparative Perspective*, Oxford: Blackwell.

Gereffi, G. (2005) "The global economy: Organization, governance and development," in N. J. Smelser and R. Swedberg (eds.) *Handbook of Economic Sociology*, 2nd edn., Princeton, NJ: Princeton University Press.

Getz, K. A. (1993) *Selecting Corporate Political Tactics*, London: Sage.

—— (1997) "Research in corporate political action: Integration and assessment," *Business and Society*, 36: 32–72.

Ghemawat, P. and Kennedy, R. E. (1999) "Competitive shocks and industrial structure: The case of Polish manufacturing," *International Journal of Industrial Organization*, 17: 847–867.

Grier, K. B., Munger, M. C. and Roberts, B. E. (1991) "The industrial organization of corporate political participation," *Southern Economic Journal*, 57: 727–738.

Haggard, S. (2000) *The Political Economy of the Asian Financial Crisis*, Washington, DC: Institute for International Economics.

Hillman, A. and Hitt, M. A. (1999) "Corporate political strategy formulation: A model of approach, participation and strategy decisions," *Academy of Management Review*, 24: 825–842.

Hillman, A. and Keim, G. (1995) "International variation in the business–government interface: Institutional and organizational considerations," *Academy of Management Review*, 20: 193–214.

Hillman, A., Zardkoohi, A. and Bierman, L. (1999) "Corporate political strategies and firm performance: Indications of firm-specific benefits from personal service in the U.S. government," *Strategic Management Journal*, 20: 67–81.

Hillman, A. J., Keim, G. D. and Schuler, D. (2004) "Corporate political activity: A review and research agenda," *Journal of Management*, 30: 837–857.

Holburn, G. and Vanden Bergh, R. (2008) "Making friends in hostile environments: Political strategy in regulated industries," *Academy of Management Review*, 33: 520–540.

Hoskisson, R. E., Eden, L., Lau, C. M. and Wright, M. (2000) "Strategy in emerging economies," *Academy of Management Journal*, 43: 249–267.

Khanna, T. and Palepu, K. (1999) "Policy shocks, market intermediaries, and corporate strategy: The evolution of business groups in Chile and India," *Journal of Economics and Management Strategy*, 8: 271–310.

Klein, K. J., Dansereau, F. and Hall, R. J. (1994) "Levels issues in theory development, data collection, and analysis," *Academy of Management Review*, 19: 195–229.

Lamberg, J. A., Skippari, M., Skippari, J. and Mäkinen, S. (2004) "The evolution of corporate political action: A framework for processual analysis," *Business and Society*, 43 (4): 335–365.

Lenway, S. A. and Rehbein, K. (1991) "Leaders, followers and free riders: An empirical test of variation in corporate political involvement," *Academy of Management Journal*, 34: 893–905.

Levitt, B. and March, J. G. (1988) "Organizational learning," *Annual Reviews of Sociology*, 14: 319–338.

Lowi, T. (1969) *The End of Liberalism: Ideology, Policy, and the Crisis of Public Authority*, New York: W. W. Norton.

Luo, X. and Chung, C. N. (2005) "Keeping it all in the family: The role of particularistic relationships in business group performance during institutional transition," *Administrative Science Quarterly*, 50: 404–439.

Meznar, M. B. and Nigh, D. (1995) Buffer or bridge? Environmental and organizational determinants of public affairs activities in American firms," *Academy of Management Journal*, 38: 975–975.

Moon, C. W. and Lado, A. A. (2000) "MNC–host government bargaining power relationship: A critique and extension within the resource-based view," *Journal of Management*, 26 (1): 85–117.

Moran, T. H. (1974) *Multinational Corporations and the Politics of Dependence: Copper in Chile*, Princeton, NJ: Princeton University Press.

Newman, K. L. (2000) "Organizational transformation during institutional upheaval," *Academy of Management Review*, 25: 602–619.

North, D. C. (1990) *Institutions, Institutional Change and Economic Performance*, New York: Cambridge University Press.

Oliver, C. (1991) "Strategic responses to institutional processes," *Academy of Management Review*, 16: 145–179.

Oliver, C. and Holzinger, I. (2008) "The effectiveness of strategic political management: A dynamic capabilities framework," *Academy of Management Review*, 33: 496–520.

Olson, M. (1965) *The Logic of Collective Action: Public Goods and the Theory of Groups*, Cambridge, MA: Harvard University Press.

Oster, S. M. (1982) "The strategic use of regulatory investment by industry subgroups," *Economic Inquiry*, 20: 604–618.

Park, T.-Y., Choung, J.-Y. and Min, H.-G. (2008) "The cross-industry spillover of technological capability: Korea's DRAM and TFT-LCD industries," *World Development*, 36: 2855–2873.

Pearce, J. L. (2001) "How we can learn how governments matter to management and organization," *Journal of Management Inquiry*, 10: 103–112.

Peng, M. W. (2003) "Institutional transitions and strategic choices," *Academy of Management Review*, 28: 275–296.

Peng, M. W. and Heath, P. S. (1996) "The growth of the firm in planned economies in transition: Institutions, organizations, and strategic choice," *Academy of Management Review*, 21: 492–528.

Peng, M. W. and Luo, Y. (2000) "Managerial ties and firm performance in a transition economy: The nature of a micro–macro link," *Academy of Management Journal*, 43: 486–501.

Peng, M. W., Wang, D. and Jiang, Y. (2008) "An institution-based view of international business strategy: A focus on emerging economies," *Journal of International Business Studies*, 39: 920–936.

Pfeffer, J. and Salancik, G. R. (1978) *The External Control of Organizations: A Resource Dependence Perspective*, New York: Harper & Row.

Powell, W. W. and DiMaggio, P. J. (1991) *The New Institutionalism in Organizational Analysis*, Chicago: University of Chicago Press.

Roland, G. (2001) "Ten years after: Transition and economics," *IMF Staff Papers: Transition Economies: How Much Progress?*, 48: 29–52.

Romer, P. M. (1994) "The origins of endogenous growth," *Journal of Economic Perspectives*, 8: 3–22.

Schatan, C. (1993) "Out of the crisis: Mexico," in D. Tussie and D. Glover (eds.) *The Developing Countries in World Trade*, Boulder, CO: Lynne Rienner.

Schuler, D. A. and Rehbein, K. (1997) "The filtering role of the firm in corporate political involvement," *Business and Society*, 36: 116–139.

Schuler, D. A., Rehbein, K. and Cramer, R. D. (2002) "Pursuing strategic advantage through political means: A multivariate approach," *Academy of Management Journal*, 45: 659–672.

Scott, R. and Meyer, J. (1994) *Institutional Environments and Organizations: Structural Complexity and Individualism*, Beverly Hills, CA: Sage.

Shaffer, B. (1995) "Firm-level responses to government regulation: Theoretical and research approaches," *Journal of Management*, 21: 495–514.

Siegel, J. (2007) "Contingent political capital and international alliances: Evidence from South Korea," *Administrative Science Quarterly*, 52: 621–666.

Stigler, G. (1971) "The theory of economic regulation," *Bell Journal of Economics and Management Science*, 2: 3–21.

Toral, P. (2008) "The foreign direct investments of Spanish multinational enterprises in Latin America, 1989–2005," *Journal of Latin American Studies*, 40: 513–544.

UNCTAD (2007) *World Investment Report 2007*, Geneva: United Nations Conference on Trade and Development.

Vernon, R. (1971) *Sovereignty at Bay: The Multinational Spread of US Enterprises*, New York: Basic Books.

Vogel, D. (1996) "The study of business and politics," *California Management Review*, 38: 146–165.

Westney, D. E. (1993) "Institutionalization theory and the multinational corporation," in S. Ghoshal and D. E. Westney (eds.) *Organization Theory and the Multinational Corporation*, New York: St. Martin's Press.

Westphal, L. E. (1990) "Industrial policy in an export-propelled economy: Lessons from South Korea's experience," *Journal of Economic Perspectives*, 4: 41–59.

Williamson, J. G. (1990) "What Washington means by policy reform," in J. G. Williamson (ed.) *Latin American Adjustment: How Much Has Happened?*, Washington, DC: Institute for International Economics.

Windsor, D. (2007) "Toward a global theory of cross-border and multilevel corporate political activity," *Business and Society*, 46: 253–278.

Xu, D. and Shenkar, O. (2002) "Institutional distance and the multinational enterprise," *Academy of Management Review*, 27: 608–618.

Yoffie, D. B. (1987) "Corporate strategies for political action: A rational model," in A. A. Marcus, A. Kaufman and D. Beam (eds.) *Business Strategy and Public Policy: Perspectives from Industry and Academia*, New York: Quorum Books.

Zardkoohi, A. (1985) "On the political participation of the firm in the electoral process," *Southern Economic Journal*, 51: 804–817.

—— (1988) "Market structure and campaign contributions: Does concentration matter? A reply," *Public Choice*, 58: 187–191.

Zollo, M. and Winter, S. G. (2002) "Deliberate learning and the evolution of dynamic capabilities," *Organization Science*, 13: 339–351.

6 Business groups and corporate governance in emerging markets

Natalya Totskaya

Introduction

Understanding business groups: the road map to success in developing countries

This chapter addresses the aspects of corporate governance specific to emerging markets, with a particular interest in governance framework within business groups. Business groups represent the dominant form of large business organizations in emerging markets around the world. In their respective national economies, business groups contribute greatly to GNP, they own a large proportion of national assets and they employ a significant percentage of the national workforce (Chung, 2005; Carney, 2008; Khanna and Rivkin, 2001). Despite the importance of groups to many national economies, research on this phenomenon is still fragmented. Broadly defining business groups as "collections of firms bound together in some formal and informal ways" (Granovetter, 1995: 454), scholars still debate groups' origins, their developmental paths and the effects of group affiliation on member firms. The portion of business group literature related to the specifics of governance mechanisms, cost and conflicts is relatively small, but growing. A review of strategy-related issues in emerging economies (Hoskisson *et al.*, 2000) has demonstrated a variety of theoretical perspectives in the studying of patterns of corporate governance. There are a number of studies on governance issues in newly industrialized markets (Khanna and Palepu, 2004; Phan, 2001; Young *et al.*, 2004) and in transition economies (Filatotchev *et al.*, 2003; Wright *et al.*, 2003). There are studies addressing corporate governance as an issue for national business policy (Carney, 2004) or as governance convergence–divergence globally (Khanna and Palepu, 2004).

In the context of interactions between the local business logic of emerging countries and global strategies of multinational enterprises (MNEs), business groups represent the essence of complexity MNEs face in entering developing countries. As the largest, strongest and most reputable players in their national markets, business groups become both partners and rivals for MNEs operating in emerging economies (Carrera *et al.*, 2003). To be competitive in emerging economies, MNEs need to understand the specifics of local business systems, including decision making, strategic motives of economic actors, societal pressures, etc. In terms of firm behavior they should be aware of potential costs and conflicts related to firm governance in less structured institutional environments. MNEs should be ready to adjust their approach to effective firm management to blend into their new and very different business environment. Understanding models and principles of corporate governance relevant to large, diversified business groups will help MNEs to assess the direction and magnitude of the adjustments in their governance system required to succeed in emerging economies.

What specific features of business groups are reflected in the corporate governance in emerging markets, and what are the implications for MNEs entering these markets? The answer to these questions is based on a synthesis of findings from prior research on business groups' origins, conduct and change. Agency and institutional theories together provide an integrated perspective for analyzing corporate governance at the firm and the country level. Agency theory helps in approaching the internal environment for corporate governance, including tensions, costs and management tools related to the specific ownership configuration of business groups. Institutional theory brings to focus external pressures that shape firm behavior in emerging markets. This chapter seeks to contribute to a better understanding of the characteristics of corporate governance in business groups. It also aims to shed light on the complexity of interactions among the elements of governance in emerging markets. The conceptual model presented in this chapter illustrates the process of formation of corporate governance in emerging markets. This model illustrates how the interactions among input factors (concentrated ownership and state activism) and formal and informal institutional relationships shape the governance system.

To answer the research questions stated above, this chapter begins with an introduction to the topic of corporate governance. The second section reviews corporate governance in light of agency perspective and internal mechanisms of governance in business groups. The third section looks at the institutional context of governance in emerging economies. The chapter concludes with a conceptual model of corporate governance in emerging markets.

Corporate governance in emerging markets

Corporate governance is the relational system that carries regulative institutions (Scott, 2001); it is built on economic, legal, sociological, ethical and psychological assumptions to accommodate various components and principles. Through the processes of institutionalization, corporate governance disciplines powerful organizational, market and societal actors. In turn, corporate governance is affected by those powerful actors. The development of corporate governance reflects institutional change; it is essential for organizational and social progress and innovation (Toms and Wright, 2002).

The importance of corporate governance has been widely accepted. In its broad meaning, corporate governance reflects the way a firm is organized and controlled. Processes, policies, and mechanisms of governance are the integral parts of a firm's economic activity; they refer to the specifics of business organization itself, and to its developmental paths. Elements of governance such as the financial system, property rights, the ownership structure, business competition and commodity markets play a vital role in economic development and in the overall well-being of any country (Claessens, 2006). The state of corporate governance not only affects firm' functioning but may also interrupt economic processes and cause crises, with wide impacts on a variety of economic actors (Johnson *et al.*, 2000). In emerging markets the relationships between the formation of the institutional environment, government structures and large, well-established business organizations are especially complex. On the one hand, they are deeply rooted in informal institutional arrangements such as societal norms and traditions, which are much stronger in developing countries than in industrialized ones. On the other hand, they are dynamic and uncertain, as developing countries may try various approaches to the creation of a market economy and integration into the global community. This is why, for emerging markets, the quality of governance may be even more essential, as their economies, political and social systems are undergoing transitions and are less steady.

In markets with underdeveloped institutions, external and internal mechanisms of corporate governance are not well balanced. Owing to the immaturity or absence of essential market institutions, external corporate governance is weak. Emerging countries are not capable of imposing a fully developed and clear set of formal rules disciplining business organizations. Given the lack of external governance, there is a need to impose additional administrative regulations within organizational hierarchies to compensate for weak, poorly functioning market institutions (Yiu *et al.*, 2007). In this regard, two primary characteristics distinguishing business groups from other business organizations become important. The first is the core group structure providing overall administrative and financial control (Khanna and Rivkin, 2006; Strachan, 1976; Yiu *et al.*, 2007); the second is the variety of ties bonding group members together. These distinctive characteristics of business groups are reflected in specific features of corporate governance within business groups, and in emerging markets in general. Group structure and ties among group members mainly define the specificity of agency relationships within business groups, and related mechanisms of control and monitoring. In addition, structural features of business groups reflect the institutional configuration of a given country, and the mode of interaction among different participants in socioeconomic exchange (Kedia *et al.*, 2006; Khanna and Yafeh, 2007; Luo and Chung, 2005).

Conflicts and controls in business group governance systems

Hierarchical ownership structure and agency relationships in business groups

The agency view on corporate governance and business groups brings to the focus of research the issues of ownership structure, relationships among owners and multiple conflicting interests. It also addresses corporate governance in terms of the mechanisms of control and coordination. Specific agency relationships within business groups are usually related to the weakness or insufficiency of external control and monitoring of group members' behavior (Yiu *et al.*, 2007). In turn, those external regulations can be attributed to the type of national legal system, with common law providing the greatest levels of owner and investor protection, and French civil law the lowest (La Porta *et al.*, 1998). In emerging countries, external regulations are in general weaker than in developed countries. The origins of a national legal system may increase the overall weakness of property rights and investment protection. In terms of business groups, this means the need to develop internal protection mechanisms. Concentrated ownership, with a hierarchical ownership structure of business groups and a multiplicity of ties among group members, serves this purpose. Ownership structure and intergroup links represent vertical and horizontal mechanisms of protection against imperfect legislation, market uncertainties and unfriendly foreign and local competition.

Vertical, often pyramidal, ownership structure determines the type and scale of agency conflicts in business groups. It also affects group external relationships with other economic actors, and national institutions. For the widely held firms that operate in developed economies, agency problems are usually associated with the conflicts of interests between owners, stakeholders and managers (principal–agent conflicts). The role of governance structures is to minimize the costs related to conflicting interests and to improve firm performance.

Principal–agent issues are less apparent in business groups with concentrated family or state ownership. It is believed that concentrated ownership helps to resolve principal–agent conflicts in group-member firms (Young *et al.*, 2004), serving as a built-in control for these types of agency problems and costs. Even if conflicts between agent and principal are much less common in business groups than in widely held companies, the potential for such conflicts still exists. On the other hand, specific features of high concentration of ownership and control in business groups trigger principal–principal conflicts between majority and minority shareholders (Chang, 2006; Millar *et al.*, 2005). For instance, concentrated private ownership and management by family members do not eliminate agency costs and the need for formal governance structures and mechanisms in family-owned business groups (Schulze *et al.* 2001). The specificity of agency problems in business groups reflects the need to consider special models of governance for business groups with concentrated ownership.

Principal–principal conflicts stem from poor legal protection of minority shareholders. Outcomes of principal–principal conflicts are multiple: on a country level they include inefficient capital allocation and lower standards of living; on a business-group level they cause some "informal" groups and coalitions to form; on a member-firm level, principal–principal issues affect firm strategies and the effectiveness of governance structures. Several studies address principal–principal issues typical of firms with concentrated ownership, and owner-managed firms. Young *et al.*'s (2008) study exemplifies principal–principal conflicts between controlling shareholders and minority shareholders both in central administrative structures of business groups and in family-controlled member firms. The level of ownership concentration and even the composition of the controlling family affect corporate governance and the performance of business groups (Bertrand *et al.*, 2008). In line with Young *et al.* (2008), these authors hypothesize that because of the "dilution" of ownership and control among powerful family members, the private interests of owners diverge: family members start tunneling resources from their business group.[1] And again, because of the weak property rights protection in the country studied (Thailand), owners cannot separate their ownership and control and properly reorganize the governance structures of their group.

The identity of concentrated ownership matters, as different types of owner impose different governance principles and related agency costs (Cuervo-Cazurra, 2006). Differences in the owners' identity affect the degree of separation between ownership, management and control within a business group. They also result in different options to access external financing and different logics of business groups' strategic behavior. Identifying family-owned, state-owned and widely held business groups, Cuervo-Cazurra proposes that more studies on owners' identity and its effects are needed, especially in relation to family-owned firms. In emerging markets, a majority of groups are privately held and a much smaller number of groups are state owned. In line with previous studies, family-owned business groups will have fewer agent–principal conflicts and related costs than state-owned ones. Principal–principal conflicts related to relationships between majority and minority shareholders will be significant; they will result in owners' entrenchment and in a lack of separation of ownership and control (Carney, 2008; Cuervo-Cazurra, 2006).

The potential for principal–agent conflicts exemplifies itself in pyramids. Morck *et al.* (2005) provide an extensive review of publications on business groups with pyramidal ownership. They notice that while in pyramids control rights and cash-flow rights are often separated, major agency problems nevertheless exist. Divergence of the interests of owners and managers in pyramids coexists with the entrenchment of both principals and agents. Concentrated pyramidal ownership increases owners' private benefits together with agency costs and conflicts (Douma *et al.*, 2006; Lins, 2003; Morck and Yeung, 2003). Owners can manipulate pyramid members' resources, efficiency and market valuation, and they use a variety of mechanisms to expropriate value from minority shareholders (Chang, 2003). On a larger scale, owners' entrenchment may affect national economic development in countries with underdeveloped institutional structures. These findings support Claessens *et al.*'s (2000) arguments that in pyramids and cross-holdings, increasing concentration of family control reflects the level of a country's economic development, together with the influence of wealthy elites on national institutional structures.

Concluding our examination of the vertical dimension of internal governance, we may say that concentrated ownership is a distinct feature of business groups, and one that defines their corporate governance. Strong owners construct governance systems that select various mechanisms to prioritize and fulfill their economic and social goals.

Horizontal ties, monitoring and interests alignment

Horizontal, "relational" ties among group members reflect another dimension of internal governance in business groups. Horizontal mechanisms of governance serve two purposes. First, alignment of group members' interests, intergroup monitoring and mutual contractual ties compensate for the lack of law enforcement in emerging markets. Second, it helps in monitoring and managing agency conflicts and costs among group affiliated firms (Khanna and Rivkin, 2001).

From the agency perspective the enforcement environment is the key factor in creating an effective business infrastructure and governance system (Berglöf and Claessens, 2006; Filatotchev *et al.*, 2003). Private business structures are often more successful in enhancing law enforcement than efforts made by government.

> Private ordering can precede and serve as a basis for public laws and a model for private and public enforcement of these laws. The balance between private ordering and private enforcement of public laws depends on the quality of public laws and the strength of enforcement institutions.
>
> (Berglöf and Claessens, 2006: 146)

In emerging countries, legal systems are often underdeveloped (Allen, 2005; Dieleman and Sachs, 2006; Guthrie, 1997; Peng, 2002), or the laws are in place but enforcement is weak (Greif and Kandel, 1995; Kedia *et al.*, 2006; McDermott, 2002). This why business groups internally impose and balance formal and informal elements of corporate governance.

Different corporate governance mechanisms vary in their effectiveness. In the case of business groups there are three main formal mechanisms of internal governance: blockholders, bilateral private enforcement and formal monitoring by banks (Berglöf and Claessens, 2006). Blockholders are of great importance, and this is reflected in governance codes and corporate law. Concentrated ownership in business groups allows powerful and authoritative dominant owners (families or state) to enforce internal codes and laws among member firms. In this regard, additional bilateral mechanisms play an essential role as they help to specify control rights and shareholder agreements, and hence bilateral mechanisms set corporate governance rules that benefit insiders, owners in particular. In a way, they may escalate the expropriation of minority shareholders, but at the same time, "rule setting" motivates all owners and investors to work together. Applicability of the third formal mechanism of governance, formal monitoring by banks, is limited within business groups as many of them do not include financial institutions as group members. Non-member banks do not perform monitoring, as access to external finances is often limited in emerging markets; groups rely on the pooling of their own resources. But formal monitoring by banks can potentially be a strong tool for maintaining overall group effectiveness when financial markets are well developed.

Among informal mechanisms of governance, reputation and self-enforcement are of great importance. They are essential when external enforcement is weak, and informal arrangements, norms and traditions are highly valued. As the external environment becomes more developed, reputation, trust and self-enforcement do not lose their significance; rather, these informal mechanisms become even stronger.

Integrating formal and informal elements, central and reciprocal monitoring in business groups correspond to external monitoring in developed economies. Monitoring in business groups helps to increase stability and growth among group members and protects them from inefficient and uncertain external markets (Carney, 2008; Luo and Chung, 2005). Various types of monitoring also create interdependence among member firms, allowing for mutual exploitation of market imperfections. Individual positions and responsibilities of different shareholders in intergroup structures often reflect the traditional distribution of authority in society at large, demonstrating strong relations between national business systems and national culture (Granovetter, 1995). The effectiveness of control of agency costs through interfirm monitoring reflects the variety of goals of business groups. It is often the case that business groups honor good performance as much as mutual support, stability and longevity (Carney, 2008; Khanna and Rivkin, 2001; Khanna and Yafeh, 2007). If these non-economic goals are important to group owners (as is often the case in Asian countries), corporate governance may focus less on economic effectiveness and more on collective benefits for the group members and value creation for society at large.

To sum up, business groups compensate for the lack of external governance structures through the creation of strong internal mechanisms (Claessens *et al.*, 2000; Yiu *et al.*, 2007). The main elements of corporate governance in groups originate from their concentrated ownership (Bertrand *et al.*, 2008; Young *et al.*, 2004) and reflect the identity of a dominant owner (Cuervo-Cazurra, 2006; Schulze *et al.*, 2001). A hierarchical ownership structure represents the vertical dimension of a governance system aimed at bringing about control in the interests of primary owners. Mitigating most principal–agent conflicts, concentrated ownership brings to the fore principal–principal conflicts as specific to business groups in emerging countries (Morck *et al.*, 2005; Young *et al.*, 2008). Interorganizational ties among member firms create the horizontal dimension of governance, providing ongoing monitoring over the alignment of interests of group members, and controlling for principal–principal costs and conflicts (Berglöf and Claessens, 2006; Filatotchev *et al.*, 2003; Khanna and Rivkin, 2001). Taken together, both dimensions contribute to the sustaining of business groups' position within the national economy; they help in lobbying for group interests in domestic and global markets. At the same time, the internal mechanisms of governance discriminate against minority investors, affecting the balance between protection and benefits for different groups of owners.

While stronger than external governance, the internal component of corporate governance in emerging markets does not manifest itself in isolation from the external institutional environment. Business groups are more than part of emerging markets' economic landscape. Groups are often the largest domestic business organizations and, taken together, group member firms own an essential part of tangible and intangible assets (Amsden, 2001; Fisman, 2001; Fisman and Khanna, 2004), and as powerful market players, groups have interests and influence beyond rivalry and good economic performance. In turn, external institutions have their interests in affecting business groups' conduct (Schneider, 2009). So, we can conclude that business groups have a "natural bond," and multidirectional interactions with the environment they operate in.

The institutional context of corporate governance in emerging markets

Business groups and national institutions

Analysis of prior research suggests that corporate governance in emerging markets emphasizes internal and often informal rules and mechanisms (Allen, 2005; Claessens *et al.*, 2000; Fisman, 2001; Kedia *et al.*, 2006; McDermott, 2002). At the same time, the institutional perspective views business groups as entities naturally integrated in their national institutional settings, including culture, traditions and social norms (Granovetter, 1995; Lee and O'Neill, 2003). The importance of social ties and informal relationships in emerging institutional environments has been strengthened by researchers who suggest that local logics are not to be ignored as factors in global economic and market development (Peng, 2003; Peng and Zhou, 2005; London and Hart, 2004; Luo and Chung, 2005). Researchers disagree on the type and particular elements of institutional environment that contribute the most to the emergence of governance. Some suggest that "countries matter so much for corporate governance" (Doidge *et al.*, 2007: 3) in terms of investor protection, law enforcement, development of financial markets and overall economic development. Others extend this view by stating that national corporate governance should be consistent with the history, culture and political and legal traditions of a country, and at the same time, governance should help exploit the benefits of economic organization with minimum agency costs (Gedajlovic and Shapiro, 1998). In view of the great embeddedness of business groups in a variety of local institutions, it is essential to understand what institutional factors affect business group governance practices, and in what way.

Mutually beneficial interactions between firms and institutions are not unique to emerging countries. For instance, in developed economies firms shape their corporate governance through private negotiations with financial institutions (Carleton *et al.*, 1998). Developing countries are known to have a much deeper and more complex connection between economic players and institutional structures. In emerging markets, business groups maintain close ties with the most influential institutions. The nation-state, represented by government, politicians and bureaucracy, is the focus of groups' external relations. National governments have induced the creation and subsequent development of business groups in a number of emerging countries in Asia and Latin America (Guillén, 2000; Keister, 1998; Yiu *et al.*, 2005). Connections between business groups and local political and bureaucratic structures are essential for the facilitated legitimization of business groups, for their sustainability in an uncertain external environment. By establishing close relationships with the state, business groups not only serve their own economic interests but also act as instruments of institutional change (Loveridge, 2006; Yiu et al., 2005). Business groups, as powerful and well-connected players, promote state efforts to create external governance mechanisms; and they can benefit from early adaptation of balanced governance practices. Considering the size, scale of operations and overall importance of business groups to their national economies, it is safe to consider that business groups represent ersatz governing structures, embedded in local institutions.

Institutional context provides a basis for the formation and further development of corporate governance systems, and the quality of institutions varies noticeably among emerging economies. Emerging markets' institutions are country specific and path dependent.

> There is evidence that corporate governance and political governance tend to be affected by historically predetermined factors (like the origin of the legal code) and, hence, cannot be easily improved. Furthermore, better governance can only mitigate the impact of external shocks, and not completely eliminate it.
>
> (Chong et al., 2005: 187)

The quality of a country's national system of corporate governance and the consistency of its economic development are related to the level of transparency on firm and country levels.

> Institutional transparency is the extent to which there is publicly available clear, accurate information, formal and informal, covering accepted practices related to capital markets, including the legal and judicial system, the government's macroeconomic and fiscal policies, accounting norms and practices (including corporate governance and the release of information), ethics, corruption, and regulations, customs and habits compatible with the norms of society.
>
> (Millar et al. 2005: 166)

Low transparency often goes along with weak corporate governance in both developed and developing countries (Claessens, 2006). In this situation, powerful shareholders can manipulate the processes of corporate governance formation and reform (White, 2004) and cause large-scale negative outcomes such as the regional economic crisis in Asia in the late 1990s (Carney, 2004). For instance, as White noticed, in Thailand, governance reforms have increased the abilities of powerful actors to further expand their power and minimize the intended effect of governance changes.

Taken together, formal and informal institutions greatly contribute to the specifics of corporate governance within business groups and at the national level.

The most important institutional factors include the development of market infrastructures such as property rights, the enforcement of law, capital markets and government involvement in economic development. These factors affect the ownership structure, which in turn shapes the characteristics of firm-level governance. Informal institutional arrangements affect national governance practices through business norms and traditions, trust, kinship-based networking and cultural values. Informal, relation-based governance manifests itself on both firm and country level, and is very visible in business groups. Entering emerging markets, MNEs need to apprehend the variety of national governance systems and learn to use particular systems for their own benefit.

Changing institutions and governance in transition

The national governance system of any country coevolves with its external environment, adding to the variety of models of governance around the world. In business groups, corporate governance is not only centered on dominant owners but also linked to powerful institutions and individual actors. Groups are also actively involved in a variety of formal and informal networks. Institutions, market controls and governance initiatives in emerging economies develop as a group. Certain elements of formal, arm's-length governance systems from developed countries become incorporated in governance practices in emerging markets. At the same time, the importance of differences in institutional arrangements and governance systems is introduced to the global economy.

There is a variety of opinions on how to shape corporate governance in emerging economies, and what elements of market institutions should be prioritized in this process. We can, however, find some common trends becoming apparent in emerging and newly industrialized countries. For instance, Allen (2005) argues for a governance model that can balance the interests of multiple actors, supporting a complex approach to the creation and accommodation of governance practices in emerging markets. Allen's position fits with the views of other scholars in terms of the flexibility and institutional adaptability of governance in developing countries (Fauver *et al.*, 2003; Krambia-Kapardis and Psaros, 2006; Mueller, 2006; Young *et al.*, 2004). The integrated use of market forces, government regulation and formal and informal governance-enhancing mechanisms all together reflect the multidimensionality of governance. Country-specific institutional contexts bring in historical roots and traditions, while the internationalization and globalization of business contribute some uniformity to formal elements of governance.

There is a strong sense in the research community that corporate governance in emerging markets should carry general, formal elements together with context-specific, informal ones. This hybrid, or transitional, system will complement relational governance specific to emerging and newly industrialized countries with principles of governance widely accepted by the developed world. A hybrid system would be beneficial for both national and international actors. It would be especially appropriate in countries and regions where resistance to change is strong, and cultural and business traditions are historically different from those in the rest of the world. Business groups, with their emphasis on relational governance and their non-transparent and concentrated ownership, fit well into a hybrid, transitional governance system. In fact, they are the major contributors to hybrid governance. Groups are interested in gaining access to external finance and obtaining recognition in international markets, so they need to incorporate some widely accepted principles and practices of governance. General aspects of corporate governance adopted in emerging countries include financial transparency and disclosure, and the independence of boards of directors (Young *et al.*, 2004). These general elements do not significantly alert the governance system within business groups, but widen the opportunities for domestic and international expansion open to groups and stand-alone firms. The adaptation of the best world practices creates some formal but not substantive similarities between corporate governance in emerging countries and that in developed countries.

To sum up on the formation of corporate governance in emerging economies, it is safe to say that the completeness and sophistication of a particular governance system depend on the level of institutional development. The principles and mechanisms of corporate governance expand from firm level to country level. They evolve from the most basic level to full-scale norms, policies and controls. Emerging markets require hybrid forms of governance owing to the uniqueness of their institutional arrangements, the greater uncertainty regarding their national economies, and the rapidly changing environment. Business groups are the pioneers in the incorporation of world best practices of governance, contributing significantly to the process of hybridization of governance.

A model of corporate governance in emerging markets

Accumulating the results of institutional and agency research, we conclude that business groups and their governance systems evolve together with the institutional structures into which they are embedded. Governance mechanisms are defined by the structure of ownership, which is highly concentrated in emerging and newly industrialized countries. Various governance systems are built on the basis of internal, firm-level elements, including vertical and horizontal relationship-based mechanisms. Relation-based governance extends beyond the boundaries of a group. In the process of their evolution, business groups become more anchored in their institutional environment, and shape external relationships. Groups enhance their governance systems by adding formal, rule-based elements from their external environment, both domestic and international. Having a wide range of mechanisms and instruments allows for greater flexibility of corporate governance, helping to balance relationships within and outside the group. In addition, it helps to maintain business groups' market position, economic power and reputation in domestic and global markets.

Overall principles of corporate governance around the world are intended to align the interests of different stakeholders, including individual and institutional actors. The major difference between governance in emerging countries and that in developed countries is defined by whose interests are served and how formalized the governance is. Separation of ownership and control in many developed economies is a generally accepted reality, and the cornerstone of corporate governance (Aguilera and Jackson, 2003; Daily *et al.*, 2003). Multiple stakeholders use different instruments and interactions to integrate their economic interests (minimize costs and maximize benefits). In emerging markets, ownership and control are rarely separated. Concentration of ownership leads to a misbalance of interests within business group, and in this situation the dominant owner is the one who benefits the most. Business groups do not necessarily measure their performance by purely economic outcomes. So, a group's governance system takes into account the need to provide mutual stability and protection against an uncertain environment. In the formation of national corporate governance we observe how the interplay among different actors, formal rules and informal relationships shapes the governance system (Figure 6.1).

The model proposed in Figure 6.1 illustrates how two main dimensions of corporate governance (state and ownership), together with institutional and other external factors, affect corporate governance. This model joins together agency and institutional approaches aiming to explain how institutional and individual forces shape corporate governance.

The ownership dimension reflects concentrated ownership as a distinct feature of business groups, and emerging markets at large. The structure of ownership centers governance mechanisms and controls on the interests of the dominant owners, who often are the members of a founding family. The owner's identity, power, and ability to access sources of capital determine the composition of vertical and horizontal elements of corporate governance. The main emphasis in this

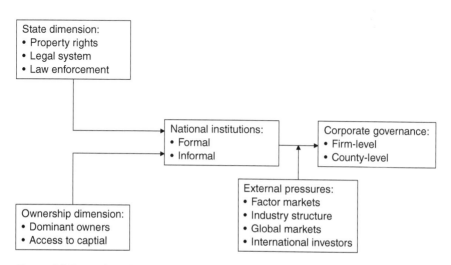

Figure 6.1 Formation of corporate governance in emerging markets.

system is given to internal instruments and controls that compensate for the lack of external regulation in emerging economies. The state dimension emphasizes the active role played by local governments in initiating industrialization and the marketization of developing countries, and in the introduction of business groups. The active position of the state in emerging markets includes efforts to create supportive market institutions and a strong enforcement environment. Distortions of reforms, bureaucratization, corruption and the black market are the downside of state activism in emerging economies.

While state and ownership are the two driving forces of national governance systems, the institutional environment performs mediating functions by shaping governance formation process. To some extent, formal and informal institutions serve as a "black box" that alters state and ownership inputs. National institutions add specific features of national culture and traditions. It is the case in emerging economies that formal institutional structures are underdeveloped; "soft" institutions prevail, bringing into focus informal networking and political connections as a substitute for weak formal ties. Business groups replace missing or imperfect institutions and enforcement, and within groups, external links compensate for the gaps in corporate control and market competition. Taken together, country-specific institutional arrangements add local logic to the complexity of interactions within a firm and bring into focus the uniqueness of local socioeconomic, political and cultural conditions. The effects of national institutions are reflected both in firm-level governance and at the national level.

External pressures condition the process of hybridization of corporate governance. They incorporate numerous processes and demands of broadly defined external environment, domestic and international. First, domestic factors of interest include changes in labor, capital, product and technology markets. Second, the structure of a national economy in terms of its size and the conditions and growth rates for new and traditional industries imposes its requirements on the practices and norms of corporate governance in different sectors of the national economy. Similar effects are expected from global markets and foreign investors, representing the third and fourth components of external pressures. Changes in the level of competition, shifts in technology and customer demands, deregulation of industries, openness of the national economy, etc. lead to the incorporation of international practices of governance.

Ownership, the state and the institutional environment are equally important contributors to the formation of corporate governance in emerging markets. While emerging economies are completing their transitions toward the market mode, ownership, the state and national institutions interplay, forming national governance systems. The exact effects caused by any of these components will differ among countries according to their specific economic, political and cultural conditions, among other factors. External pressures will add variability to models of governance, mixing and matching globally accepted best practices with particular demands for openness in, and the internationalization of, local markets.

Discussion and conclusions

Summary of findings

Corporate governance around the world, including in emerging markets, has been widely discussed in management. Depending on their backgrounds, scholars have approached this subject from many theoretical perspectives. Researchers have taken into account multiple factors affecting the formation and effectiveness of governance systems. The scope of studies has varied from shareholder to firm, industry and national economy. Within the body of the corporate governance literature, studies of business groups represent the meso level of governance analysis. Business groups as large business organizations exemplify local corporate governance. Owing to the complex nature of business groups, it becomes clear that no single-theory approach covers the whole spectrum of relationships, motives and mechanisms contributing to corporate governance. There is a need to integrate the economic logic of business behavior with the broader social context of corporate governance and emerging markets research. One way of doing this is by bringing together agency theory and the institutional perspective.

This chapter has placed at the center of its analysis features of corporate governance specific to business groups and emerging markets. Business groups dominate emerging and newly industrialized economies, performing several essential functions. Researchers agree that business groups tend to substitute for underdeveloped market structures. Groups also act as instruments of institutional transformation in emerging economies, bringing about major changes in management practices, technological developments and principles and practices of corporate governance.

The efficiency of corporate governance in business groups is based on the high concentration of ownership. The two dimensions of corporate governance are the vertical ownership structure and horizontal ties among group members and with the external environment. Being a distinctive characteristic of business groups, ownership concentration itself substitutes for the lack of legal protection of property rights in emerging markets. In the presence of powerful owners, the system of corporate governance in business groups is built around the owner's goals and interests, and mainly consists of internal regulation and control mechanisms. Agency costs and conflicts in business groups differ from those in companies with dispersed ownership. Principal–principal conflicts, and expropriation of minority shareholders' assets, are much more significant in business groups than are agent–principal conflicts and costs. The focus of corporate governance in group-affiliated firms is broader than in corporations whose ownership is widely istributed. Groups align economic and non-economic interests and carry out societal functions in the countries to which they belong.

Contributions

This chapter makes several contributions in the domains of business groups, corporate governance and local–global interactions. First, it integrates agency and institutional streams of corporate governance research with studies of business groups. As a result, this chapter structures our understanding of corporate governance attributes, both among member firms and in the central administrative structures of business groups. Second, the chapter introduces a model of the formation of corporate governance in emerging markets. This model proposes that there is an interplay between ownership and state as main inputs to corporate governance in emerging economies, conditioned by the national institutional environment and by various external factors. Third, the chapter brings into focus relational governance as a response to the changing, uncertain and sometimes hostile environment found in developing countries. Relational ties and informal networking are as essential to the well-being of business groups as they are for nation-states in promoting best governance and shaping institutional transformations. Fourth, the chapter encourages discussion of the features of corporate governance associated with greater variability of institutional environments and the coexistence of "global" and "local" approaches to corporate governance.

Implications for MNEs

In the context of escalating processes of globalization, MNEs are actively expanding in international markets, entering newly industrialized, emerging and less developed economies. This chapter will help MNEs to be more aware of national business practices and of the greater embeddedness of national governance systems in country-specific institutional environments. The model proposed provides MNEs with a better understanding of local contexts, so that global companies will be able to fine-tune their approach to corporate governance, enhancing related mechanisms and practices. MNEs will be able to adjust to their new markets, new competitors and new customers faster; they will comply better with the requirements of local regulations and business traditions. The direct outcomes of such adjustment to local logic will include learning, more effective operations and higher performance. Indirect benefits will include having a better reputation and greater societal acceptance stemming from the involvement in local networks, including efficient interactions with business groups.

Directions for future research

Interactions between companies from emerging and developed economies offer abundant opportunities for future studies. Social context needs to become fully incorporated into research on corporate governance. At the institutional level it is still to be determined what the role of national culture in national governance systems is, and what particular dimensions of culture are critical to the formation of corporate governance. Further research is required on particular variables and effects of the proposed model. Refinement of variables and model testing will be the next step in this process. While researchers are aware of the importance of the owner's identity as regards firms' goals and decision making, it is still unclear what the relations between owner or shareholder identity and mechanisms of corporate governance are. These and other studies will help to focus the proposed theoretical model more clearly, shape and test the relations between variables, and deepen our knowledge of corporate governance in different contexts.

Note

1 The term "tunneling," or "transferring," is used in corporate governance to describe the process of expropriation of resources across business-group member firms. The controlling shareholders can move resources (usually profits) from the firms where they have low cash-flow rights to the ones where these shareholders have high cash-flow rights. Tunneling is an example of expropriation from minority shareholders in business groups.

References

Aguilera, R. V. and Jackson, G. (2003) "Cross-national diversity of corporate governance: dimensions and determinants," *Academy of Management Review*, 28 (3): 447–465.

Allen, F. (2005) "Corporate governance in emerging economies," *Oxford Review of Economic Policy*, 21 (2): 164–177.

Amsden, A. (2001) *The Rise of "the Rest": Challenges to the West from Late-Industrializing Economies*, Oxford: Oxford University Press.

Berglöf, E. and Claessens, S. (2006) "Enforcement and good corporate governance in developing countries and transition economies," *World Bank Research Observer*, 21 (1): 123–150.

Bertrand, M., Johnson, S., Samphantharak, K. and Schoar, A. (2008) "Mixing family with business: A study of Thai business groups and the families behind them," *Journal of Financial Economics*, 88: 466–498.

Carleton, W. T., Nelson, J. M. and Weisbach, M. S. (1998) "The influence of institutions on corporate governance through private negotiations: Evidence from TIAA-CREF," *Journal of Finance*, 53 (4): 1335–1362.

Carney, M. (2004) "The institutions of industrial restructuring in Southeast Asia," *Asia Pacific Journal of Management*, 21: 171–188.

—— (2008) *Asian Busiess Groups: Context, Governance and Performance*, Oxford: Chandos.

Carrera, A., Mesquita, L., Perkins, G. and Vassolo, R. (2003) "Business groups and their corporate strategies on the Argentine roller coaster of competitive and anti-competitive shocks," *Academy of Management Executive*, 17 (3): 32–44.

Chang, S. J. (2003) "Ownership structure, expropriation, and performance of group-affiliated companies in Korea," *Academy of Management Journal*, 46 (2): 238–253.

—— (2006) "Business groups in East Asia: Post-crisis restructuring and new growth," *Asia Pacific Journal of Management*, 23: 407–417.

Chong, A., Izquierdo, A., Micco, A. and Panizza, U. (2005) "Political and corporate governance and pro-cyclicality in capital flows: Evidence from emerging market countries," *International Finance*, 8 (2): 167–198.

Chung, C.-N. (2005) "Beyond *Guanxi*: Network contingencies in Taiwanese business groups," *Organization Studies*, 27 (4): 461–489.

Claessens, S. (2006) "Corporate governance and development," *World Bank Research Observer*, 21 (1): 91–122.

Claessens, S., Djankov, S. and Lang, L. H. P. (2000) "The separation of ownership and control in East Asian corporations," *Journal of Financial Economics*, 58: 81–112.

Cuervo-Cazurra, A. (2006) "Business groups and their types," *Asia Pacific Journal of Management*, 23: 419–437.

Daily, C. M., Dalton, D. R. and Cannella, A. A. (2003) "Corporate governance: Decades of dialogue and data," *Academy of Management Review*, 28 (3): 371–382.

Dieleman, M. and Sachs, W. (2006) "Oscillating between a relationship-based and a market-based model: The Salim Group," *Asia Pacific Journal of Management*, 23 (4): 521–536.

Doidge, C., Karolyi, G. A. and Stulz, R. M. (2007) "Why do countries matter so much for corporate governance?" *Journal of Financial Economics*, 86: 1–39.

Douma, S., Georg, R. and Kabir, R. (2006) "Foreign and domestic ownership, business groups, and firm performance: Evidence from a large emerging market," *Strategic Management Journal*, 27: 637–657.

Fauver, L., Houston, J. and Naranjo, A. (2003) "Capital market development, international integration, legal systems, and the value of corporate diversification: A cross-country analysis," *Journal of Financial and Quantitative Analysis*, 38 (1): 135–157.

Filatotchev, I., Wright, M., Uhlenbruck, K., Tihanyi, L. and Hoskisson, R. E. (2003) "Governance, organizational capabilities, and restructuring in transition economies," *Journal of World Business*, 38: 331–347.

Fisman, R. (2001) "Estimating the value of political connections," *American Economic Review*, 91 (4): 1095–1102.

Fisman, R. and Khanna, T. (2004) "Facilitating development: The role of business groups," *World Development*, 32 (4): 609–628.

Gedajlovic, E. R. and Shapiro, D. M. (1998) "Management and ownership effects: Evidence from five countries," *Strategic Management Journal*, 19: 533–553.

Granovetter, M. (1995) "Coase revisited: Business groups in the modern economy," *Industrial and Corporate Change*, 4: 93–130.

Greif, A. and Kandel, E. (1995) "Contract enforcement institutions: Historical perspective and current status in Russia," in E. Lazear (ed.) *Economic Transition in Eastern Europe and Russia: Realities of Reform*, Stanford, CA: Hoover Institution Press.

Guillén, M. F. (2000) "Business groups in emerging economies: A resource-based view," *Academy of Management Journal*, 43: 362–380.

Guthrie, D. (1997) "Between markets and polities: Organizational responses to reform in China," *American Journal of Sociology*, 102: 1258–1304.

Hoskisson, R. E., Eden, L., Lau, C. M. and Wright, M. (2000) "Strategy in emerging economies," *Academy of Management Journal*, 43: 249–267.

Johnson, S., Boone, P., Breach, A. and Friedman, E. (2000) "Corporate governance in the Asian financial crisis," *Journal of Financial Economics*, 58 (1–2): 141–186.

Kedia, B. L., Mukherjee, D. and Lahiri, S. (2006) "Indian business groups: Evolution and transformation," *Asia Pacific Journal of Management*, 23 (4): 559–577.

Keister, L. A. (1998) "Engineering growth: Business group structure and firm performance in China's transition economy," *American Journal of Sociology*, 104: 404–440.

Khanna, T. and Palepu, K. (2004) "Globalization and convergence in corporate governance: Evidence from Infosys and the Indian software industry," *Journal of International Business Studies*, 35: 484–507.

Khanna, T. and Rivkin, J. W. (2001) "Estimating the performance effects of groups in emerging markets," *Strategic Management Journal*, 22 (1): 45–74.

—— (2006) "Interorganizational ties and business group boundaries: Evidence from an emerging economy," *Organization Science*, 17: 333–352.

Khanna, T. and Yafeh, Y. (2007) "Business groups in emerging markets: Paragons or parasites?" *Journal of Economic Literature*, 45 (June): 331–372.

Krambia-Kapardis, M. and Psaros, J. (2006) "The implementation of corporate governance principles in an emerging economy: A critique of the situation in Cyprus,"
Corporate Governance, 14 (2): 126–139.

La Porta, R., Lopez-de-Silanes, F., Shleifer, A. and Vishny, R. W. (1998) "Law and
finance," *Journal of Political Economy*, 106 (5): 1113–1155.

Lee, P. M. and O'Neill, H. M. (2003) "Ownership structures and R&D investments of
U.S. and Japanese firms: Agency and stewardship perspectives," *Academy of Management Journal*, 46 (2): 212–225.

London, T. and Hart, S. L. (2004) "Reinventing strategies for emerging markets: Beyond
the transnational model," *Journal of International Business Studies*, 35: 350–370.

Loveridge, R. (2006) "Developing institutions – 'crony capitalism' and national capabilities: A European perspective," *Asian Business and Management*, 5: 113–136.

Lins, K. V. (2003) "Equity ownership and firm value in emerging markets," *Journal of
Financial and Quantitative Analysis*, 38 (1): 159–184.

Luo, X. and Chung, C. N. (2005) "Keeping it all in the family: The role of particularistic
relationships in business group performance during institutional transition," *Administrative Science Quarterly*, 50 (3): 404–439.

McDermott, G. A. (2002) *Embedded Politics: Industrial Networks and Institutional
Change in Postcommunism*, Ann Arbor: University of Michigan Press.

Millar, C., Eldomiaty, T. I., Chong, J., Choi, C. J. and Hilton, B. (2005) "Corporate governance and institutional transparency in emerging markets," *Journal of Business
Ethics*, 59: 163–174.

Morck, R. and Yeung, B. (2003) "Agency problems in large family business groups,"
Entrepreneurship Theory and Practice, 27 (4): 367–383.

Morck, R., Wolfenzon, D. and Yeung, B. (2005) "Corporate governance, economic
entrenchment, and growth," *Journal of Economic Literature*, 43 (3): 655–720.

Mueller, D. C. (2006) "The Anglo-Saxon approach to corporate governance and its applicability to emerging markets," *Corporate Governance*, 14 (4): 207–219.

Peng, M. W. (2002) "Towards an institution-based view of business strategy," *Asia
Pacific Journal of Management*, 19: 251–267.

—— (2003) "Institutional transitions and strategic choices," *Academy of Management
Review*, 28 (2): 275–296.

Peng, M. W. and Zhou, J. Q. (2005) "How network strategies and institutional transitions
evolve in Asia," *Asia Pacific Journal of Management*, 22: 321–336.

Phan, P. H. (2001) "Corporate governance in the newly emerging economies," *Asia
Pacific Journal of Management*, 18 (2): 131–136.

Schneider, B. R. (2009) "A comparative political economy of diversified business groups,
or how states organize big business," *Review of International Political Economy*, 16
(2): 178–201.

Schulze, W., Lubatkin, M. H., Dino, R. N. and Buchholtz, A. K. (2001) "Agency relationships in family firms: Theory and evidence," *Organization Science*, 12 (2): 99–116.

Scott, W. R. (2001) *Institutions and Organizations*, Thousand Oaks, CA: Sage.

Strachan, H. W. (1976) *Family and Other Business Groups in Economic Development:
The Case of Nicaragua*, New York: Praeger.

Toms, S. and Wright, M. (2002) "Corporate governance, strategy and structure in British
business history, 1950–2000," *Business History*, 44 (3): 91–124.

White, S. (2004) "Stakeholders, structure, and the failure of corporate governance reforms
initiatives in post-crisis Thailand," *Asia Pacific Journal of Management*, 21: 103–122.

Wright, M., Filatotchev, I., Buck, T. and Bishop, K. (2003) "Is stakeholder corporate governance appropriate in Russia?" *Journal of Management and Governance*, 7 (3): 263–290.

Yiu, D., Bruton, G. D. and Lu, Y. (2005) "Understanding business group performance in an emerging economy: Acquiring resources and capabilities in order to prosper," *Journal of Management Studies*, 42: 183–206.

Yiu, D. W., Lu, Y. and Burton, G. D. (2007) "Business groups: An integrated model to focus future research," *Journal of Management Studies*, 44 (8): 1551–1579.

Young, M. N., Ahlstrom, D. and Bruton, G. D. (2004) "The globalization of corporate governance in East Asia: The 'transnational' solution," *Management International Review*, 44: 31–50.

Young, M. N., Peng, M. W., Ahlstrom, D., Bruton, G. D. and Jiang, Y. (2008) "Corporate governance in emerging economies: A review of the principal–principal perspective," *Journal of Management Studies*, 45 (1): 196–220.

Part III
Empirical perspectives

7 Entrepreneurship, firm size and knowledge transfer to developing and emerging countries

Claude Marcotte

Introduction

Until the 1990s, multinational corporations (MNCs) from developed countries were considered by researchers and policy makers to be the most effective vehicles for the transfer of organizational and technological knowledge to developing and emerging countries. This perception was particularly evident in the literature on international technology transfer.[1] In their exhaustive review of the literature, Reddy and Zhao (1990: 286) reported that "[t]here is little debate in the literature that the primary agent of technology transfer from the home country is the multinational corporations." Their article did not even address the role of small and medium-sized firms (SMEs) in technology transfer, possibly because their involvement was still negligible, or because smaller organizations were perceived as less effective than MNEs in enabling recipient firms to learn new organizational and technological skills.

The literature on international business has reinforced this notion of the primacy of large organizations in the cross-border transfer of knowledge. Thus, Dunning referred to the total stock of knowledge in MNCs as the "knowledge capital ingredient of direct investment" (1970: 147). In his approach, knowledge is considered to be at the root of international activities, and is seen as part of the firm's capital, on the same level as more tangible assets or resources. More recently, that "knowledge ingredient" was integrated into his extended version of the eclectic paradigm of international production (Dunning, 1993: 98–101). Both forms of knowledge identified by Polanyi (1966) – the codified and tacit forms – were part of the ownership-specific advantages that Dunning attributed to large international firms. The tacit dimension of organizational knowledge has particularly attracted the attention of researchers in international business. Thus, Kogut and Zander (1993) hypothesized that large organizations exist because they specialize and capitalize on their competitive advantage in transferring tacit knowledge. Unlike codified knowledge, which can be recorded in symbolic forms such as blueprints and drawings, tacit knowledge is made of the unique expertise and skills that have been acquired by organizations over the years and have not been recorded in documents. This form of knowledge is specific and in some way "personal" to each firm: it is made of very specific expertise that has been learned and shared more or less consciously by the management and employees and that cannot be transferred purely via codified instructions. The members of the supplier firms have to teach their personal knowledge and skills to their counterparts in the receiving firms, making the process more personalized, complex and costly.

Because of the "sticky," hard-to-transfer nature of tacit knowledge (Von Hippel, 1994), the organizational and contextual differences between the knowledge suppliers and knowledge receivers constitute important determinants of the transfer effectiveness. In the case of suppliers from developed economies and receivers from developing and emerging countries, the most frequent factors that seem to impact the transfer process are the cultural differences, the institutional ambiguity and the gap in managerial and technological skills (Marcotte and Niosi, 2000). Considerable human and financial resources must then be devoted by the partners to the transfer process if it is to be effective. That being so, large MNCs would then be at an advantage in transfers involving institutionally and culturally distant partners. Their considerable tangible and intangible resources – for example, the number of international managers, the amount of financial capital and the breadth of tacit knowledge – would give them an advantage over their smaller competitors.

Are large organizations actually more effective than smaller ones in dealing with the complex transfer issues originating from institutional and cultural distance, as the literature on international knowledge transfer and international business suggests? Of course, no definite answer to that question can be provided. However, some recent developments in international entrepreneurship and SME internationalization may qualify the views generally held in international business. Somewhat paradoxically, these developments have brought out the predominance and advantages of tacit knowledge and localized learning in smaller organizations (Audretsch and Thurik, 2001; Acs *et al.*, 2009). In these theoretical formulations, globalization and the dominance of MNCs are not considered as prime factors of international competitiveness. Thus, Audretsch and Thurik (2001) argued that "the so-called death of distance resulting from globalization has shifted the comparative advantage of high-cost locations towards economic activity that cannot be easily and costlessly diffused across geographical space." Local and regional characteristics, with their rich source of tacit knowledge, constitute better opportunities for the creation and diffusion of innovations, and are better exploited by SMEs. In this context, SMEs, being characterized by personalized and mostly tacit knowledge and skills, might be in a better position to perceive and correctly interpret the informal and tacit institutional norms in less developed countries. This would facilitate the transfer of knowledge to these countries.

For some other researchers, on the contrary, SMEs' reliance on tacit knowledge and the institutional barriers to the international diffusion of that type of knowledge play a constraining role on smaller firms' capacity to transfer their expertise abroad, especially when the recipient firms are located in less developed countries. Is the constraining effect more important than opportunity creation for smaller organizations? A nuanced answer to that question requires more conceptual and empirical research in institutional theory and entrepreneurship. In comparison with the international business literature focused on large organizations' involvement and effectiveness in international knowledge transfer, the research on the role of SMEs in this area of activity has been much less abundant.

The objective of this chapter is to review the literature on the specificities of knowledge transfer to developing and emerging countries by Western SMEs, and to illustrate some of the conceptual positions with case results. The chapter proceeds as follows. First, I present the arguments in the literature that explain why smaller organizations might be less effective than MNCs in transferring their knowledge abroad. Some of these arguments are based on the institutional approach. Second, I analyze the counterarguments based on the potential entrepreneurial opportunities for Western SMEs in developing and emerging countries. To put these counterarguments into perspective, a brief review of the literature on the international dimensions of entrepreneurship and knowledge transfer is presented. The case of knowledge transfer to China is used to illustrate the opportunity-based view. In the last section we draw on these considerations of constraints and opportunities for SMEs in international technology transfer to examine the concept of "micromultinationals," recently created to designate the more globalized SMEs.

The constraining role of institutions and tacit knowledge in internationalization: SMEs as less effective transferors of knowledge

Institutional constraints on SME internationalization

From a strictly institutional perspective it may be argued that the institutional and cultural specificities in developing and emerging countries constitute important barriers to the effective transfer of organizational and technological knowledge by Western firms (Munir, 2002). A central element of the institutionalist approach is that organizations sharing the same environment will also share the same values and managerial practices. Thus, the focus of this approach is on organizational homogeneity rather than variation (DiMaggio and Powell, 1983). The adoption of similar values and practices is explained by organizations' concern over legitimacy and credibility. The international management researchers who have examined the impact of institutional differences have usually interpreted the institutional view as a theory of the adaptation of the firm (Doz and Prahalad, 1993; Dacin *et al.*, 2002). As is mentioned in the second chapter of this book, the analysis of the international activities of the firms requires that one take into consideration the complexity inherent in the relations between organizations that differ in terms of institutional contexts. These contexts shape different rationalities and logics. The changing economic, cultural, political and social conditions in developing and emerging countries constitute significant challenges for Western firms.

The rules and norms of the recipient country's institutional environment consti-tute boundaries of legitimate organizational practices for knowledge transfer. By adapting to existing practices and institutional norms – formal as well as informal – Western transferors acquire much-needed legitimacy in the unstable context of less developed countries. Smaller Western firms, being limited in specialized personnel and financial resources, would be even more vulnerable than MNEs to political, institutional and market changes in developing and emerging countries (UNCTAD, 1993: 36). They would have to adapt to the context of the recipient countries without much chance to capitalize on their key strengths, such as flexibility, proac-tiveness and innovativeness. Rather than innovate in the host country, they will seek to transfer those parts of their managerial and technological knowledge that are closest to those that exist in local organizations. For SME owners, cost and risk minimization will then be a priority. The result is that their partners in less developed countries will then learn less than if they had associated with MNEs.

The predominance of tacit knowledge in SMEs

Two internal "shortcomings" of SMEs are likely to contribute to their lessened effectiveness in knowledge transfer: their reliance on tacit knowledge and their lack of resources. Much of the know-how in small firms seems to remain tacit (UNCTAD, 1993; Eden *et al.*, 1997; Buckley, 1997). Thus, Buckley reported that

> [t]he channel of written instructions is used much less frequently in SMEs than MNEs, partly because of lack of personnel to codify the technology and partly because many of the skills in SMEs are acquired through per-sonal experience. Sending technical experts abroad to aid in technology transfer is much more difficult for SMEs (the high opportunity cost of tech-nical personnel is crucial here) and written instructions are used much less frequently. Manuals and technical handbooks are used by a minority of SMEs and even blueprints and drawings are only used in 51% of cases.
>
> (1997: 75)

Eden *et al.* (1997: 63) argued that SMEs are less effective than larger organiza-tions in transferring their technology. The major reason is the shortage of finan-cial and human resources. Smaller organizations cannot devote as many employees or as much funding to aiding the transfer process, and thus cannot address the organizational and technological gaps of their partners in less developed countries. In addition to the shortage of resources, a lack of manage-rial expertise in the area of international business has also been observed in SMEs (Buckley, 1997). It is usually the owners themselves who launch and supervise international projects. It is very difficult for them to find the time to collect sufficient information about the complex issues involved in dealing with unstable institutional contexts. The lack of managerial expertise and resources in SMEs might explain why they are less likely than large organizations to manage the transfer process properly when problems occur.

Tacit knowledge as a source of entrepreneurial opportunities for Western SMEs

Entrepreneurship theory and international technology transfer

Entrepreneurship theory has progressed tremendously in the role assigned to knowledge in the process of opportunity recognition and exploitation. It has evolved from a strict Schumpeterian economic approach, whereby knowledge was implicitly conceived as being easily codifiable, to a cognitive conceptualization of the entrepreneurial activity based on the workings of tacit knowledge.

To Schumpeter (1961), an entrepreneur was a person who carried out new combinations, which could take the form of new products, processes, markets, organizational forms or sources of supply. Entrepreneurship was, then, the result of new combinations of tangible resources. Entrepreneurs were highly determined leaders who had the capacity to act when they perceive new possibilities or opportunities. These opportunities were perceptible to a large number of persons in a given society; however, a very small percentage of individuals actually pursued such opportunities.

In Schumpeter's framework, knowledge in organizations appeared to take the form of codified or readily codifiable elements that are easily discovered and imitated by competitors. The monopoly situation that innovators temporarily enjoyed then came to an end. Organizations could not exploit one particular innovation for a long period of time, whether through in-house production or technology transfer. They had to be continually on the defensive and keep innovating at a faster pace than their competitors. Interfirm cooperation and technology transfer were not yet considered as profitable ways to prolong the competitive advantages of innovators, nor were they conceived as profitable organizational innovations. It must be emphasized that Schumpeter's theory was largely developed in an era when less consideration seemed to be given to the institutional and political roots of economic activity. National differences in institutional and cultural structures may determine the ways in which economic and business systems are implemented. For example, Whitley (1999) identified six ideal-types of business systems, based on the degree of ownership-based coordination of economic activities and the extent of alliance forms of organizational integration. By understanding and using these contextual differences as business opportunities, entrepreneurial firms may increase their competitive advantage over less flexible and proactive international firms.

By contrast with Schumpeter, Baumol (1993) clearly perceived the entrepreneurial potential of international technology transfer. The latter was considered to be an innovative and entrepreneurial activity. Then, with the complementary developments in the opportunity-based approach, which draws largely on cognitive concepts (Venkataraman, 1997; Shane and Venkataraman, 2000), and in the knowledge spillover theory of entrepreneurship (Audretsch and Thurik, 2001; Acs *et al.*, 2009), both the content and the process of knowledge creation and transfer have become central topics in entrepreneurship research. That research was largely influenced by the work of Hayek (1945) on the unequal diffusion of knowledge in society, and that of Kirzner (1973) on alertness and learning,

The content and process of knowledge transfer by SMEs

The specialized skills in smaller firms have been attributed to their capacity to capitalize on their tacit knowledge, which is viewed by the proponents of the "SME advantage" as a source of competitive advantage rather than a constraint (Chew and Yeung, 2001). Rather than being only a source of teaching and transaction costs, tacit knowledge may also constitute a source of opportunity and competitive advantage. Foreign partners located in developing countries are often looking for this type of complementary knowledge in order to understand and use blueprints and related documents effectively. In fact, one of the major complaints from Chinese partners involved in technology transfer agreements was that not enough tacit knowledge was provided by firms from industrialized countries (Lan and Young, 1996). Smaller entrepreneurial organizations have been described as possessing certain characteristics that may be advantageous in international technology transfer. The more innovative ones distinguish themselves by their highly specialized technological and human assets. Many innovating SMEs have developed technologies that are very attractive on the international market. In a study on technology transfer to developing countries by Canadian SMEs, Niosi and Rivard (1990) found that most of these enterprises could be described as small oligopolists, occupying a large proportion of the domestic market in their respective niches. Moreover, the technology transferred to developing countries by SMEs is usually sophisticated and up to date, and not some "scaled-down" version.

If their distinctive competency lies in highly specialized, tacit and niche-based organizational and technological skills, then are SMEs able to teach these skills to their partners in developing countries? As I have said, because of shortage of resources it should be the case that SMEs transfer less comprehensive packages of knowledge than MNCs. That proposition was confirmed in a study of technology transfer to India (Desai, 1997). However, in a study of technology transfer to China by Canadian firms, it was found that smaller firms were able to transfer packages of knowledge – tacit as well as codified – that were as complete as those transferred by MNCs (Marcotte and Niosi, 2000, 2005). Tacit knowledge was transferred using technical assistance and in-house training of employees in China. Being used to communicating their knowledge and skills through demonstration and modeling rather than through written documents, employees in small firms were in a good position to teach these elements of tacit knowledge to their colleagues in the host country. Their less formalized, more personal approach appeared to compensate for the relative scarcity of financial and human resources in SMEs. Especially in the case of the more innovative ones that are likely to transfer their technology abroad, it may be asked whether their domestic experience in operating under conditions of tacit knowledge, limited resources and with a limited buffer against environmental uncertainty, rather than constraining them, might actually better prepare them to communicate effectively with their partners in developing areas and adjust to the highly uncertain context of these countries.

Besides this direct, face-to-face communication style, smaller firms also differ from larger enterprises in their flexibility and capacity to react quickly to environmental changes in their foreign investment in developing countries (Marcotte and Julien, 1995). The latter are usually characterized by different cultural values such as collectivism and high power distance (Hofstede, 1980). The managerial and technical differences that frequently exist in these firms also require adaptation on the part of transferors. In a previous study on technology transfer to China, Marcotte (1999) found that Canadian managers who acknowledged these differences and interpreted them correctly were able to transfer their technology more effectively, whatever the size of the firms. Moreover, even though Canadian SMEs reported having more difficulties than large firms due to the organizational and technological gap of their Chinese partners, they were able to be as effective as their larger counterparts in transferring new knowledge.

The effectiveness of knowledge transfer refers to the actual learning accomplished by the recipient firms. The learning process entails a constant interaction between tacit and codified elements of knowledge. Nonaka and Takeuchi (1995) conducted extensive research on this interaction in Japanese companies that succeeded in creating "knowledge spirals" in which there was a constant transformation of tacit into explicit forms of knowledge and vice versa. These spirals were present during both the acquisition and the transfer of knowledge. Similarly, internationalizing firms seem to go through a learning process in which both forms of knowledge are at work. Some research endeavors in the area of international entrepreneurship are aimed at discovering the idiosyncratic and multifaceted aspects of knowledge transformation and entrepreneurial learning. For example, Marcotte and Niosi (2000, 2005) studied the issues of knowledge and learning during technology transfer to China by Canadian manufacturing firms of various sizes. The results tended to validate their model based on evolutionary and cognitive theories. The transformation of tacit into explicit knowledge and back into tacit knowledge was done gradually and involved three phases of learning: learning by doing, by insight and by knowledge creation. The first phase was characterized by short-term problem solving having more to do with know-how and trial and error than know-why and in-depth understanding of the organizational changes associated with the new technology. The second phase involved more "double-loop" learning and conscious efforts on the part of the recipient firms to understand the principles underlying the new technology and to make the necessary organizational changes in order to benefit more from the technology. The third phase entailed more research and development and the creation of new tacit knowledge that could be used in turn by recipient firms to share and transfer the technology.

The SMEs as well as the larger firms were going through the same phases. Learning in recipient firms was not significantly associated with the size of their

Canadian transferors. Recipient firms that acquired their technology from Canadian SMEs learned to adapt or modify the technology in the same proportion as those who received it from large firms.

The decision-making process in small international firms has been described in the literature as highly personalized – reflecting the preferences and values of the owner – and somewhat irrational (Buckley, 1997; Dichtl *et al.*, 1984). Rather than being based on factual and objective assessments of alternatives, decisions regarding, for example, foreign locations and selection of partners in the transfer process might be largely influenced by the owners' personal affinities and intuitions. Decisions in smaller organizations are typically embedded in their local institutional contexts and not sifted through the principles of formal strategic planning. To what extent does that personalized and localized form of rationality fit with the type of logics and rationality of developing countries? Although a direct answer to that question is difficult to find, the results mentioned above on SMEs transfer capabilities suggest that the fit may be as good as that offered by MNCs.

Regarding the "irrationality" of the decision-making process in SMEs, it might be more fruitful to examine whether a different type of rationality, of an entrepreneurial nature, is at work in these organizations, without making a value judgment as to the logic of this approach. Small business owners rarely apply rigorously the principles of formal strategic planning. Learning by doing and trial and error are very important in this personalized approach. Rather than concurrently and comprehensively evaluating the different alternatives – collecting all the pertinent information on these alternatives, then analyzing and calculating the advantages and disadvantages of each one before choosing the best one – most of these owners use an active and dynamic approach. They choose the alternative that appears to be an interesting and affordable opportunity, taking into consideration their personal affinities with a certain way of doing things, with certain potential partners or with certain regions of the world. In our study on joint ventures implemented by Quebec SMEs in developing countries (Marcotte and Julien, 1995), we found that one of the important reasons why these firms had invested in these ventures was that the owners had previously formed a friendship with the owner of the partner firm. Apfelthaler (2000) reports cases of Austrian owners who invested in the United States because of their personal preferences for that country and not because they had rigorously analyzed alternative markets. They had the feeling that it was in the United States that they could realize their dream of becoming international.

Do these observations make small business owners "irrational" decision makers? Not necessarily, since there are different shades and forms of rationality. In the case of small business owners the decision-making process often has a character of intuition, and sometimes involves emotions and passion as well as reason. It is a less detached and objective form of rationality than that of the formal strategic model. But in any economic system there might be a place for both types of decision making.

In comparison with large organizations, SMEs are more likely to tend to opt for partnership with local firms when they invest in developing countries

(UNCTAD, 1993). The knowledge sharing and learning involved in joint ventures and other forms of strategic alliances may contribute significantly to enhancing the capabilities of local firms. Working within an international entrepreneurship framework, some researchers (e.g. Etemad 2003) have emphasized the innovation opportunities involved in the collaborative and synergistic learning process involving two or more small firms sharing fundamentally the same vision, even when the cultural and institutional expressions of that vision differ. That learning process might be a source of competitive advantage at the organizational and national level if an appropriate niche can be exploited by the partners to the transfer.

SMEs are increasingly involved in foreign direct investment, international strategic alliances and technology transfer (Marcotte, 2002). While their international activities were typically limited to developed countries until the 1990s, their presence in developing areas is now well documented. For example, in a 2005 study, Canadian SMEs had transferred their technology to three different countries before entering China, and in many cases the previous transfers had been done in various developing economies.

Concluding remarks: the rise of micromultinationals?

The objective of this chapter was to review the literature on the specificities of knowledge transfer to developing and emerging countries by Western SMEs. Both the constraints and the opportunities for international transfer of knowledge were analyzed. The highly uncertain institutional context of less developed countries and the complexities relating to the transfer of tacit knowledge were presented as serious limitations to the capacity of SMEs to be effective transferors of knowledge. On the other hand, the predominance of tacit knowledge and highly specialized skills in SMEs, combined with their flexibility and personalized management styles, could also be conducive to heightened adaptability to uncertain international contexts and effective knowledge transfer.

While the issue of constraints versus opportunities is far from settled, the results that I present here on knowledge transfer to China indicate that SMEs can transfer complete packages of knowledge and can be as effective as larger organizations in teaching organizational and technological skills to their foreign partners. Moreover, their growing involvement in foreign operations in both developed and developing countries, mostly through collaborative agreements with local partners, has given rise to the concept of micromultinationals (Dimitratos *et al.*, 2003; Ibeh *et al.*, 2004), to designate their capacity to be leaders and small oligopolists in their respective niche markets. Typically, these micromultinationals operate in knowledge-intensive sectors such as software, telecommunications and computer-related services. It is difficult to obtain precise and up-to-date figures on the prevalence of these types of SMEs. In a report by the Organisation for Economic Co-operation and Development (OECD, 1997) it was estimated that 5 to 10 percent of manufacturing SMEs were extensively internationalized – they were present in more than five countries and two continents.

These SMEs were drawing at least 40 percent of their turnover from international activities. Another 10 to 20 percent were active in up to three countries.

It appears difficult to predict the extent to which Western SMEs will continue to expand their international operations in less developed countries, especially in the current context of financial and economic problems. Access to financial resources is a key problem for internationalizing SMEs, and that access is being made more and more difficult. Will the international demand for their specialized, knowledge-intensive products and services be affected to the point of nullifying their remarkable expansion into new and less developed markets in the last decades?

Note

1 Technology transfer is a rather misleading concept in that the transfer activities are not restricted to the technological elements of knowledge. They usually also entail organizational, cultural and institutional dimensions of cross-border knowledge sharing. For this reason, the more generic term "knowledge transfer" will be used in this chapter.

References

Acs, Z. J., Braunerhjelm, P., Audretsch, D. B. and Carlson, B. (2009) "The knowledge spillover theory of entrepreneurship," *Small Business Economics*, 32: 15–31.

Apfelthaler, G. (2000) "Why small enterprises invest abroad: The case of Austrian firms in the U.S.," *Journal of Small Business Management*, 38: 92–98.

Audretsch, D. B. and Thurik, A. R. (2001) "What's new about the new economy? Sources of growth in the managed and entrepreneurial economies," *Industrial and Corporate Change*, 10: 267–315.

Baumol, W. J. (1993) *Entrepreneurship, Management and the Structure of Payoffs*, Cambridge, MA: MIT Press.

Buckley, P. (1997) "International technology transfer by small and medium-sized enterprises," *Small Business Economics*, 9: 67–78.

Chew, Y. and Yeung, H. (2001) "The SME advantage: Adding local touch to foreign transnational corporations in Singapore," *Regional Studies*, 35 (5): 431–448.

Dacin, M. T., Goodstein, J. and Scott, W. R. (2002) "Institutional theory and institutional change: Introduction to the special issue," *Academy of Management Journal*, 43: 45–57.

Desai, A. V. (1997) "The case of India," in P. J. Buckley, J. Campos, H. Mirza and E. White (eds.) *International Technology Transfer by Small and Medium-Sized Enterprises: Country Studies*, New York: St. Martin's Press.

Dichtl, E., Leibold, M., Koglmayr, H. G. and Muller, S. (1984) "The export-decision of small and medium-sized firms: A review," *Management International Review*, 24: 49–60.

DiMaggio, P. and Powell, W. (1983) "The iron cage revisited: Institutional isomorphism and collective rationality in organizational fields," *American Sociological Review*, 48: 147–160.

Dimitratos, P., Johnson, J. E., Slow, J. and Young, S. (2003) "Micromultinationals: New types of firms for the global competitive landscape," *European Management Journal*, 21 (2): 164–174.

Doz, Y. and Prahalad, C. (1993) "Managing DMNCs: A search for a new paradigm," in S. Ghoshal and D. Westney (eds.) *Organization Theory and the Multinational Corporation*, New York: St. Martin's Press.

Dunning, J. H. (1970) "Technology, United States investment and European economic growth," in C. P. Kindleberger (ed.) *The International Corporation*, Cambridge, MA: MIT Press.

—— (1993) *Multinational Enterprises and the Global Economy*, Reading, MA: Addison-Wesley.

Eden, L., Levitas, E. and Martinez, R. (1997) "The production, transfer and spillover of technology: Comparing large and small multinationals as technology producers," *Small Business Economics*, 9 (1): 53–66.

Etemad, H. (2003) "Managing relations: the essence of international entrepreneurship," in H. Etemad and R. Wright (eds.) *Globalization and Entrepreneurship*, Cheltenham, UK: Edward Elgar.

Hayek, F. (1945) "The use of knowledge in society," *American Economic Review*, 35 (4): 519–530.

Hofstede, G. (1980) *Culture's Consequences: International Differences in Work-Related Values*, London: Sage.

Ibeh, K., Johnson, J. E., Dimitratos, P. and Slow, J. (2004) "Micromultinationals: Some preliminary evidence on an emergent 'star' of the international entrepreneurship field," *Journal of International Entrepreneurship*, 2: 289–303.

Kirzner, I. (1973) *Competition and Entrepreneurship*, Chicago: University of Chicago Press.

Kogut, B. and Zander, U. (1993) "Knowledge of the firm and the evolutionary theory of the multinational corporation," *Journal of International Business Studies*, 24: 625–645.

Lan, P. and Young, S. (1996) "International technology transfer examined at the technology component: A case study of China," *Technovation*, 16 (6): 277–286.

Marcotte, C. (1999) "Connaissances, apprentissage et succès lors du transfert de technologie en Chine," doctoral dissertation, Université du Québec à Montréal.

—— (2002) "Beyond exporting: The growing involvement of small and medium-sized enterprises in foreign direct investment," in A. B. Ibrahim and W. Ellis (eds.) *Entrepreneurship and Small Business Management: Text, Readings and Cases*, 4th edn., Dubuque, IA: Kendall/Hunt.

Marcotte, C. and Julien, P. A. (1995) "Partage d'information et performance de coentreprises implantées par les PME québécoises dans les pays en développement," *Revue Internationale PME*, 8 (2): 175–201.

Marcotte, C. and Niosi, J. (2000) "Technology transfer to China: The issues of knowledge and learning," *Journal of Technology Transfer*, 23: 43–57.

—— (2005) "Small and medium-sized enterprises involved in technology transfer to China: What do their partners learn?" *International Small Business Journal*, 23: 27–47.

Munir, K. A. (2002) "Being different: How normative and cognitive aspects of institutional environments influence technology transfer," *Human Relations*, 55 (12): 1403–1428.

Niosi, J. and Rivard, J. (1990) "Canadian technology transfer to developing countries through small and medium sized enterprises," *World Development*, 18 (10): 1529–1542.

Nonaka, I. and Takeuchi, H. (1995) *The Knowledge-Creating Company: How Japanese Companies Create the Dynamics of Innovation*, Oxford: Oxford University Press.

OECD (1997) *Globalisation and Small and Medium Enterprises*, vol. 1, Paris: Organisation for Economic Co-operation and Development.

Polanyi, M. (1966) *The Tacit Dimension*, Garden City, NY: Doubleday.

Reddy, N. M. and Zhao, L. (1990) "International technology transfer: A review," *Research Policy*, 19: 285–307.

Schumpeter, J. (1961) *The Theory of Economic Development*, New York: Oxford University Press.

Shane, S. and Venkataraman, S. (2000) "The promise of entrepreneurship as a field of research," *Academy of Management Journal*, 25: 217–226.

UNCTAD (1993) *Small and Medium-Sized Transnational Corporations: Role, Impact and Policy Implications*, New York: United Nations Conference on Trade and Development.

Venkataraman, S. (1997) "The distinctive domain of entrepreneurship research," *Advances in Entrepreneurship, Firm Emergence and Growth*, 3: 119–138.

Von Hippel, E. (1994) "Sticky information and the locus of problem solving: Implications for innovation," *Management Science*, 40: 429–439.

Whitley, R. (1999) *Divergent Capitalisms: The Social Structuring and Change of Business Systems*, Oxford: Oxford University Press.

8 A comparison of foreign acquisitions in the Brazilian electricity industry

What determines success?

Marcos Bosquetti, Rick Molz and Taïeb Hafsi

This chapter uses the Montreal Local–Global model of local–global interaction as an analytical template with which to understand two acquisitions in the Brazilian electricity industry. It compares the strategic approaches taken in two different acquisitions. The first is the acquisition of a Brazilian electricity distribution and supply company by a Portuguese multinational corporation (MNC), the second a similar acquisition by a French MNC. At first glance, the two acquiring MNCs adopted similar strategic approaches in positioning their new Brazilian subsidiary in the local environment, but achieved different results. This ten-year longitudinal comparative study integrates findings of systematic research on MNCs' strategy in the Brazilian electricity sector. It illustrates the uneasy interaction between a developing country's traditional logic and MNCs' economic logic, and highlights key lessons about the determinants of success when dealing with such an acquisition.

This chapter is grounded in the Molz–Raţiu (forthcoming) model of local global interaction. The model is grounded in institutional theory and argues that there are different dominant logics. Most of the Organisation for Economic Co-operation and Development (OECD) countries have a dominant logic built around neoclassical economic rationality, while developing and emerging country firms have a dominant logic based on local traditions. These two different logics are apparent in the interaction between multinational corporations from the OECD countries and local actors in emerging and developing countries. The OECD economic logic is built around concepts of efficiency and effectiveness in generating surplus, while the traditional logic of the emerging and developing countries is built around anthropological conceptualizations of traditional culture. In emerging and developing countries' traditional logic, greater emphasis is placed on community-based values and property rights to organize and sustain human relationships. Decisions are often slow and based on respect for traditional criteria. Local social networks are built around clans and community. This is in contrast with the economic logic of the developed OECD countries, which is built around the supremacy of the market for achieving economic objectives. Property rights are defined in relation to a market logic and organized to generate economic surplus within a clear, formal and stable institutional structure. Decision criteria are based on economic cost–benefit analysis, results and performance. The global OECD economic logic does not refer to specific national or local roots, and social networks are global, concerned with achieving economic objectives.

This chapter applies the Molz–Raţiu model in comparing two acquisitions of Brazilian electricity utilities. The first acquisition was made by a French multinational corporation and the second was made by a Portuguese multinational corporation. Thus, both MNCs are from OECD countries. Using the Molz–Raţiu model, this chapter explores the concept of dominant economic logic and local traditional logic in the interaction involved in these two MNC acquisitions of Brazilian electricity utilities. First, we intend to present an overview of Brazilian society's culture and values, then one of the Brazilian electricity industry. In subsequent sections we examine the multinational companies and their acquisition strategies in Brazil. Finally, we discuss the positioning strategies of the newly acquired companies in the Brazilian market, before offering a few conclusions.

The Brazilian Way

In his book *Brazil Is Not for Amateurs* (2002), the Brazilian researcher Belmiro Castor points out the peculiarities of the political, economic and social conditions that justify the title of his book. Castor (2002: 47) states that Brazil is a "nation accustomed to ambiguity." He argues that as a general rule, accuracy and precision are not strong points in Brazilian culture and states that "Brazil is the motherland of imprecision, of the *almost*, the *maybe*, the *who knows* and *God willing*. Nothing or almost nothing is precisely defined, everything *depends*" (ibid.: 48).

According to Castor, the Brazilian tradition of systematic research is relatively poor and frequently leads to "opinion-ism" (I think this, I think that) and "find-ism" (I find this, I find that); or, at the extreme opposite, leads to the uncritical use of models or interpretative tools developed for utilization in the simpler, more controllable settings found in relatively stable and mature economic, social and political systems (2002: 49).

Castor's research shows that the problem goes far beyond the quality of Brazilian statistics. He argues that many self-proclaimed experts fail to understand the plain facts of the country because they are accustomed, on the one hand, to browse with familiarity and ease in the symbolic world of equations, formulae and algorithms, and on the other, to display an "abysmal ignorance of how real people subsist, how they earn a living and how they spend their income" (2002: 50).

Castor argues that no matter the depth and length of a study about Brazil, one is unlikely to reach clear and uncontroversial conclusions about what the country and its people really are and how they succeeded in building a country where few things seem permanent. He states that what he found about the political, economic and social conditions of Brazil "is more like a succession of eternal provisionals, which defy and confound conventional ways of thinking" (2002: 52).

Castor's findings illustrates some manifestations of a developing country traditional logic, which is, according to Molz and Raţiu (forthcoming), built around community-based legitimacy, the integration of complex and contradictory interpretations of resources, and an intuitive but concrete epistemology.

The Brazilian electricity sector

In Brazil the 1990s were a decade marked by changes in economic policy, changes that had the objective of stabilizing the currency, opening up markets to competition, reducing the indebtedness of the country and repositioning the role of government in formulating policies and regulations instead of being the owner of enterprises.

This period also saw the beginnings of changes in the Brazilian electricity sector. Until 1993, companies under the virtually total control of state or federal governments operated in markets protected by regional monopolies, tariffs and a nationally uniform minimum guaranteed return on investment. Following the trends in the electricity sector reform worldwide, the laws governing the system were changed in 1993. The objective was to restore the economic and financial balance of the companies and treat them as businesses. In particular, previous controls on prices and guaranteed indebtedness caused confusion and prevented sound economic management of the firms. The 1993 electricity laws also abolished the pay equalization and guaranteed pricing. Between 1995 and 2006, electricity prices increased in real terms by more than 100 percent for households and more than 50 percent for industrial and commercial customers (Bosquetti and Fernandes, 2006).

From 1995 to 2000 the main changes in the electricity sector were the deployment of bidding for new concessions of public services; separation of the activities of generation, transmission, distribution and supply of electricity; the creation of two new agents, the independent power producer and a consumer free to choose his or her supplier; the establishment of the Agência Nacional de Energia Elétrica (ANEEL), the independent electricity industry regulator; the creation of a wholesale energy market; and the implementation of a priority program of thermoelectricity to accelerate the expansion of electricity supply. The year 2000 was characterized by a number of problems related to the clarity of the new rules of the game. In May 2001, simultaneous shortages in the southeast and northeast regions led the nation to face its largest electricity rationing program, which lasted until February 2002 (Bosquetti and Fernandes, 2006).

Changes in the economic and political contexts had also great impact on the electricity sector. In 1999 the government implemented a free-floating exchange rate, doubling the value of the US dollar in Brazil, and consequently the local denomination of debts of the electricity companies with foreign exchange exposure. Also in 2002, during the presidential election campaign the "Brazil risk" went up around 800 points in the first quarter of the year to a peak of 2,300 points in October, which led to another doubling of the exchange rate value of the US dollar. In 2003 the new government published a report entitled

"Institutional Model of the Electricity Sector," laying the foundation of a revitalization for the sector. The new model disappointed the expectations of "going back" to the previous model and kept the bases of the 1993 model, seeking private-sector participation and the encouragement of competition. The most significant changes introduced at this time were the creation of a new agent responsible for the energy and environmental planning, and an increase in government control over the national system operations and the wholesale market (Bosquetti and Fernandes, 2006).

The year 2003 was also marked by disruptions related to privatizations in the electricity sector, and excess electricity generation capacity, a side effect of the rationing program, leading to the completion of new generation and transmission projects and changed consumer behavior for added energy saving.

The period 2004–2006 has been marked by a yo-yo between threats of electricity supply crisis and excess capacity. This oscillation reflects the impact of weather on the predominant hydroelectric generation system in Brazilian electricity sector. As the reform of the new electricity sector model had not been consolidated, the 2004 national program of public–private partnership failed to attract enough investment to the electricity sector. As a result, the electricity sector remains a constraint on the development of the Brazilian economy (Bosquetti and Fernandes, 2006).

Key success factors in the Brazilian electricity sector

In their two-decade longitudinal study of the Brazilian electricity sector, Bosquetti and Fernandes (2006) have identified three key success factors (KSFs) for a player to succeed in entering the Brazilian market.

The first KSF is *familiarity with the Brazilian electricity sector*. It is related to knowledge of the political, economic and regulatory aspects of the sector, which implies enough intimacy to understand the modus operandi of the sector and to learn how to maximize opportunities and minimize the threats of the context in which the company is operating. According to Bosquetti and Fernandes (2006), since about 1990 the Brazilian electricity sector has been marked by uncertainties and disruptions, as described earlier. The authors argue that this KSF is perhaps the most important among the three identified in their study.

The second KSF is *operational excellence*. This is a typical factor of public service companies that optimizes the price/quality ratio to offer regulated products and services.

The third key success factor is *integration technique*. Bosquetti and Fernandes (2006) argue that owing to the nature of the product, a vertical integration of all the value-chain activities (generation, transmission, distribution and supply of electricity) provides synergy and facilitates risk management, mainly between the power generation business (energy supply) and the distribution business (guarantee of the consumer market) in the sector.

These three KSFs in the Brazilian energy sector will be applied in this comparative study as a complementary tool of the Molz–Rațiu model to analyze and understand MNCs' entry strategy into the Brazilian electricity market, the different outcomes and their way of dealing with the challenging local–global interaction.

The French MNC

The French MNC is among the largest companies in the sector of generation, transmission, distribution and supply of electricity. As one of the largest electricity generation companies worldwide, it provides electricity for forty-two million customers in five continents, thirty-eight million of them in Europe. The organization employs 160,000 people and is composed of a portfolio of seventy-five subsidiaries and investments established in Europe and in other competitive markets for electricity and natural gas. The French MNC offers solutions to the market that combine electricity, gas and related services through a vertical integration strategy across the energy-sector value chain.

The technical skills acquired over decades of monopoly operation in the French market looked appropriate for making inroads into the Brazilian market. The objective of the French MNC was to consolidate its position as world market leader, firmly anchored in Europe and growing its presence in emerging markets, increasing its profitability in all its businesses. Its internationalization strategy began in the 1990s and has intensified, with a growing number of international acquisitions of electricity companies and equity investments in power generation.

Currently its international presence is restricted to the United Kingdom, Germany, Italy and Spain, where its massive foreign investments are concentrated on integrated business in the electricity value chain; to Belgium, Switzerland, Austria, Hungary, Poland, Slovakia, China, Vietnam, Morocco and Mali, where it also has investments in power generation from renewable energy sources; and to South Africa, Laos, the United States, Thailand, Japan and the United Arab Emirates, where it has business consultancy and engineering services. Almost all its acquisitions and partnerships have been financed from its own cash-flow resources.

The French MNC's internationalization to Brazil, 1996–2006

As part of its strategy for internationalization to Brazil, in 1996 the French MNC acquired one of the largest Brazilian state-owned distribution companies and gave it the mission of growing business along the energy-sector value chain to meet Brazil's growing demand. The acquired company provided electricity to three million consumers in its area of concession in Brazil and employed 3,500 people. Supplying electricity to one of the richest areas in Brazil, it was expected to be profitable.

The Brazilian subsidiary invested in generation businesses and started a gas and telecom business in 1997, but sold them in 2001. It contracted debts in foreign currency, which ended up harming its financial results during the foreign exchange currency crisis in 1999 and the period of the Brazilian presidential campaign of 2002. Before the presidential elections the French MNC injected US$1 billion into its Brazilian subsidiary and approved the implementation of an action plan proposed to recover profitability and efficiency through downsizing, reducing operating costs and reducing commercial losses.

Despite its financial strategy, which included swap transactions to protect against exposure to currency risk, the Brazilian subsidiary ended 2003 with a consolidated debt of US$2 billion. The French parent company decided in 2006 to dispose of almost all its assets in the Brazilian energy sector and bitterly withdrew from the Brazilian market.

The Portuguese MNC

The Portuguese MNC is among the ten largest European players in the energy sector, and the third largest MNC in the Iberian Peninsula. It operates in the generation, distribution and supply of electricity in Europe and Latin America and also has significant presence in the Portuguese gas sector. This MNC employs 15,000 people and has a portfolio of eleven investments in subsidiaries established in six countries. It has an international strategy similar to that of the French MNC described earlier. The Portuguese MNC's objective was to consolidate its position in the Iberian Peninsula and grow its presence in emerging markets by increasing its profitability in all its businesses. Its strategy of internationalization also started in the mid-1990s and has been enhanced through acquisitions of distribution companies and equity investments in power generation, but to a lesser extent than the French MNC.

The Portuguese MNC has massive foreign investments in integrated electricity businesses in Spain and Brazil. It has also investments in power generation from renewable energy sources in France, Belgium, Poland and the United States. It has a relevant presence in the Iberian Peninsula gas sector. Currently, its main international strategy is focused growth in Spain and Brazil by executing generation projects and strict analysis of new opportunities.

The Portuguese MNC's internationalization to Brazil, 1998 to the present

The Portuguese MNC started its strategy of internationalization to Brazil in 1998 after acquiring a state-owned distribution company that supplies electricity to one of the most industrialized regions in Brazil. As part of its strategy the Portuguese MNC acquired another state-owned distribution company in 1999, doubling the number of customers, and started investing in power generation. Today, its Brazilian subsidiary holds investments along the Brazilian energy sector value chain, consolidating activities concerned with the generation, distribution and supply of electricity in six major states of Brazil, serving 3.5 million customers and employing almost 3,000 people. It has achieved significant growth through the acquisition of companies and investments in power generation. It is interesting to note that, unlike the French MNC's acquisition, both distribution businesses acquired by the Portuguese MNC in Brazil suffered very low levels of commercial loss.

Regarding risk management to debts and foreign exchange exposure and operational efficiency, the Brazilian subsidiary of the Portuguese MNC contracted debts in both foreign and Brazilian currency. It took out long-term loans from Brazilian funds for infrastructure development, even though doing so was more expensive than using funds from its parent company. It has also modernized its distribution system and invested heavily in training to improve operational efficiency, achieving profitability across all its businesses and thereby demonstrating success in its Brazil strategy.

Strategic approaches to positioning a Brazilian subsidiary

This section presents and compares the relevant strategic approaches of the French and the Portuguese MNCs to positioning their Brazilian subsidiary. The two MNCs had similar strategic intent: to grow their business in Brazil; both were involved in the same electricity market, faced the same turbulence in the political and economic contexts, and had the same regulator (watchdog), but came up with very different outcomes. While the Portuguese MNC achieved success in its internationalization to Brazil, the French MNC failed and retired from the market.

The main differences between the strategic approaches of the MNCs are related to the following issues: (1) the composition and role of the board of directors and its relationships with the parent company; (2) familiarity with the Brazilian electricity sector and understanding of its modus operandi; (3) diversification of the growth strategy in Brazil; (4) debts and foreign exchange exposure risk management; and (5) operational efficiency.

Composition of the board of directors

The key difference in the composition of the board of directors between the cases is the Portuguese approach to understanding the Brazilian context and electricity sector. Since the establishment of its subsidiary in Brazil, the Portuguese company has had three of its nine board members take a seat on both the parent's and the subsidiary's boards. Moreover, two of the nine board members in its subsidiary are external members with long-term experience in the Brazilian electricity sector. By contrast, the French MNC composed its Brazilian subsidiary's board of directors without any external members.

Parent–subsidiary relationship

The analysis of the MNC–Brazilian subsidiary relationship (the role played by the parent company's board of directors) was based on a seven-point scale for the level of distribution of power (authority) between boards of directors proposed by Muritiba (2005). The seven points in the scale are (1) absent, (2) collector, (3) approver, (4) counselor, (5) democratic, (6) centralizer, and (7) operational. Thus, the scale ranges from decentralization at one extreme (an absent board of directors) to the other extreme of centralization (an operational board of directors). According to Muritiba (2005), when the parent company's board of directors play their roles in the extremes of this distribution of power, the subsidiary faces no support from the parent company, or too much interference in its decisions and operations. Muritiba suggests that the balance would be the ideal of facilitating and improving the decision-making process and the board's relationship.

In this comparative case study the Portuguese parent board of directors played a more balanced role, mostly as *councilor* and *democratic* (levels 4 and 5 in Muritiba's scale), than the French one, which tended more to the decentralization extreme, mostly as *absent* (level 1).

Familiarity with the Brazilian electricity sector

Regarding familiarity with the Brazilian electricity sector, which is considered a key success factor in the strategy of internationalization to an emergent economy, the Portuguese MNC seems to have learned more about Brazil than the French one. At the end of the longitudinal study the Portuguese company demonstrated greater intimacy in understanding the modus operandi of the Brazilian electricity sector than the French MNC. It seems to be related to the strategic approach it took regarding the composition of its boards of directors and to the more balanced roles they played in the parent–subsidiary relationship.

Growth strategy in Brazil

In terms of implementing their growth strategy in Brazil, while the French company dispersed its focus, adopting a multi-utility business concept by starting and then winding up gas and telecom businesses in a very unstable and infant competitive market, the Portuguese company focused its efforts purely on the electricity business. It built and developed its business along the Brazilian electricity sector supply chain by acquiring another distribution company, which means more customers, guaranteeing a market for its investments in generation projects in partnership with national and international players, and thereby managing its risks more effectively.

Operational excellence

Operational efficiency is another key success factor, not only in businesses in the electricity sector but also in any business concerned with infrastructure. Again, both MNCs were attracted by the opportunity to accelerate their return on investment by improving the operational efficiency levels of their Brazilian subsidiary.

In the case of the French MNC, the company it acquired had the highest level of commercial and technical losses in the Brazilian electricity sector, which appeared to offer more room for improving performance. However, it failed in its two large programs designed to reduce those losses, which in fact was a consequence of social problems in its concession area, problems that became even worse as the economic and social context changed. As regards its downsizing and workforce reduction strategy, in the short term it achieved better levels of performance, especially in the ratio of number of customers per employee. However, in the medium and long term, workforce morale declined and performance fell back to the sector's average ratio.

The Portuguese company was more successful in its strategy to improve the operational efficiency of its Brazilian subsidiary. It invested in information technology to integrate business and resources planning processes, implementing management control systems similar to those employed in the parent company. It also invested in training and the development of competencies in the workforce in Brazil and in exchanging key people from parent and Brazilian subsidiary to transfer knowledge and business practices, accelerating the learning curve and building the parent–subsidiary relationship at different levels of the company hierarchy.

Risk management

Regarding risk management of debts and foreign exchange exposure, the French MNC financed its Brazilian subsidiary from its own cash-flow resources, which ended up harming the subsidiary's financial results because of the foreign exchange currency crisis and the Brazil Risk, with credibility crises reducing by two-thirds the value of the national currency against the US dollar. The Portuguese company balanced its source of investment with Brazilian currency by contracting long-term loans from Brazilian funds for infrastructure development to manage its risk to foreign exchange exposure.

Outcomes of the strategy of internationalization to Brazil

Despite the French MNC's greater experience in internationalization strategy as compared with the Portuguese MNC, the French failed to achieve their strategic intent, while the Portuguese internationalization strategy to Brazil is considered a successful case in the Brazilian electricity sector.

Discussion

Institutional scholars have proposed a split in the environment in which firms operate, although as two sides of the same coin (Scott, 2001): an economic/technical environment that rules decision making according to rational efficiency principles, and an institutional environment comprising the social and political pressures arising from the company's context and affecting its decisions.

Depending on the industry, context and strategy, companies can comply with one environment or the other. The electricity industry is strongly affected by both the technical and the institutional context, but the strength of each can vary from one country to another.

The outcomes of the French MNC's strategy in Brazil were very poor, especially when compared with its performance in other countries, such as the United Kingdom. The British subsidiary tripled its number of customers and is now one of the top three players in the generation, distribution and supply of electricity and gas, even though the MNC entered that market almost two years later than it did the Brazilian one, employing a similar strategic approach and applying the same competences. However, while it has had remarkable success in the United Kingdom, in Brazil it has been a failure. Therefore, a brief comparison of the institutional context in the United Kingdom and Brazil respectively during the time frame of this study highlights the distinctive nature of the Brazilian case and its dominant logics as well as the specific factors that played in favor of the Portuguese MNC compared to the French one in the Brazilian electricity market.

The institutional context in the United Kingdom during the period 1995–2005 was predominantly technical, with a clear focus on market efficiency. The newly opened British electricity market has had a clear and consistent definition of the "rules of the game" – regulations to ensure that demand for electricity is satisfied and that license holders are able to finance their activities, promote competition in generation and supply, and protect the interests of customers in terms of prices and quality of service (Fernandes *et al.* 2006).

The institutional context in Brazil, on the contrary, has been predominantly institutional and political. It is characterized by strong pressure for social legitimacy and uncertainties and interruptions in the privatization process and the opening up of the electricity market. There were no clear and consistent "rules of the game" for the Brazilian electricity market. Lack of a national integrated energy planning framework led to an electricity supply crisis. The institutional context of that time frame was marked by a currency exchange crisis and a lack of credibility in the Brazilian economy.

The results achieved by the French MNC's subsidiaries at the end of the period are meaningful. The subsidiary operating in the UK market found a context that was predominantly technical, with institutional landmarks clearly defined, so that it could drive its effort toward goals related to its technical competence. On the Brazilian side the French MNC's subsidiary seems to have failed in part because the technical approach did not work in an environment characterized by loose regulation and strong political forces, although it followed the same model as in Britain. For instance, it experienced great difficulty in recovering debts from consumers and playing by the Brazilian electricity industry's rules of the game. As a consequence, its integrated growth strategy in generation and distribution businesses failed to be implemented in the Brazilian institutional context. Therefore, it failed to develop the parent company's technical integration competence and market risk management in the Brazilian electricity industry.

Considering the three key factors of success (KSFs) identified in the context of the Brazilian electric sector, the French MNC emphasized organizational skills to leverage KSFs 2 and 3 (operational excellence and technical integration) but it seems to have lacked the skills to leverage FCS 1 (familiarity with the Brazilian electric sector), perhaps because of the cultural gap or through assuming that all countries that have adopted the British model of market liberalization operate the same way. Perhaps the French MNC's successful entry strategy in OECD countries, such as the United Kingdom and Germany, among other countries with a dominant logic built around neoclassical economic rationality, has reinforced and nurtured its technical competences, namely operational excellence (KFS 2) and integration technique (KSF 3), in a recursive way, as observed by Teece *et al.* (1997) in their study of interaction among competence, strategy and performance.

Lack of clear and consistent "rules of the game" in the Brazilian electricity market, and economic and political instability, are a reflection of the dominant elements of the local model of a developing country in the Molz–Raţiu (forthcoming) model of local global interaction, which makes Brazil a "nation accustomed to ambiguity" (Castor, 2002: 47) and therefore a challenge for MNCs from OECD countries such as France and Portugal.

This study shows that the OECD economic logic, which rules decision making according to rational efficiency and effectiveness principles, seems to be *not enough* to cope with social and political pressures arising from the institutional context of a developing country.

Comparing the French and the Portuguese MNC interactions with Brazil, it is possible to see, through the lens of the Molz–Raţiu (forthcoming) model of local global interaction and the three KSFs (Bosquetti and Fernandes, 2006) for a player to succeed in entering the Brazilian market, how the two MNCs are singularly different in their way of dealing with the dominant elements of the local model of a developing country.

The key difference between the two MNCs seems to be the attention and effort put on the first KSF (familiarity with the Brazilian electricity sector). This KSF is related to the knowledge of the political, economic and regulatory aspects of the sector, which implies that enough intimacy is needed to understand the modus operandi of the country and sector and to learn how to maximize opportunities and minimize the threats of the context in which the company is operating.

The composition of the subsidiaries' board of directors and the type of relationship they had with their parent company are evidence of their awareness regarding the dominant elements of the local model. Indeed, the ability to execute their growth strategy in Brazil and their output after almost a decade of operation in the Brazilian electricity market seems to be purely a consequence of mastering the first KSF.

Organizations develop strategies to cope with their environment and evaluate their performance according to their strategic intent (Hamel and Prahalad, 1989). As a result, over time they create organizational competencies relevant to their strategy. However, the strength of these competencies will vary according to their alignment with institutional context and success in strategy implementation.

The Portuguese MNC seems to have paid much more attention to this first KPI than the French MNC. One strong reason for this key difference is the colonial and cultural linkages between the Portugal and Brazil. Brazil was discovered and colonized by Portugal and its official language is Portuguese. Therefore, the cultural and linguistic linkages and networks are important factors in explaining the success of the Portuguese MNC in Brazil. Rubens Ricupero (2001) points out the Brazilian dilemma regarding globalization, which seems to be a kind of second wave of colonization in which the OECD countries with more intimacy and understanding of the local model can have a competitive advantage and a better chance of success in the uneasy interaction between a developing country's traditional logic and MNC economic logic, as discussed in the Molz–Raţiu (forthcoming) model of local–global interaction.

A final word: although the findings of this comparative case study lead to the discussion above, they do not rule out other possible interpretations of the determinants of acquisition success and failure when dealing with an interaction of this kind, such as a different level of risk appetite, changes in the MNC's strategic intent, and even some conflicts in the parent–subsidiary relationship not captured by the fieldwork of this case study.

Conclusion

This ten-year longitudinal comparative study applied the Montreal Local–Global model of local global interaction as an analytical template through which to understand two acquisitions in the Brazilian electricity industry. It illustrates the uneasy interaction between a developing country's traditional logic and MNC economic logic, and highlights key lessons about the determinants of an acquisition's success when such an interaction is involved.

This chapter has compared two similar cases of acquisitions occurring at the same time and in the same industry, but with very different results, in a country "not for amateurs" known for its "Brazilian Way." This chapter's contribution resides in three main aspects.

First, it illustrates the application of the Montreal Local–Global model of local–global interaction by pointing out how susceptible MNCs are to the winds of the institutional context in which their subsidiaries operate.

Second, the findings of this comparative study show that despite being larger and having more experience in international business than the Portuguese MNC, the French corporation missed the first of the three KSFs necessary for a player to succeed in entering the Brazilian market, or paid much less attention to it than the Portuguese MNC (Bosquetti and Fernandes, 2006). In other words, the French MNC seemed to have insufficient intimacy with Brazil to understand the modus operandi of the country and sector and to learn how to maximize opportunities and minimize the threats of the context in which its subsidiary was operating. In this comparative study the Portuguese MNC seems to have a strong advantage, not only because of Portugal's colonial and cultural linkages with Brazil, but also because the MNC seems to have paid much more attention to this first KPI than the French MNC, perhaps because it knew more about the Brazilian Way than the French corporation did.

Third, the use of key success factors (KSFs) as a complementary tool has proved to be a useful way to apply the Molz–Raţiu (forthcoming) model of local–global interaction. Furthermore, this study has reinforced the importance of culture and local traditions as key elements of different dominant logics by pointing out the first KSF – familiarity with the Brazilian electricity sector – as a prerequisite for the development of the other two KSFs – operational efficiency and integrated technique.

Fourth, both MNCs studied here offer practical lessons about the composition of boards of directors and the parent–subsidiary relationship as being among the determinants of acquisition success when dealing with such an uneasy inter-action between a developing country's traditional logic and MNC economic logic.

References

Bosquetti, M. A. and Fernandes, B. H. (2006) "Internacionalização e competência organ-izacional. O caso de uma empresa francesa no setor elétrico brasileiro," paper pre-sented to Workshop em Internacionalização de Empresas, São Paulo: Universidade de São Paulo.

Castor, B. V. J. (2006) *Brazil Is Not for Amateurs: Patterns of Governance in the Land of "Jeitinho"*, Philadelphia: X-Libris.

Fernandes, B. H. R., Bosquetti, M. A. and Mills, J. F. (2006) "Competence development and performance measurement: A cross country study of energy companies," papere presented to the Fifth International Conference on Performance Measurement and Management, London, 25–28 July.

Hamel, G. and Prahalad, C. K. (1989) "Strategic intent," *Harvard Business Review*, May–June, 67 (3): 63–76.

Molz, R. and Raţiu, C. (forthcoming) Work in progress.

Muritiba, S. N. (2005) "Participação dos conselhos de administração em decisões de estratégia no âmbito da governança corporative," dissertation presented to the Faculty of Economy, Management and Accounting, University of São Paulo – USP, São Paulo: FEA/USP.

Ricupero, R. (2001) *O Brasil e o dilema da globalização*, 2nd edn., São Paulo: SENAC.

Scott, W. R. (2001) *Institutions and Organizations*, 2nd edn., Thousand Oaks, CA: Sage.

Teece, D. J., Pisano, G. and Shuen, A. (1997) "Dynamic capabilities and strategic man-agement," *Strategic Management Journal*, 18 (7): 509–533.

9 The behavior of multinational enterprises in developing countries

Having a sense of the "good" through "smart partnerships" in Malaysia

Rabia Naguib

Introduction

Past and present Malaysian governments have often sought to direct the course of economic development while at the same time ensuring a more equitable distribution of costs, opportunities and rewards among the diverse ethnic and racial factions typical of a multiracial population. One way of doing so was through a "smart partnership" between the public and the private sectors. The concept of "smart partnership" came out of a dialogue among members of the Commonwealth Partnership for Technology Management (CPTM) and Malaysian Industry-Government Group for High Technology (MIGHT) in Kuala Lumpur in 1993. In this perspective, "smart partnership" refers to the business principles of **S**ustainable, **M**easurable, **A**chievable, **R**ealistic and **T**ime bound objectives. It also refers to the idea of sharing fairly and equitably, and is based on the philosophy of a win–win strategy.[1] Through different agencies and policies the Malaysian government interacts with businesses and seeks to be assured that they will respect certain regulations and requirements. A smart partnership is meant to be synergistic and to create the basis of long-term dynamic stability. According to Mahathir[2] (2000: 35), smart partnerships

> are about government, organizations, and people working together for long-term mutual gains to help bring about global harmony and cooperative prosperity. They require the following ingredients for success: a shared vision, common goals, clear understanding of each partner's strengths and weaknesses, willingness to compromise, and to be patient and tolerant. Its originality lies in the practice and not the principle.

The Malaysian government clearly understands that it needs to formulate its core development philosophy and strategy according to its particular circumstances, culture and history. The political leaders, through their understanding of the historical and social context of their country and of its specific needs, have played a critical role in shaping the way forward for the development of Malaysia. In such a context, where social and economic needs are clearly identified and the local reality is complex and dynamic, what are the challenges facing MNEs through their subsidiaries? How do these companies manage the different and often conflicting pressures they are subjected to? How do they reconcile global efficiency requirements with local needs?

Using empirical research conducted in the context of Malaysia (Naguib, 2004), this chapter aims to present results related to the behaviour of multinational firms in terms of social responsibility and local adaptation. To date, the business context of Malaysia remains underresearched. It therefore represents a very rich and interesting field of study. In terms of methodology, using case studies is highly appropriate. It allows the investigation of this specific context in an in-depth and descriptive way. Thus, I will start by introducing the research context through a brief description of Malaysia, followed by a brief review of the literature, enabling me to identify a framework for analysis. Then I will present three case studies investigating the behavior of the subsidiaries of three well-known and successful MNEs, namely Nestlé, Unilever and Alcom. This comparative study will help us to address and highlight the questions raied above and to illustrate in different ways the concept of smart partnership as practiced in Malaysia.

Research context

Multinational subsidiaries are confronted with two distinct sets of isomorphic pressures, and with the need to maintain their legitimacy in regard to both the host country and the parent company. Therefore, they find themselves in a situation of "institutional duality." The institutional context of the host country can influence the practices of multinational subsidiaries, in particular through direct pressures exercised by regulatory components. These translate as laws and regulations promoting some types of behavior and restricting others (Scott, 2001). The subsidiary therefore adopts particular practices as a way of becoming isomorphic with local organizations in the same activity sector. But, in fact, foreign subsidiaries are not expected to be entirely isomorphic, especially if the parent company is powerful and the subsidiary less dependent on the host country (Meyer and Zucker, 1989).

The other side of the coin is that countries looking to develop find themselves subject to strong pressures, both internally and externally. They must either let their way of development be dictated by others, adopting policies set by international institutions at the risk of altering or destroying their traditional institutional frameworks and losing their sovereignty; or else draw on their national culture and their own system of norms and values to tease out a suitable development model (Cheng *et al.*, 1998; Coates, 1987). Stiglitz (2002) notes that countries that have managed globalization in their own way, like those in Southeast Asia, have been in a better position overall to benefit, and to share out the benefits equally, than other countries. They have been able to control the terms of engagement with the global marketplace. In contrast, countries whose globalization was managed for them by the International

Monetary Fund and other international financial institutions have done less well. He concludes that the problem is not globalization itself, but the way in which it is managed.

The case of Malaysia is instructive in this regard. In addition to being for a while a "success story," in terms of economic development, Malaysia displays the features of an institutional context in which companies are expected to consider the country's norms, values, cultural and social traditions, and religious beliefs. That explains the choice of this country as a field study.

Context background and characteristics

Malaysia was formerly dependent on the production and export of two commodities, rubber and tin. Wide fluctuations in the prices of these commodities meant uneven growth for the country. Even after oil palms and cocoa were introduced, the prospect for economic growth and higher income for Malaysians was poor (Mahathir, 2000). A decision was thus made to industrialize by manufacturing goods for local consumption and for exports. But Malaysia had neither the expertise nor the capital needed to set up industrial plants. It was therefore decided that initiatives should be set up in order to attract foreign investment. The strategy proved very successful in creating jobs and generally developing the country. As noted in *The Economist* (2003: 13):

> In the 30 years from 1970 to 2000, Malaysia's economic growth, despite the Asian Crisis of 1997–98, averaged about 7 percent. ... Malaysia had been admirably agile in reinventing itself. Under the British, Malaya was a highly successful commodity economy, its tin, rubber and palm oil helping to fill the colonialists' pockets far out of proportion to the country's size. Then it turned itself into a manufacturer. Now it is changing again. ... Probably the most significant change is the new emphasis on services.

With independence in 1957, Malaysia inherited an economy dominated by the export of natural resources, especially minerals, rubber, palm oil and forestry products. In the period 1960–1970 the government embarked upon an economic development strategy of import substitution. It sought to enlarge the country's economic base beyond the export of natural resources by encouraging domestic manufacturing enterprises through tax incentives and subsidies. At the same time, it sought to attract foreign direct investments by creating "industrial estates" or free trade zones, and by providing improved services in utilities and transportation (United Nations, 2006a).

In 1971, Malaysia's government introduced a policy of affirmative action aimed at restoring the ethnical imbalances and at helping the Bumiputras ("Sons of the Soil") – who lived in the rural areas, had little access to education and owned less than 2 percent of the country's corporate assets, even though they make up 60 percent of the population – to increase their share in the economy to 30 percent. Through the introduction of the New Economic

Policy (NEP), "ethnic restructuring and poverty alleviation were elevated to primacy among the goals of Malaysia's development effort" (Rudner, 1994: 394). The government, emulating in part the Japanese experience, incorporated these social concerns while becoming an active partner with private business interests in order to ensure the furtherance of its economic growth and development strategy.

Malaysia's national development

Under Mahathir's leadership, the Malaysian government provided support for greater economic diversification and, coupled with its policies of deregulation and liberalization of the financial system, these actions helped transform the country into a middle-income emerging market by the end of 1995 (Liu, 2001).

Despite periods of political turmoil, successive governments in Malaysia have continued to follow strategically designed five-year plans. After the National Development Policy (1991–2000), which followed the NEP, Mahathir's government developed "Vision 2020" to share and show the Malays the way forward. The general direction of this strategy has been to shift the economy toward a broader base while emphasizing international competitiveness. Governments have also encouraged movements toward more capital-intensive and technologically sophisticated industries (United Nations, 2006b).

The heavy dependence on foreign direct investment (FDI) in gross domestic capital formation, especially for manufacturing investments, has sometimes limited the development of domestic entrepreneurship, while enhancing the dominance of foreign finance capital. International financial liberalization succeeded in temporarily generating massive capital inflows into East Asia, but it also exacerbated systemic instability and somewhat trimmed the scope of governmental interventions, which had previously been responsible for the rapid pace of economic growth and development. These problems became dramatically apparent when Malaysia was hit by the regional financial crisis in 1997–1998. In the decade just preceding the crisis, the average economic growth rate had been 8.7 percent, but it suffered a sharp 7.5 percent contraction afterwards (Jomo, 2001).

However, Malaysia weathered the crisis better than many other South Asian and East Asian economies. In part this was due to its stricter controls over foreign borrowing, as well as stricter central bank regulations. Indeed, Malaysia's short-term foreign debt and its current account deficits in proportion to its international reserves were far less than in South Korea, Thailand and Indonesia (World Bank, 2000). The speed of recovery of Malaysia from the financial crisis was also due in part to a high savings rate (over 41 percent of GNP in 1998), a relatively low public debt, a cooperative labor force (no labor unions exist) and relative political stability, all of which helped maintain sound macroeconomic policies. The strength of exports, particularly exports of electronics, semiconductors and related components, was also an important factor in Malaysia's rapid economic recovery.

Methodology

This chapter draws upon two main theories, institutional theory and corporate social responsibility (CSR), to analyze the behavior of MNEs in local contexts in regard to their degree(s) of adaptation. Although several researchers (Ghoshal and Bartlett, 1990; Bartlett and Ghoshal, 1998; Prahalad and Doz, 1987; Gupta and Westney, 2003) have studied the behavior of MNEs, pointing out the need for these enterprises to be both global and local, most of these studies considered only three imperatives: economic, technological and political. This is perhaps understandable, as they were more interested in the organizational capacities of MNEs in terms of resources devoted to creating sustainable competitive advantages that allow them to produce added value and increase profitability.

In this chapter, however, we are primarily interested in unpacking the behavior of MNEs in terms of their capacity for local adaptation and participation in sustainable development, which includes adding value to host countries and contributing to their growth while still ensuring profitability and legitimacy. Looking beyond the firm's need for profitability and a unified corporate strategy (standardization), we are also interested in highlighting the "fit" or "alignment" between their organizational characteristics and those of the task environment (adaptation). We consequently highlight the need for "balance" or "equilibrium" in the survival strategies for MNEs. It has been well established in the literature (Kim and Hwang, 1992; Dunning, 1998, 2003) that MNEs are forced to maintain a constant balance between myriad pressures coming from different directions – a situation that points to the complexity of managing MNEs and the challenges their managers and directors face on a day-to-day basis. Therefore, there is a need for a multilevel analysis to study the behavior of MNEs, taking into consideration simultaneously firm-specific, industry-specific and country-specific factors (Naguib, 2004).

Institutional theory places greater emphasis on the social and cultural aspects of the overall environment. Those aspects constitute institutional pressures that push organizations to adopt isomorphic or similar behaviors (DiMaggio and Powell, 1983; Meyer and Scott, 1992). Current thinking on CSR takes us to the heart of the relationship between the corporation and society (Carroll, 1999; Freeman, 1984). The issue of what role companies should play within a society is reviewed, leading to a discussion of the responsibilities companies should assume and for which it should be hold accountable. Friedman (1962) held that

> [t]here is only one social responsibility of business, to use its resources and engage in activities designed to increase its profits so long as it stays within the rules of the game, engages in open and free competition, without deception and fraud.

However, other economists and sociologists, and philosophers in particular, see corporate responsibility as going beyond the basic function of conducting commercial activities. Since society provides tangible and intangible resources that benefit the company, the latter has a moral and ethical obligation to take respons-ibility for the various actors that allow it to exist, maintain its operations and make profit (Bird, 2001). For-profit enterprises create wealth by exploiting the resources of the social body in which they operate (OCDE, 2001). Therefore, they have to distribute that wealth equally among the participants and stakehold-ers in their activities. That legitimizes the introduction of the principles of dis-tributive justice, fair trade, corporate ethics, citizenship and sustainable development into the study of organizations.

Given the nature of the present research questions and the lack of previous studies in the context of Malaysia, exploratory research using a qualitative approach was necessary. Also, the present study uses multiple sources of evid-ence, which is characteristic of the case-study approach (Eisenhardt, 1989; Yin, 1994). As Yin (1994) clearly pointed out, one of the most important sources of case-study information is the interview, whereas the most important use of docu-ments is to corroborate and augment evidence from other sources. In this study, interview data were utilized as the main evidence to describe the company-level processes. Documentary evidence was retrieved to construct a picture of the industry-level dynamics and changes in the institutional context.

Obviously, Malaysia displays the features of an institutional context in which enterprises are expected to consider the country's norms, values, cultural and social traditions, and religious beliefs. In the light of this recognition, six subsid-iaries of MNEs operating in the Malaysian context were surveyed, using second-ary data and semi-structured interviews. A total of forty-five managers (mainly expatriates) were interviewed in the course of this study (Naguib, 2004). In this chapter I have chosen to present from my sampling frame three cases: Nestlé (Anglo-Swiss), Unilever (Anglo-Dutch) and Alcom (Canadian). These cases are very representative and revealing of the behavior of the subsidiaries of MNEs caught between the pressures for internalization and standardization from the parent company and local adaptation from the host country. Being of different nationalities and operating in different industries, they also highlight the impact of such factors on the degree of adaptation of the subsidiaries of MNEs. Overall, these cases allow us to examine the involvement of some MNEs in smart part-nerships with the Malaysian government and therefore to assess the dynamic interaction between the global and the local in this specific context.

Comparative case analysis

This section presents three case studies of MNEs operating within an emerging market context. In the first, we consider the Anglo-Dutch giant Unilever in the food and beverage sector. This is followed by an analysis of another major player of European pedigree in the food sector, the Swiss firm Nestlé. Finally, we con-sider a manufacturing company from not just a different continental context but also a different industry, the Canadian-owned Aluminium Company (Alcom).

The three case studies chosen illustrate in an interesting way the interaction between different factors influencing the strategies and behavior of the subsidiaries of MNEs regarding the degree of their local adaptation. These firms are subject to pressures coming from the parent company, from the sector of industry in which they are operating as well as from the host country. Therefore, a multi-level analysis is necessary, and different factors (organizational, sectoral and contextual or social) need to be taken into consideration all together. As these factors vary from one firm to another, variation in their behaviors can be normally expected.

According to some researchers, the social and contextual factors play a crucial role in explaining the variation between the subsidiaries of MNEs. In this vein, Kostova (1996: 316) used the concept of institutional distance, defined as the difference between the institutional profiles of the countries of the parent company and of the subsidiary, to support this argument. The present study shows that even though the three firms are operating within the same context, with similar institutional distance, they still vary regarding their degree of local adaptation and social responsibility. Some researchers argue that industrial and sectoral factors are more decisive and influential in explaining this variation. The example of Unilever and Nestlé, which operate in the same field of industry and still show variation in their behaviour, is quite revealing. Organizational factors, which were mainly highlighted by the contingency theory, cannot completely explain the variation. Also, we need a more integrative and explorative approach in order to better understand the behavior of MNEs in developing countries, which I propose to do initially through the presentation of three cases.

Case 1: Unilever Malaysia

As Anwar Ibrahim, Deputy Prime Minister of Malaysia, put it in 1997 (p. 2):

> Unilever has demonstrated that fruitful and mutually beneficial relationships can result when multinational corporations are prepared to put down roots, adapt and operate within national goals and aspirations. While other companies have come and gone, Unilever has become an integral part of the Malaysian corporate and social scene. It has helped the local economy to grow and has reaped the rewards of the growth of Malaysian economic endeavour.[3]

There was another instructive statement in the same year by Chim Howe Lai, chairman of Unilever (Malaysia): "Unilever has adopted from the beginning a multidomestic strategy opting for a total integration with the community in which it operates. Unilever Malaysia has participated in Malaysia's socio-economic development plans."

The Anglo-Dutch MNE Unilever is one of the world's largest consumer goods enterprises. With dual headquarters in London and Rotterdam, Unilever employs more than 160,000 people. The enterprise's primary activity is the manufacture and sale of products in over ninety countries around the world. However, the Unilever story in Malaysia began when the company started exporting vast quantities of soap and other consumer goods to the then British colony. In the 1930s the soap market became static, with the emergence of locally manufactured soaps. Unilever then started exploring the possibility of setting up a factory there in order to compete more effectively and to take advantage of the supply of cheap coconut oil. This first initiative was interrupted by the Japanese invasion of Malaysia in 1940.

After World War II, and within a strategy of global expansion seeking to meet consumers' demand worldwide and to source for raw material, Unilever set up a factory in Kuala Lumpur in 1947. Then costing RM 12 million, the factory, built to produce soap and margarine, was the largest in the country. It created job opportunities for hundreds of Malaysians. Unilever has always been aware that in order to succeed in the host country, it had to become a genuine corporate citizen of that country (Bartlett and Ghoshal, 1989). In 1956 the company invested $1 million to expand the factory to meet the increasing demand for its products locally and abroad.

In 1957, Unilever was among the first private companies to support the government's Central Apprenticeship Board Scheme, a program planned by the International Labour Organization (ILO) to train more skilled technicians. In 1958 the company created the Bumiputra Pilot Scheme and offered to train 1,000 Malay youths over a period of two years at its own expense, anticipating the participation of other large companies. Unilever has offered many training programs that have benefited the country. Many employees had the opportunity to learn leadership and management skills through the sponsored Outward Bound School training. Also, under the Lever Executive Training Program, hundreds of local executives were sent for skill upgrading courses overseas. Furthermore, in support of the government's policies aimed at forging a Malayan identity after independence, Unilever undertook an initiative to "Malayanize" the company by gradually promoting local employees to executive positions previously held by Europeans.

In 1959, Unilever sponsored an art exhibition, "The Malayan Way of Life," aimed at encouraging new talent to contribute to Malayan identity. Tun Razak, then Deputy Prime Minister, was quoted as saying, "You have demonstrated that business need not just be a question of manufacturing or selling, but can also contribute to the life of the Malayan community and to cultural needs of our growing nation." In addition, Unilever was one of the first companies to stamp "Made in Malaya" on its products. Attracted by this practice, the Minister of Labor suggested that all locally made goods should carry this stamp to encourage people to buy them. This led to the setting up of a Made-in-Malaysia Trade Fair in 1964.

In 1979, in compliance with the Bumiputra ownership target of the New Economic Policy, which sought to bring about an equal distribution of wealth among ethnic groups, the company embarked on an equity restructuring exercise. This led to the issue of 30 percent of its capital to two Bumiputra institutions in 1981, Permodolan Nasional (23 percent) and Lembaga Tabung Haji (7 percent), each with a director on the board of Unilever Malaysia.

Attracted by the stable government, the expanding population and rising purchasing power, the company continued to expand its investment, use local raw materials whenever possible, and broaden its product range. By 1967, Unilever's investment in Malaysia had totaled $18 million and the company had grown from a two-plant factory manufacturing soaps and edible fat and oil products to a multi-product business entity. In 1982 the company built an oleochemical plant in a new industrial estate in Bukit Raja. In 1987 a new detergent powder plant with manufacturing facilities for liquids and detergent bars was added to the Bukit Raja operations. Following this, a new ice cream factory worth RM 25 million and equipped with state-of-the-art facilities was opened in 1993.

In 1994 a significant turning point for the company came when it changed its corporate name from Lever Brothers to Unilever (Malaysia) Holdings Sdn Bhd. By adopting the global name the company reiterated its status as a multinational multilocal business entity. This status reflects the Malaysian thrust toward globalization while maintaining a unique local identity.

Unilever Malaysia was considered by the then chairman of the mother company as "a jewel in the Unilever crown, for product innovation and adaptation, and customer service excellence." Unilever Malaysia ranks as one of the prized operations in Asia. It has earned a market leader position in Malaysia, has developed a deep understanding of local culture and has maintained a good reputation over the years. Over its fifty years in Malaysia, Unilever "has demonstrated a highly workable philosophy of combining local integration in many respects with a corporate temperament and identity that has propelled the company into the industry" (Tabaksblat, 1997). Unilever's long-standing operations in Malaysia, spanning almost six decades, are considered by the corporate executive of the company to be an affirmation of its status as a good producer, marketer, employer, partner and "citizen" of Malaysia, participating to its development. The motto of the company is "We value our past. We believe in our future. We excel by being the best."

However, in 2001 Unilever Malaysia announced a restructuring of its activities in order to focus on its core strengths and to save on investments in factories, labor and other associated costs. Long known for manufacturing a wide variety of consumer goods such as detergents, cleaning liquids, shampoos and the like, the company decided to outsource its products from both local manufacturers and Unilever sister companies. It decided to concentrate on its strengths, such as brand management, consumer understanding, customer development and marketing to capture a larger slice of the fast-moving consumer goods market.

Meanwhile, 550 employees of the closed-down Bukit Raja factory had to look for another job. For the head manager of the company, the result of this restructuring exercise would be an improvement in business prospects and being able to offer Malaysian consumers innovative and high-quality goods at competitive prices, as well as being more responsive to changes in demands (Yap, 2001).

Thus, Unilever asserts its involvement toward its partners and the pursuit of long-term value creation for its shareholders. Given the nature itself of the products and services it offers to its customers, seeking to "feed" and to "clean," Unilever seeks to be socially involved. It supports UN Global Compact,[4] produces a separate social and environmental report, and states:

As a responsible business, we seek to understand and manage our social, environmental and economic impacts, working in partnership with our suppliers and customers, with governments and NGOs, and increasingly with the consumers who are at the heart of everything we do.

(Unilever, 2006)

In Malaysia, more specifically, the corporate executives have to adapt to, and try to meet, the local requirements, such as ensuring that all the products offered are halal (even toothpastes and shampoos). Also, in its efforts to be a responsible corporate citizen, in 2000 Unilever Malaysia launched an annual community project aimed at enabling education, the Unilever EduCare Program, working in cooperation with the Ministry of Education. The theme for the project is meant to change from year to year depending on the current needs of the students. The project started with the theme "Wheeling to Education," and 1,000 students from some rural areas benefited from a donation of 1,000 bicycles to enable them to continue their studies. Overall, Unilever's commitment to Malaysian society ranges from offering scholarships, sponsorships and contributions to old people's homes and orphanages to supporting charities and foundations.

In terms of quality, products marketed by Unilever Malaysia adhere to international quality standards set by Unilever worldwide. The MNE strongly believes that without quality, its growth is not assured. In 1990 it introduced the Supplier Improvement Program (SIP) as part of its quality improvement initiative. Unilever Malaysia has also been certified ISO 9000 (quality products), ISO 18,000 (Occupational Health and safety management systems) and ISO 14,000 (environment).

In the early 1990s, when environmental consciousness was on the rise, Unilever Malaysia became one of the first Malaysian enterprises to take serious steps to minimize the impact of its business on the environment. Its then technical director recognized that "it is no longer just a matter of filling the stomachs of the people to make them happy. They want a better quality of life, and a better and healthier environment." Many local managers interviewed in Unilever Malaysia expressed their concern, in a long-term perspective, for environmental and social responsibility issues. In their opinion there is a direct link and a strong causality between the sustainable development of the company and the sustainable development of society and the surrounding environment. Also, in order for their companies to grow and prosper, business leaders need to help the local community to grow and prosper. Thus, corporate executives are fully aware that by helping others they actually help their company to survive and grow.

Case 2: Nestlé Malaysia

If Unilever Malaysia has chosen the slogan "We value our past, we believe in our future," Nestlé Malaysia is using the motto "Together we win. Meeting targets matters" – seeking to grow while helping and benefiting from national growth.

Nestlé was established in Switzerland in 1867 by Henri Nestlé, a chemist who developed and started manufacturing a milk food product for babies whose mothers were unable to breastfeed. The founder used his name, Nestlé, which in German means "little nest," as his company logo – a nest with a mother bird feeding her young. The company grew and continued to expand through some major mergers and acquisitions. Nestlé became the largest food company in the world, marketing over 8,500 brands and 30,000 products. It operates nearly 500 factories across five continents and employs over 200,000 employees worldwide.

Nestlé first set foot in Malaysia in 1912, as the Anglo-Swiss Condensed Milk Company, with the setting up of a distribution office in Penang. Its growth and expansion made a move to Kuala Lumpur necessary in 1939. In 1962, Nestlé set up its first plant, in Petaling Jaya, to manufacture sweetened condensed milk. Since then the company has expanded to operate seven factories and six sales offices in Malaysia. Nestlé was publicly listed on the Kuala Lumpur Stock Exchange in 1989. It is 60 percent owned by the Swiss parent company, while 21 percent is held by the Bumiputras and 19 percent by public investors. In his 2004 annual statement the chairman of Nestlé Malaysia pointed out that

> [o]perating in multicultural and multiracial Malaysia offers Nestlé an inval-uable source of understanding, learning and innovation. We respect the rich and diverse heritage, the unity and harmony, which is uniquely Malaysian. As we continue to nourish the nation, we will meet the varying needs of our consumers.[5]

The following year, in 2005, the chairman also outlined his vision of continued smart partnerships:

> With higher disposable incomes and changing demographics setting the tone for the food sector in Malaysia, Nestlé is well poised to take advantage of these new opportunities as they occur. ... Beyond just being a provider of quality food and beverages, we have grown with the nation and its people for more than 93 years, touching lives by being actively involved in the social, economic and environmental development of the nation. We will continue to nourish Malaysia and work together towards achieving its long-term vision.[6]

Given the need for integration and the nature of its activities, based on food and beverages, where tastes, flavors and needs vary within and between coun-tries, Nestlé has to adopt "[g]lobal thinking and strategies but local action and commitment" (Lopez, 2001b). It has to combine "global presence" with "local flavor." Thus, Nestlé illustrates the necessity for many MNCs to think globally and to adapt locally following a transnational strategy as described by Bartlett and Ghoshal (1986, 1998).

In this perspective, in 2000 Nestlé launched a program called GLOBE (Global Business Excellence). This program is meant to "unlock Nestlé's potential" and to make it easier to improve its performance and operational efficiency. Nestlé's CEO stated:

[W]e want to harmonize and simplify our business process architecture across the Group. The intention is to enable Nestlé to realize the advantages of being a global leader, while minimizing the drawbacks of size. Our purpose is to optimize our industrial infrastructure whilst maintaining decentralization in all areas where proximity to consumers and clients is a key element of success.

(see Brabeck-Letmathe, 2001)

In sum, the main objectives of this program are to standardize business processes to leverage the size of Nestlé as a competitive strength, and to unite and align Nestlé on the inside to be globally competitive on the outside and benefit from the "e" world, with a focus on customer channels and consumers. Nestlé Malaysia has been chosen as a pilot market for the Asian zone for the implementation of the GLOBE initiative (Berita Nestlé, 2001). Regarding this decision, the company's managing director stated that "the group has identified Malaysia as a key base … which reflects Nestlé Malaysia's competitiveness and strengths" (The Star, 2001).

While seeking integration and standardization worldwide, Nestlé also has to respond to cultural and religious needs and to respect local laws and regulations. In Malaysia, Nestlé has had to comply with the halal requirements of local Muslim consumers and with the halal certification imposed by the government.[7] Nestlé states that it conforms to halal requirements for three reasons:

- *Corporate responsibility to Muslim consumers* – allowing it to promote its image as "a responsible corporate citizen committed to fulfilling its obligation to the country and its consumers."
- *Good business sense* – seeking a competitive advantage in order to increase its market share. Nestlé manufactures and markets more than 300 halal products in Malaysia and boasts of being "one of the first manufacturers whose products have been certified halal."
- *Export – expanding the Muslim market worldwide.* Given the "fantastic opportunities" for halal products in West Asia, Nestlé was keen to develop this market further (Lopez, 2001a). It did indeed succeed in making Malaysia a "center of halal excellence" for Nestlé. Its managing director reiterated this point in the 2005 Annual Report: "[I]n view of the importance of the 'halal' status in the export of food products, Nestlé welcomes the Government's efforts to develop Malaysia into a 'halal' hub."

This case study demonstrates how Nestlé learned to reap benefits from what could be seen as local and social constraints. By adapting its products to the consumers' needs and by conforming with the government regulations, it became a leading and profitable enterprise in Malaysia.[8] In 2004, Nestlé's annual report recorded a turnover of RM 2.9 billion, a profit before tax of RM 297.2 million and a net profit after tax of RM 220.4 million. In 2008 the net profit exceeded RM 320 million and the company spent RM 210 million on increasing domestic capacity and developing further products for export. The profitability of Nestlé is correlated with the economic growth of the country. This equation led Nestlé's directors to be fully aware of the importance of promoting sustainable development for their own company's sustainable and profitable growth, as they mentioned many times in the interviews.

Moreover, as part of its social involvement, in 2002 Nestlé launched a campaign patterned after the World Health Organization's "Global Healthy Schools initiative" to address the eating habits of the children in primary schools. The campaign was carried out in collaboration with the Ministry of Education. In 2006, Nestlé Malaysia embarked on an initiative to develop its production executives into front-line managers through an Executive Diploma in Manufacturing Management (EDMM). This initiative is a customized qualification between Nestlé and the Open University Malaysia. It is aimed at "developing specific Nestlé workplace competencies," According to Sullivan O'Carroll, Nestlé Malaysia's managing director, this collaboration with a local university supports "the Government's vision for an enhanced, knowledgeable and educated workforce." He also admitted that

> there is a need to invest in human capital development so as to have a workforce which continually upgrades its competencies to meet the challenges of a global market, yet is specialized enough to meet the specific needs of the company. ... We believe it is essential to create opportunities for Nestlé personnel to develop themselves.
>
> (*The Star*, 2006)

Overall, the Nestlé Malaysia case study illustrates another example of the "smart partnership" policy adopted in Malaysia, which translates into a concrete collaboration between the public and the private sectors, promoting mutual interests and a win–win perspective. This strategy is a good catalyst for sustainable development at the national and organizational levels.

Case 3: Aluminium Company of Malaysia (Alcom)

Alcom is a subsidiary of the Canadian group Alcan, a leader in the aluminum industry. Established in 1902, the Alcan group is one of the largest and most international aluminum companies in the world. It has operations and sales offices in over thirty countries. Alcan was the pioneer of the aluminum industry in Malaysia. It was established in 1960. "Alcom, as the pioneer aluminium company in Malaysia, has been an important contributor to the industrial development of the country throughout the past four decades" (Glenn Lucas, 2000, who had been managing director of Alcom since 1960).

From small Alcan Malay beginnings, Alcom has grown into a modern and sophisticated semifabricating company with an annual turnover exceeding RM 300 million and total investments of RM 247 million. At Alcom, commitment to Malaysia's industrial development was evident from the very start, as evidenced by a statement from the Ministry of International Trade and Industry (2000):

Certainly the company would have grown in tandem with the growth of Malaysia itself, since its incorporation almost 3 years after the country achieved Independence. Companies such as Alcom would have been part and parcel of the industrial development of Malaysia, and would have contributed to, as well as benefited from the industrialization process.

Alcom is considered to be the largest manufacturer of aluminum products in Malaysia. These products are used in building and construction, electrical and electronics, transports, packaging and other consumer durables. Alcom has also acquired a dominant position in the ASEAN market. Almost half of the company's annual production is exported to markets such as Japan, China, Hong Kong, South Korea, Taiwan, the Middle East, Europe and Southeast Asia.

Since its establishment as AlcanMalay, the company has had the strong backing of the Malaysian government, which provided tax incentives under the Pioneer Industries Ordinance.[9] Malaysian Industrial Development Finance also provided a long-term loan to the venture. The Alcan Group supplied the majority of the capital as well as engineering and technology. With a growing economy, demand for aluminum products increased progressively. The local management had to expand capacity to keep pace and achieve profitability.

In 1969, AlcanMalay was listed on the Kuala Lumpur Stock Exchange following an issue of 40 percent of its shares to the Malaysian public. The participation came mainly from customers and employees, and the name of the company was changed to Alcan Malaysia Berhad. In compliance with the government's New Economic Policy, Alcom restructured its equity shareholding in 1975, resulting in Alcan's stake falling from 55.2 percent to 34.5 percent. Meanwhile, Malaysian ownership increased to 53 percent, with organizations such as Lembaga Tabung Haji. To reflect the majority Malaysian ownership, the company's name was changed to Aluminium Company of Malaysia (Alcom) in 1976.

In 1982 a new plant was built in Bukit Raja at a cost of RM 120 million, transforming Alcom into the largest and most modern aluminum operation in Southeast Asia and expressing the trust by the shareholders in the long-term future of the company and the Malaysian economy. However, because of a threatening recession and the fluctuation of the prices of raw materials, the company experienced some financial difficulties and operating losses during the mid-1980s. In contrast, 1989 marked a return to profitability and the announcement of a program designed to improve product quality and range. In the same year, exports overtook domestic shipments, in line with the Malaysian policy of promotion of export-oriented industries. Also, the turnaround of the company coincided with the beginning of a prolonged period of growth in Malaysia's economy.

In fact, Alcom benefited from Malaysia's economic growth and more especially from the implementation of many national-class and prestigious construction projects. These included the Petronas Twin Towers, KL International Airport and Telekom Tower, for which Alcom won supply contracts. During this period, Alcom made strategic decisions to invest an additional RM 100 million to increase its production capacity. In search of better returns, Alcom also adopted a strategy of diversifying into downstream activities and increasing value added products. The company was certified ISO 9002 in 1994 and 14,001 in 1995, and has developed a solutions-oriented and customer partnering approach that has helped it to grow.

In 1997, Alcom was affected by the financial crisis that struck Malaysia and its neighbors, yet it was able to withstand the difficulties. In 1998, under the initiative of Alcan, Alcom implemented the Full Business Potential (FBP) program, which consists of a performance improvement process aimed at identifying and achieving optimal returns from existing assets. Through this program the company realized significant cost savings and productivity improvements. The economic recovery in Malaysia and in the East Asian region generally, combined with the evolution of the ASEAN Free Trade Area (AFTA), have stimulated greater demand for aluminum products and have helped the company to develop further. In this case the Malaysian Incorporated Strategy, which seeks to strengthen public–private sector networking, proved effective. Such a "smart" partnership "has enabled the country, and the private sector, to face and overcome mutually the challenges and negative impact of the financial and economic crisis," according to a Malaysian official. In 2003, Alcan increased its ownership position in Alcom from 36 percent to 60 percent (Alcan, 2006):

> Alcan is pleased to further reinforce our strategic relationship with Alcom and demonstrate our commitment to meeting the increasing demands for value-creating and quality light gauge aluminum products in Southeast Asia. This is another example of Alcan's focus on high-value opportunities that maximize value for all Company stakeholders as well as strengthen our competitive position in growth markets such as Asia.

Alcom and its Canadian parent proclaim themselves to be particularly committed to social responsibility and sustainable development. Alcan's board of directors ensures that the company is managed in the interest of its shareholders as a whole, while taking into account the interests of other stakeholders. According to the MNE's CEO (Alcan, 2004):

> There is no doubt in my mind that sustainability makes good business sense. It creates value today and preserves it for tomorrow. It drives us to become a better employer, a better investment, a better neighbour, and a better company with superior value-added products."

In addition to being a member of the World Business Council for Sustainable Development (WBCSD),[10] Alcan also became a participant in the UN Global Compact in 2004. Indeed, the MNE

> has been successful at constructing an image of itself as a socially and environmentally concerned company. It has undertaken a major overhaul of its public image by committing to lowering its emissions beyond Kyoto levels, donating

large sums of money to environmental organizations, lobbying the US Government for more recycling programs, publishing sustainable reports.

(Girard, 2005)

Alcan won a United Nations Environmental Programme (UNEP) Award for Excellence in sustainable development. The award was the result of an original program promoting the benefits of recycling and fostering entrepreneurial spirit among schoolchildren around the world. Alcan's International Micro-Business Network (IMBN) was responsible for the program, which is one of the company's sustainability initiatives. As part of the Micro-Business project worldwide, Alcom introduced a recycled paper project in Malaysia in May 1999 to involve schoolchildren in environmental issues and entrepreneurship. The project was implemented with the support of educational, technical and physical expertise from Alcom until the school was able to run the project on its own. Projects include the recycling of paper and shopping bags, making greeting cards using handmade paper, and the collection of aluminum cans. According to Alcom's director,

> Our aim is to work with the community to promote sustainable development in terms of helping children to make choices in harmony with the environment while at the same time develop their entrepreneurial spirit and creativity. The whole idea of recycling and making paper products is to get the children to understand that paper can be reused. That will help reduce the number of trees cut down annually, and at the same time, the school earns some money. Many organizations in the country are working towards environmental awareness and we see our role as complementing their efforts.

Overall, this case study illustrates another example of smart partnerships between the public and private sectors on the one hand, and the interaction between the global and local on the other hand.

In summary, the three case studies show different levels of adaptation within the same context or institutional profile. Moreover, even though they are operating in the same industry, Unilever and Nestlé nevertheless exhibit different levels of adaptation. Unilever has been highly responsive and socially embedded, adopting a proactive strategy from the beginning and showing more social responsibility. By contrast, Nestlé moved from a global to a transnational configuration, becoming more locally responsive and socially embedded by following a reactive strategy. Alcom seems to be socially responsible more by organizational choice than by institutional obligation, given the nature of the industry in which it is operating, which does not require much adaptation. It is following an interactive strategy and a pragmatic approach to social responsibility.

Finally, through the three case studies presented we can notice that MNEs can adopt a "glocal" strategy (being globally efficient and locally responsive) by following one of three approaches to corporate social responsibility: being proactive, reactive or interactive.

Practical implications

Recent events around the world have made it clear that it is no longer enough simply to "do things right," as the emphasis has shifted to how to "do the right thing." Most enterprises have to think in sustainable development terms. For the president of Alcan Inc., "Sustainability is ... a permanent feature of the contemporary business landscape. A feature that challenges us to innovate by finding new and better ways of dealing with our increasingly complex and interconnected world" (Alcan, 2004).

MNE managers are, therefore, well aware of the importance of taking all the economic and social partners involved in their operations into account, and developing the image of a responsible corporation. Their firm's legitimacy and reputation depend on it. Nestlé learned that lesson the hard way, as one of its executives admits. These days, he says, image is increasingly measured by the company's level of social responsibility.

That image is crucial for attracting investors, recruiting skilled employees, selling products to consumers, offering services to clients and continuing to qualify for the operating permits issued by national and local authorities in host countries. All things considered, although the global impact holds sway in strategy development at MNEs, strong pressure at the local level can also compel a firm's attention in that process. Customer demands, the claims and regulatory requirements of local communities, and a national government watching over its country's development can all exert enormous pressures. Those pressures or local demands, far from constituting a brake on the firm's activities, can be seen as opportunities. By conforming to specific local needs and adapting its products to customer demands, Nestlé could and did make a profit, reconciling its social and its economic responsibilities.

As evidenced elsewhere in this chapter, directors, managers and key decision makers in MNEs are expected to be constantly juggling two sets of reasoning: one economic, which encourages standardization and globalization, fostering the company's efficiency; and the other social, requiring that the firm pay attention to local realities. Thus, "think globally, act locally" becomes more than just a motto characterizing transnational companies. Managers are expected to make it their leitmotiv, continually adjusting operations to balance the global with the local, and the uniform with the specific (Prahalad and Doz, 1987; Prahalad and Hamel, 1990).

In summary, by taking into consideration both economic and social needs of the local contexts within which they are operating, MNEs increase the chances of improving the management processes of their subsidiaries and their performance. Also, MNEs in emergent markets are required to be partners in the national development process and, besides generating added value for their business, to add value to the host country by being more socially responsible.

Conclusion

This chapter highlights the importance of the sociocultural environment, which is often blurred in the literature on strategic management by an emphasis on the task environment. It suggests how management processes and the relation with governments of the host countries can be improved when managers become aware of the local realities and cultural specifics. Managers need to be better equipped to make enlightened decisions, developing strategies that respect local realities as well as global pressures, maintaining a balance between the economic and the social. Using examples of companies operating in the context of Malaysia, I focused on three cases of subsidiaries of MNEs having to reconcile the global with the local. Finally, I advance the position, based on opinions expressed by executives in the companies I studied, that management is still a matter of "good sense." One might add here that management is also a matter of having a "sense of the good," so that in addition to "doing things well," managers will be in a position to "do the right thing" in a socially responsible way.

Notes

1 Smart News, "Langkawi Smart partnership International Dialogue," 29–31 July 2004, www.psfuganda.org/smart.php.
2 Dr. Mahathir Mohamad is the fourth prime minister of Malaysia. He was elected in 1981 and stepped down as prime minister in 2003. Many attribute the country's success to his dynamic leadership.
3 *Fifty Great Years in Malaysia*, Unilever, 1997.
4 The global compact is an agreement, based on ten principles relating to human rights, environmental protection, labor rights and corruption, designed to promote responsible corporate citizenship: www.unglobalcompact.org.
5 Nestlé Malaysia Annual Report 2004.
6 Nestlé Malaysia Annual Report 2005.
7 ASEAN Free Trade Area, promotes regional tariff reduction. It was originally initiated in 1992 by six ASEAN members (Brunei, Indonesia, Malaysia, the Philippines, Singapore and Thailand). Vietnam joined in 1995, Laos and Myanmar in 1997, and Cambodia in 1999.
8 Through Milo, Nestlé holds a 90 percent share of the chocolate drink market. In terms of revenue contribution, Milo's domestic sales accounted for 20 percent of the RM 2.2 billion turnover posted for the financial year 2000. Exports to Thailand, the Philippines, Indonesia, Singapore, West Asia and the United States contributed another 8.7 percent.
9 Halal certification, produced by the Islamic Affairs Division of the Prime Minister's Department, is a recognition letter designed for administration purposes to indicate the state of "halal" (acceptable), applied to food products, drinks and consumer items for Muslims. It is based on the Islamic law practiced in the country.
10 Nestlé has been the target of strong international criticism and has fueled many watchdog organizations' critics and debates. According to Co-op America, Nestlé's reputation is not good because of how it carries out its operations, ranging from the marketing of infant formula to the production of its chocolate and bottled water. For example, Baby Milk Action, a UK-based non-profit group, is opposing Nestlé in response to its baby-formula marketing campaigns. It is still calling for the continued boycott of all Nestlé products and brands owing to the company's refusal to comply with the World Health Assembly's baby-food marketing guidelines.

References

Alcan (2004) "Sustainability: A critical component of successful business models in the 21st century," notes from an address by Travis Engen, president and chief executive officer, Alcan Inc., at Globe 2004, Vancouver, 31 March. Online, available at: www.wbcsd.org/plugins/DocSearch/details.asp?DocTypeId=-1&ObjectId=NjAzOQ&URLBack=result.asp%3FDocTypeId%3D-1%26SortOrder%3D%26CurPage%3D339.

—— (2006) "Alcan increases ownership stake in Aluminium Company of Malaysia." Online, available at: www.alcan.com/web/publishing.nsf 10 August 2003 (accessed May 2006).

Bartlett, C. A. and Ghoshal, S. (1986) "Tap your subsidiaries for global reach," *Harvard Business Review*, 64 (4): 87–94.

—— (1989) *Managing across Borders: The Transnational Solution*, Boston: Harvard Business School Press.

—— (1998) *Managing across Borders: The Transnational Solution*, 2nd edn., Boston: Harvard Business School Press.

Berita Nestlé (2001) "Nestlé Malaysia leads programme Globe in Zone AOA," *Berita Nestlé*, 68 (1).

Bird, F. (2001) "Good governance: A philosophical discussion of the responsibilities and practices of organizational governors," *Canadian Journal of Administrative Sciences*, 18 (4): 298–312.

Brabeck-Lemathe, P. (CEO Nestlé SA) (2001) Annual Report.

Carroll, A. B. (1999) "Corporate social responsibility: Evolution of a definitional construct," *Business and Society*, 38 (3): 268–295.

Cheng, T.-J., Haggard, S. and Kang, D. (1998) "Institutions and growth in Korea and Taiwan: The bureaucracy," *Development Studies*, 34 (6): 87–111.

Coates, N. (1987) "The 'Confucian ethic' and the spirit of Japanese capitalism," *Leadership and Organization Development Journal*, 8 (3): 17–22.

DiMaggio, P. J. and Powell, W. (1983) "The iron cage revisited: Institutional isomorphism and collective rationality in organizational fields," *American Sociological Review*, 48: 147–160.

Dunning, J. H. (1998) "Location and the multinational enterprise: A neglected factor?" *Journal of International Business Studies*, 29 (1): 45–65.

—— (2003) "Some antecedents of internationalization theory," *Journal of International Business Studies*, 34: 108–115.

Economist, The (2003) "Changing of the guard: A survey of Malaysia," *The Economist*, 5 April.

Eisenhardt, K. (1989) "Building theories from case study research," *Academy of Management Review*, 14 (4): 532–550.

Freeman, E. R. (1984) *Strategic Management: A Stakeholder Approach*, Boston: Pitman.

Friedman, M. (1962) *Capitalism and Freedom*, Chicago: University of Chicago Press.

Ghoshal, S. and Bartlett, C. A. (1990) "The multinational corporation as an interorganizational network," *Academy of Management Review*, 15 (4): 603–625.

Girard, R. (2005) "Can Alcan claim to be the best? It's [*sic*] corporate and social responsibility in question," *Polaris Institute Researcher*, July. Online, available at: www.polarisinstitute.org/files/Alcan.pdf.

Jomo, K. S. (2001) *Malaysian Eclipse: Economic Crisis and Recovery*, London: Zed Books.

Kim, W. and Hwang, P. (1992) "Global strategy and multinationals' entry mode choice," *Journal of International Business Studies*, 23 (1): 29–53.

Liu, O. (2001) "Malaysia: From crisis to recovery," Occasional Paper 207, International Monetary Fund, Washington, DC.

Lopez, J. (2001a) "Nestlé to invest RM 150 million to beef up operations," *The Star*, 1 May.

—— (2001b) "Transparency and accountability within business sector: the way we do our business," paper presented by the managing director, Nestlé Malaysia, at a conference entitled "Integrity in Business: The Way Forward," Corporate Governance Malaysia.

Mahathir, M. (2000) *Selected Speeches*, vol. 2: *Globalisation, Smart Partnership and Government*, Petaling Jaya, Malaysia: Pelanduk Publications.

Meyer, J. W. and Scott, W. R. (1992) *Organizational Environments: Ritual and Rationality*, updated edition, Beverly Hills, CA: Sage.

Meyer, M. W. and Zucker, L. G. (1989) *Permanently Failing Organizations*, Newbury Park, CA: Sage.

Ministry of International Trade and Industry (2000) Aluminium Company of Malaysia: 40th Anniversary Celebrations, Tuesday, 18 July. Online, available at: www.miti.gov.my.

Naguib, R. (2004) "Interface Organisation – environnement, cas des entreprises multinationales opérant dans un pays en développement: contexte de la Malaisie," PhD thesis, HEC Montréal.

OCDE (2001) *Responsabilité des entreprises: Initiatives privées et objectifs publics*, Paris: Organisation de Coopération et de Développement Économique.

Prahalad, C. K. and Doz, Y. L. (1987) *The Multinational Mission: Balancing Local Demands and Global Vision*, New York: Free Press.

Prahalad, C. K. and Hamel, G. (1990) "The core competence of the corporation," *Harvard Business Review*, 68 (3): 79–91.

Rudner, M. (1994) "Malaysian development in retrospect and prospect," in M. Rudner (ed.) *Malaysian Development: A Retrospective*, Ottawa: Carleton University Press.

Scott, W. R. (2001) *Institutions and Organizations*, Thousand Oaks, CA: Sage.

Star, The (2001) "Unilever to stop producing goods in revamp exercise," 5 May: 5c.

—— (2006) "Customized qualification," *The Star*, 15 June. Online, available at: http://thestar.com.my/education/story.asp?file=/2006/7/16/education/14815501

—— (2008) "Malaysia's GDP to grow 5.8% this year, says UN body," *The Star*, 28 March. Online, available at: http://biz.thestar.com.my/news (accessed 16 July 2009).

Stiglitz, J. (2002) "Globalism's discontents," *The American Prospect*, 13 (1) (1–14 January): A16–A22.

Tabaksblat, M. (1997) "Unilever: Fifty years in Malaysia" (chairman of Unilever NV).

Unilever (2006) www.unilever.com/ourvalues/environmentandsociety (May).

United Nations (2006a) *United Nations Millennium Development Goals Report*, New York: United Nations.

—— (2006b) *Malaysia: International Trade, Growth, Poverty Reduction and Human Development*, Kuala Lumpur: United Nations Development Programme.

World Bank (2000) "Malaysia: Social and structural review update," East Asia Recovery and Beyond.

Yap, L. (2001) "Unilever to stop producing goods in revamp exercise," *The Star*, 5 May.

Yin, R. (1994) *Case Study Research: Design and Methods*, 2nd edn. Beverly Hills, CA: Sage.

10 Environment, strategy and leadership patterns as determinants of firm performance

The case of a developing country

Taïeb Hafsi and Bernard Gauthier

Introduction

The three dimensions of environment, strategy and leadership are the basis of the dominant strategic management framework (Schendel and Hofer, 1978). Based on Andrews's (1987) formalization of the concept of corporate strategy, the idea of strategic management emphasizes the process by which the interaction and fit between environment, the organization's resources and choices, and the nature of leadership, in particular top management's values, lead to higher performance. These dimensions may be seen as antecedents of performance. In the case of developing countries, can we expect the same relation? In their study of management theory and practice in developing countries, Kiggundu *et al.* (1983) suggested that those theories in which the organization can behave as a closed system should apply to developing countries. Where the organization cannot behave as a closed system, they found that there were significant differences from what happens in developed countries. As neither strategy nor leadership nor environment can strictly be considered internal to the firm, we should expect differences.

In developed countries, much research has been devoted to the bilateral relationships between performance and each of the factors strategy, leadership and environment. Despite thorny methodological issues, related to our ability to build appropriate constructs and measure them properly (Prescott and Venkatraman, 1990), the contingency theory, in particular, which posits congruence between environment and structure as a determinant of performance, has been tested in a variety of situations and circumstances. The congruence of strategy, structure and environment has also received wide support in numerous circonstances (Rumelt, 1991; Venkatraman and Prescott, 1990; Venkatraman and Grant, 1986; among many). Finally, Porter's early work (1980) has popularized a number of strategies that are supposed to improve performance, while Miller (1996) and Hrebeniak and Joyce (1985) have suggested the conditions of environmental determinism and of strategic choice in which these strategies provide the best performance. Linking leadership to performance has been more difficult to operationalize. Hambrick and Mason's work (1984) has provided an important lead with the idea of relating demographic characteristics to performance, and has been joined by numerous followers (Geletkanycz and Hambrick, 1997; Finkelstein and Hambrick, 1995; Westphal and Zajac, 1995; Daily and Dalton, 1992; Reuber *et al.*, 1992). Other significant work has found a fit between strategic choices and leadership profiles (Golden and Zajac, 2001; Michel and Hambrick, 1992; Zajac and Shortell, 1989).

Although the importance of each of these factors on firm performance is widely recognized, rarely have all of environment, strategy and leadership characteristics been related, in a large sample test, to performance, though the possibility has been discussed in case research (Andrews, 1987; Schendel and Hofer, 1978). Even more rarely has such research been performed in a developing country setting (Hafsi and Farashahi, 2005; Hoskisson *et al.*, 2000; Sim and Teoh, 1997; Kiggundu *et al.*, 1983). It is to fill such a gap that this research has been conducted and its results proposed here.

In this chapter we use a unique set of microeconomic data on a relatively large sample of Cameroonian firms, gathered during the 1992–1995 period,[1] to describe the nature of these firms' institutional and competitive environment, their strategic responses and the characteristics of their top managers. Then we study the relationships that exist between the performance of these firms and three sets of variables describing environment, strategy and leadership characteristics. We show that there are clear firm behaviors that can be described by configurations of these variables, and such configurations explain their performance.

In the first section of the chapter a theoretical review is proposed to highlight the strategic management conceptual framework to which we intend to contribute, and the specific contributions of our research. Then, in the second section, the nature of the context within which Cameroonian firms evolve, the generic strategies that they have developed to respond to such a context, and the demographic profiles of the managers who were responsible for their conduct are described. Finally, in the third section these dimensions of context, strategy and managerial characteristics are used to explain Cameroonian firms' performance.

Theoretical framework

In this section the relationships among environment, strategy and leadership, and the links of these factors to performance, are investigated by reviewing the strategic management literature. We first review what has been reported in the literature about the importance of environment, resources and leadership as predictors of performance, and attempt throughout to assess the meaning of these findings for firms in developing countries, in particular in Cameroon. We conclude that although environmental, strategic and leadership factors may be seen as antecedents of firms' performance in developing countries, institutional instability in these countries may reduce the influence of traditional industry factors and make entrepreneurial creation and sociopolitical skills more significant in generating competitive advantage and economic performance.

Environment

The influence of environment on a firm's strategic behavior and structural arrangements is well documented in the strategic management literature (Venkatraman and Prescott, 1990; Butler and Carney, 1986; Miller, 1982; Chandler, 1962). The fit between environment, strategy and structure has often been shown to be a predictor of performance (Rumelt, 1991; Khota and Orne, 1989; Gomez-Mejia and Balkin, 1987). Miller (1981) and Mintzberg (1978) have suggested that these dimensions come in configurations that are themselves related to performance. The evidence confirming both contingency theory and configurational theory propositions is now overwhelming, even if there are still many methodological issues that cast a shadow on the precision of the findings (Miller, 1996; Shaker and Covin, 1993; Venkatraman and Prescott, 1990). However, there has been relatively little research done on the topic in relation to firms in developing countries (Hafsi and Farashahi, 2005). For example, Uskiden and Pasadeos (1995) have compared *Administrative Science Quarterly* and *Organization Science* from 1990 to 1992, and found mostly Western-centric research. Of the fifty-three articles published by ASQ, forty-eight were from and about the United States and the other five about Europe. Yet, very early, Negandhi (1971) and others (see Kiggundu *et al.*, 1983 for a synthesis) have shown that developing countries' general environment is so overwhelming that one may be faced with patterns that are at odds with Western-based theories.

Most of the environmental influences are generally seen as task related and competition borne (Porter, 1980). Competition dynamics are often presented as based on factor-market imperfections, and their differentiated exploitation by individual firms (Barney, 1990). It is, for example, widely accepted that *high barriers to entry, a small number of competitors, a low elasticity of demand, a low cross-elasticity with substitutes, low relative power of suppliers and buyers and product differentiation all contribute to differences in firm performance.* Factor-market imperfections are also generated by institutional factors (Oliver, 1997). Regulations, norms and cognitive-cultural factors all contribute to bending traditional economic rationality into normative rationality (DiMaggio and Powell, 1983). This is even more the case in developing countries. The general environment is more fluid, and, in particular, sociopolitical factors dominate traditional task environment factors (Scott, 2001; Martinez-Vasquez and McNab, 2000; Peng and Heath, 1996).

The situation in developing countries such as Cameroon is also unusual (Hadjimanolis and Dickson, 2000; Kiggundu *et al.*, 1983). In particular, industry dynamics are often highly politicized and competition may be severely constrained (Brautigam, 1997). In addition, the public sector may be dominant and private-sector initiative may not be easy to predict. Whether there are barriers to entry or to exit is the object of specific bargaining among key actors. The very nature of what may constitute differentiation is subtle, and hidden to the unfamiliar observer. For example, differentiation may be related to access to public markets, or public favors, for political reasons. In general the situation is highly fluid and unstructured, so that there is a need for a more "developmental" perspective (Allen, 1988).

Strategy

These environmental influences are often seen as deterministic (Hrebeniak and Joyce, 1986). Yet strategic choice is possible and has a bearing on a firm's performance (Oliver, 1997; Porter, 1994). A resource perspective (Wernerfelt, 1984) suggests that resource selection and deployment may result in sustainable firm performance variations where factor-market imperfections in the form of barriers to resource acquisition, imitation or substitution are generated (Shoemaker and Amit, 1994; Barney, 1986; Penrose, 1959). *In developing countries these barriers are also sociopolitical, with government playing a central role, and government access being a key meta-resource.*

The Chamberlin–Penrose (CP) theory (Barney, 1986; Penrose, 1959; Chamberlin, 1933; Robinson, 1933) emphasizes the unique assets and resources of the firm and their impact on the firm's strategy and returns. This perspective is interesting, particularly because it has been revived recently with the popularity of the resource-based view of the firm (Wernerfelt, 1984, 1995). This perspective is consistent with the traditional strategic management model (Ansoff, 1965; or Learned *et al.*, 1965). More specifically, the CP resource-based perspective suggests that "certain ... resource and asset differences may allow some firms to implement strategies that alter an industry's structure in ways that uniquely benefit these firms. For this reason, firm heterogeneity can represent an important source of competitive advantage for firms" (Barney, 1986: 793).

Sustainable competitive advantage is the outcome of discretionary rational managerial choices, selective resource accumulation and deployment, strategic industry factors and factor-market imperfections. Whether resources are scarce, unique, inimitable, durable, idiosyncratic, nontradeable, intangible or nonsubstitutable makes the difference in terms of sustainable advantage and firms' enduring performance. In developing countries, factor-market imperfections that are related to the nature of the general environment abound, and provide ample space for strategic choices (Gauthier, 1996). *The competitive advantage of a firm may come more often from its sociopolitical stakeholders' relations skills than from other, more traditional resources.*

However, in developing countries, national resource and structural problems also have a bearing on the behavior of firms (Mathews, 2000; Gauthier, 1995). In particular, it has frequently been shown that infrastructural factors may be an impediment to the competitiveness of firms (Gauthier, 1995; Ibghy and Hafsi, 1992). Basic utilities or transportation means may be critical for the development of firms, forcing some of them to commit important resources to be able to maintain an acceptable technical-economic performance (see Ouedraogo, 2003). Infrastructural factors frequently combine with regulatory factors to make the difference between success and failure. Also, institutional instability may lead to added uncertainty. For example, regulation may be hastily improvised to affect fundamentally the structure of industry, dramatically modifying barriers to entry and competition. As a result, firm success in many developing countries could be more related to the ability to affect regulation or to benefit from it, and thus to socially and politically related factors, than to technical-economic and competitive factors (Scott, 2001; Neelankavil *et al.*, 2000; Tsang, 1998; Stiglitz, 1998).

Evolutionary theories, most notably those of the Austrian school (Jacobson, 1992; Kirzner, 1981), suggest that profit is not the result of monopoly power but rather the result of entrepreneurial discovery and innovation. According to these theories, the goal of strategy formulation is not to limit competitive forces, but rather to discover new ways to generate returns. These ideas are particularly relevant to developing countries' situation, because of firm age, size and lack of resources. We can therefore propose that *entrepreneurs in Cameroon, as in many developing countries, still attempt to avoid competition through discovery* (Glueck *et al.*, 1980), which may explain the amazing growth of the informal sector in these countries (Gauthier, 1996; Arellano, 1994; De Soto, 1990).

Alertness to opportunities is the distinctive competence of entrepreneurs, whether in Cameroon or elsewhere. However, one would expect the opportunities to emerge as much from the needs of consumers as from government regulations (Arellano, 1994; Brautigam, 1997). The market is described as rarely in equilibrium (Schumpeter, 1950; Mises, 1949), and this is exacerbated because "an enormous amount of ignorance stands in the way of complete coordination of the actions and decisions of the many market participants" (Jacobson, 1992; Kirzner, 1979). The field in Cameroon could be expected to generate innumerable opportunities for profitable exchanges that go unnoticed, except by a few. *Entrepreneurial profit is thus expected to be related to access to superior information, especially from government sources.*

Also, in many developing countries, "invisible" assets have frequently been mentioned by researchers (Woodworth, 2000; Goldsmith, 1996) as the name of the game, even though the term has to be understood in a wider sense, and in particular includes a large array of intangible sources of competitive advantage, some politically related (e.g. the support of powerful individuals), others ethnically related (access to the resources and support of a powerful group), still others market related (e.g. access to information about government coming decisions). The same could apply to Cameroon.

In recent years, most developing countries have gone through a massive process of institutional change whereby traditional values have been peeled off the make-up of firms and individuals because they have been seen as inimical to economic growth. As new institutions take time to develop, a situation of institutional void may be experienced in some cases, which will affect the normal functioning of these countries. The ability to deal with economic and social interactions and to resolve conflict peacefully has also been severely weakened in the process. This weak institutional structure of many developing countries is an increasingly dominant factor in the determination of firms' performance (Stiglitz, 1998). Economic and institutional theorists have suggested that the key to understanding the lack of economic development is the "governability" of the country (Hafsi and Faucher, 1996), which may be conceived as being the result of a fit between purpose, institutional arrangements and leadership characteristics. Governability alone does not ensure success. Firms also have to be competitive in their markets, competitiveness being again the result of a combination of strategy, structural arrangements and leadership characteristics. Applying this to the context of Cameroon, one would expect governability issues to be dominant competitive factors (Wallis and Dollery, 2001; Klingner, 1996). Thus, *the traditional teachings related to the effects of industry structure will probably not hold.* Rather, *infrastructural, regulatory and sociopolitical conditions will be at least as important as competition in determining firms' performance.*

Leadership

Furthermore, managerial characteristics – in particular, the characteristics of the top management team – have also been shown to be predictors of organizational behavior and performance (Knight *et al.*, 1999; Boeker, 1997; Hambrick and Mason, 1984). The argument is that top management background – in particular, values and experiences – is associated with firms' strategies and performance (Pegels *et al.*, 2000). The relationship between firm performance and leadership characteristics has been widely studied (Hafsi and Fabi, 1996). Such factors as age, experience, education and even social origin, together with psychological characteristics, are related to performance. Hambrick *et al.* (1993) have also shown that demographic and psychological characteristics are themselves related.[2] We would expect these authors' propositions to apply to the situation of Cameroon. In particular, *the age of managers may be positively related to sales growth but negatively related to profit. Their education and experiences may be related to profit and stability. Finally, social and ethnic origins may be related to profit and growth performance.*

A recent study has shown that in Cameroon, age, education, social origin, property status, experience and family background combine into four patterns of managerial profile that are consistently related to strategic behavior (Hafsi *et al.*, 1997). In general, in fluid environments top managers have more profound influences as they affect the values and beliefs and institutionalization of corporate behavior (Selznick, 1957).

To summarize this discussion, the performance of firms in developing countries can be conceived as being determined by environmental, strategic and entrepreneurial characteristics. An environment characterized by institutional instability may reduce the influence of traditional industry structural factors and make entrepreneurial creation more effective. Sociopolitical skills may be seen as a critical resource, probably a kind of meta-resource that makes other resource acquisition and deployment choices more relevant and more effective as a source of competitive advantage. Finally, top managers' characteristics mediate between the peculiar environmental conditions of business and strategic choices. We would expect these three important factors to coalesce in a limited number of configurations. Tentatively, on the basis of these conclusions we can construct the model shown in Figure 10.1 to explain the performance of firms in

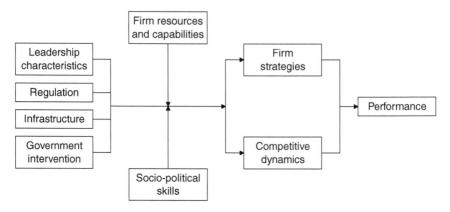

Figure 10.1 A model to explain firm performance in Cameroon.

Cameroon. This figure shows that basic environmental factors (in particular, infrastructure, regulation and government intervention) and leadership characteristics determine competitive dynamics, and firm strategies (in particular, resource acquisition and deployment choices) that lead to good performance. The relationship is moderated by the firm's resources and capabilities, in particular the available sociopolitical skills.

In this research we use this model as a guide to check the relationships between firm performance patterns and the three of environment, strategy and leadership patterns. In the next section the data and methods used are described in more detail.

Data and methods

The sample

The data used in this study were collected within the framework of the Regional Program of Enterprise Development (RPED), an important research project coordinated by the World Bank. Surveys were conducted in seven African countries undergoing adjustment programs. The Cameroon study was realized by the authors in collaboration with researchers and associates at École Supérieure des Sciences Économiques et Commerciales (ESSEC) of Douala. The survey was performed in June and July of 1993 and 1994 among manufacturing enterprises in Cameroon.

A stratified sample of 202 firms in the two main industrial regions of Douala and Yaoundé[3] and in four industrial sectors – wood and furniture, textile and clothing, metal and small machinery, and food and beverages – was studied. These geographical regions and industrial sectors account for the vast majority of manufacturing activities in Cameroon.

As shown in Table 10.1, 34 firms in the sample were classified as micro enterprises (1–4 employees), eighty-one were small (5–29 employees), fifty-four were medium-sized (30–99 employees) and thirty-three were large (100 employees or more). Forty firms in the sample could be categorized as informal, meaning either not legally registered, or registered as a personal enterprise, and satisfying one of the two following criteria: (1) they do not keep annual accounts; or (2) they have an apprenticeship scheme.[4] Most informal firms were micro in size (0–4 full-time employees). It is also important to mention the very large average size of firms in the food and beverage sector, in particular brewing and palm oil transformation. Some 56 percent (11,524 employees) of all full-time workers are to be found in this sector.[5]

Two limits should be mentioned. First, the probability for a firm to be included in the sample is related to its size and visibility. Larger firms may therefore be overrepresented. Second, the structural adjustment program (SAP) in Cameroon may have led to a high level of firm exit and creation, while our sample captures only those firms still active in the market, thus overstating firm dynamism. Table 10.1 presents the distribution of the 202 firms by size and sector and other sample characteristics.

Detailed information was collected on sales, employment, wages, finance and strategy. The survey also provided information on firms' constraints and the effects of government policy. The questionnaire[6] was divided into eleven sections, of which the nine content-related ones are: firm creation, general characteristics of the firm, competition, technology, the labor market, financial markets, infrastructure, regulation and general firm support.

The questionnaire was administered by a group of professors and research associates under the supervision of a principal researcher (one of the coauthors here). Each questionnaire was completed by the researcher in one or more interviews with the top officer (usually the general manager) or the owner-entrepreneur of the firm, both of whom appeared eager to collaborate in the research.[7] In addition to the questionnaire, a mini-case study, based on interviews with key officers, was written on fifty of the participating firms.

Table 10.1 Distribution of firms by size and sector

Sectors	Micro (1–4)	Small (5–29)	Medium (30–99)	Large (100+)	Total
Food and beverages	4	24	16	13	**57**
Wood and furniture	10	17	6	10	**43**
Textiles and clothing	9	18	7	4	**38**
Metal and machinery	11	22	25	6	**64**
Total	**34**	**81**	**54**	**33**	**202**

The variables

To investigate the relationships between performance and the environmental, strategic and leadership factors described in the model, and to search for patterns, we rely on three sets of explanatory variables, as summarized in Table 10.2. These variables are as follows.

Environmental variables

Environmental variables describe, first, the competitive dynamics of the industries or, more realistically, of the country as a whole (*number of competitors, size of main competitors, entry and exit of competitors, the effect of such movements*). They also represent the macro and regulatory environment (*taxation levels, interest rates, the accessibility of credit, the cost of credit, the price of imported raw materials, local demand variation* and *the relative cost of labour*), and finally the infrastructural situation (*electricity service level, telecommunication service level, road facility level, security level, the overall infrastructure situation, firms' expenditures on infrastructure*).

Strategy variables

Strategy variables have been chosen to show the "pattern of ... resource deployment" (Prescott and Venkatraman, 1990). Taking into account the quality of the responses obtained, fourteen out of twenty-five functionally related variables were selected. They include six marketing variables, including *advertising and promotion expenses*, and five other variables describing the distribution and sales channels (*direct sales to foreigners, sales through private agencies to foreigners, direct sales to local private users, sales to local private intermediaries: retailers and wholesalers, sales to local public retailers and wholesalers*). They also include four operation variables (*mode of operation, movement of personnel, size of employment, degree of specialization*) and three variables highlighting financial and technology policies (*borrowing in local currency, foreign borrowing, royalty expenses*). These variables are similar to those used in research published in *Strategic Management Journal* from its beginnings to 1996.

Entrepreneurial characteristics variables

The fifteen variables classified as entrepreneurial characteristics were *sex, age, geographical origin, father's employment, mother's employment, length of education, major at university* (if applicable), *managerial education, experience before start-up, experience as an apprentice, experience in the economic sector, other firms under control, vocational training in business administration, vocational training in a related technical field* and *vocational training in accounting*. These variables are similar to those used in previous research (Daily and Dalton, 1992; Reuber *et al.*, 1992; Hambrick and Mason, 1984).

Table 10.2 Independent variables

Environmental variables		Strategy variables		Entrepreneur variables	
i	Number of competitors	i	Advertising and promotion expenses	i	Sex
ii	Size of main competitors	ii	Direct sales to foreigners	ii	Age
iii	Entry and exit of competitors	iii	Sales through private agencies to foreigners	iii	Geographical origin
iv	Taxation levels	iv	Direct sales to local private users	iv	Father's employment
v	Interest rate	v	Sales to local private intermediaries	v	Mother's employment
vi	Credit accessibility	vi	Sales to local public intermediaries	vi	Length of education
vii	Credit cost	vii	Mode of operation	vii	Major at university
viii	Price of imported raw materials	viii	Movement of personnel	viii	Managerial education
ix	Local demand variation	ix	Size of employment	ix	Experience before start-up
x	Relative cost of labor	x	Degree of specialization	x	Experience as an apprentice
xi	Electricity service level	xi	Borrowing in local currency	xi	Experience in the economic sector
xii	Telecommunication service level	xii	Foreign borrowing	xii	Other firms under control
xiii	Road facility level	xiii	Royalty expenses	xiii	Vocational training in business administration
xiv	Security level			xiv	Vocational training in a related technical field
xv	Overall infrastructure situation			xv	Vocational training in accounting
xvi	Firm's infrastructure expenditures				

These three sets of explanatory variables are then used to explain the following performance variables, as follows.

Performance variables

Performance variables were seen as an indication of the firm's capacity to adapt and survive (Chakravarthy, 1986; Venkatraman and Ramanujan, 1986). As shown in Table 10.3, we included in the model such variables as *growth in revenue, profit to sales ratio* and *debt to assets ratio* in relation to financial performance, *growth of personnel, capacity utilization* and *exports* in relation to operational performance, and *investment to sales ratio* as an indication of the firm's ability to survive in the long run.

The choice and classification of some of these variables may be subject to debate. In particular, distinguishing between strategy and performance variables is a treacherous exercise. For example, *growth of personnel* or *exports* may also be used as strategy variables. They were included as performance variables because, in our research, they were seen by managers as a measure of their success in the Cameroonian environment. *Growth of personnel* is generally seen as an organizational effectiveness variable, because of the firm's close links with the surrounding community. Similarly, *exports* is also seen as an organizational effectiveness variable because exports enhance the firm's ability to reduce its dependence on local politics.[8]

Empirical analyses

To identify the patterns that characterize Cameroonian firms' behavior and the relationship of such behavior to performance, we proceeded in two steps:

1   We looked for patterns of generic strategies, environment conditions and leadership characteristics that make up or explain the actual behavior, using a factor (principal component) analysis.
2   Then the factors obtained were used as independent variables in a regression analysis to explain performance.

Table 10.3 Dependent variables

Type of variables	Actual variables in the model
a Financial	i Growth in revenue ii Profit to sales ratio iii Debt to assets ratio
b Operational	iv Growth of personnel v Capacity utilization vi Exports
c Long-run performance	vii Investment to sales ratio

The use of principal component analyses was selected in view of its usefulness in situations where a large number of variables are to be introduced in a model and when these variables are correlated (Miller and Friesen, 1984), which is the case here. Principal component analysis is based on the idea that there may be factors that explain the behavior of all the variables retained. In other words, the analysis is used to identify a small number of common factors, say q of them, that linearly reconstruct the p original variables:

$$Y_{ij} = X_{i1}B_{1j} + X_{i2}B_{2j} + \ldots + X_{iq}B_{qj} + E_{ij}$$

where Y_{ij} is the value of the ith observation on the jth variable, X_{iq} is the ith observation on the qth common factor, B_{qj} is the set of linear coefficients called the factor loadings, and E_{ij} is similar to a residual but known as the jth variable's unique factor. Because everything except the left-hand side variable is to be estimated, the model has an infinite number of solutions. Various constraints are introduced along with a definition of "reconstruct" (here, minimum residual variance summed across all equations), to make the model determinate.

The principal component analysis, together with the special combinations of variables, provides an indication of the basic forces that underlie all the variables. This may be interpreted as the underlying patterns that make up strategy. This R clustering, as opposed to the Q clustering (see Miller and Friesen, 1984), focuses on variables rather than firms, and is thus intended to identify common factors, generic rather than actual behavior or characteristics. The latter would probably be unique combinations of the generic environments, strategies and leadership characteristics identified. Miller and Friesen have argued that given that strategy is situational, these patterns are not as useful as clusters of firm's actual strategic behavior, but we still believe that in an environment such as Cameroon, where strategic choice is reduced and environmental determinism high (Hrebeniak and Joyce, 1985), generic behavior is interesting and relevant. From such generic behavior one can come up with hypotheses about firms' actual strategic behavior.

Finally, the relationship between performance and all the environment, strategy and entrepreneurial characteristics is reconstructed by regressing the performance data available on the factors identified previously. This is a procedure that is now becoming widely accepted and has been used in many strategic management articles (Kim and Lim, 1988; Venkatraman and Grant, 1986; Miller and Friesen, 1984). The factors themselves are the basic representations of the original variables; it is therefore legitimate to replace these variables with the factors identified.

Such a procedure increases the efficiency and power of the regression procedure by increasing the degrees of freedom. More importantly, since the factors are representative of generic patterns, it is the correct procedure for identifying the relationship between (generic) strategy and performance. Each of the performance variables is regressed on the factors, and the results are then compared and discussed.[9]

166 T. Hafsi and B. Gauthier

Results of data analyses

Using principal component analyses we have obtained a set of factors that are summarized in Table 10.4. Table 10.5 presents a summary of performance variable statistics.

We then tried to explain performance (growth of sales and labor, and profit/sales ratio) using the factors developed earlier as independent variables. To do so, stepwise regressions with each of the group of factors were run on each of the performance variables – *growth of sales revenue, growth of personnel, profit to sales ratio, capacity utilization* – and also on quasi-performance variables such as *investment over sales ratio, debt to assets ratio* and *exports*. Also, four industry dummy variables (public versus private, local versus foreign, size of industry, type of industry) were included to track the sources of performance better. Results are provided in Table 10.6.

We observe first that there is a high level of explained variance of sales growth. Adjusted R2 is generally over 30 percent, and reaches as high as 67 percent for the overall growth of sales, with a large number of factors showing significant contributions at the 0.05 level. Looking in detail, we see that the overall sales growth is explained significantly by such factors as *formal training of managers, age and informal training of managers, overall regulatory conditions, taxation, entrepreneurial strategies in consumer markets* and *strategies of supply to private-sector industrial markets* and to *public-sector consumer*

Table 10.4 Factor identity summary

Code	Meaning
A. Environmental factors	
i Infra 1	Overall infrastructure constraints
ii Infra 2	Telecommunications
iii Comp 1	Increase of competition trend
iv Comp 2	Reduction of competition trend
v Comp 3	Size of competitors
vi Reg 1	Financial environment
vii Reg 2	Overall regulatory conditions
viii Reg 3	Taxation
B. Strategy factors	
i Stra 1	Focus on public-sector intermediate or industrial mkts
ii Stra 2	Focus on private intermediate or industrial markets
iii Stra 3	Production-based focus on consumer markets
iv Stra 4	Export focus
v Stra 5	Focus on public-sector consumption markets
vi Stra 6	Production-based supply to the public sector
C. Leadership factors	
i Ent 1	Formal training
ii Ent 2	Experience (age and informal training)
iii Ent 3	Social (sociogeographic) origin
iv Ent 4	Sex

Table 10.5 Performance variables: summary statistics (means and *t*-ratios by size and sector)

	# Obs	All	Size				Sector			
			Micro	Small	Medium	Large	Wood	Metal	Food	Textiles
GSALES	133	-5.7	-17.4* (-1.851)	-0.2 (1.421)	-14.5 (-1.387)	+9.1* (1.815)	-10.8 (-0.815)	-2.5 (0.711)	-6.8 (-0.173)	-4.3 (0.198)
GSALES912	135	-0.2	-20.5** (-2.253)	+3.3 0.786	+4.2 (0.812)	-0.5 (-0.034)	-1.6 (-0.205)	-0.8 (-0.129)	+8.5 (1.589)	-12.8 (-1.565)
GSALES923	132	-4.5	-13.2 (-1.108)	-2.4 (0.453)	-20.6* (-1.721)	+26.5** (3.243)	-8.1 (-0.492)	-1.9 (0.467)	-8.7 (-0.593)	+1.0 (0.621)
GLABOUR	146	-7.6	-4.9 (0.529)	-7.2 (0.141)	-12.2 (-1.102)	-3.9 (0.594)	+1.2* (1.846)	-5.3 (0.650)	-17.8** (-2.631)	-6.1 (0.272)
GLABOUR912	139	-0.3	+3.6 (0.498)	-7.2 (-1.170)	+7.7 (1.407)	-1.1 (-0.124)	+10.2* (1.690)	+0.3 (0.113)	-4.9 (-0.791)	-8.5 (-1.095)
GLABOUR923	145	-9.6	-4.2 (0.996)	-84.0 (0.380)	17.3* (-1.721)	-6.3 (0.496)	-7.6 (0.390)	-6.0 (0.944)	-17.7* (-1.922)	-5.8 (0.664)
PPS	168	+0.8	+1.8 (0.186)	+5.7* (1.837)	-1.9 (-0.694)	-7.6* (-1.740)	+6.1 (1.176)	+1.1 (0.074)	-4.1 (-1.357)	+2.0 (0.254)
CAPAC	191	+194.6	+307** (3.108)	+191.2 (-0.173)	193.5 (-0.042)	+85.2** (-2.887)	+134** (-1.956)	+219.6 (1.049)	+177.7 (-0.631)	+244.3 (1.497)
INVS	184	+5.2	+14.8** (2.852)	+4.7 (-0.300)	+0.1* (-1.644)	+3.7 (-0.457)	+10.4* (1.826)	+4.5 (-0.334)	+4.4 (-0.295)	+1.3 (-1.198)
DEBTR	193	+30.4	+16.0** (-1.980)	+24.1 (-1.570)	+37.1 (1.170)	+53.2** (2.870)	+26.4 (-0.630)	+27.7 (-0.540)	+31.0 (0.100)	+38.6 (1.190)
EXPORT	199	+9.1	+4.1 (-1.350)	+2.5** (-3.400)	+7.5 (-0.580)	+35.0** (7.450)	+22.7** (4.440)	+7.4 (-0.710)	+3.9* (-1.930)	+4.2 (-1.430)

Notes

T-statistics appear in parenthesis and are calculated using a regression of the performance indicator on a constant and a dummy variable for the sector or size category. * Statistically significant at a 10% confidence level. ** Statistically significant at a 5% confidence level.

Table 10.6 Regression results: entrepreneur, environment and strategy variables (first part)

VARIABLES	GSALES (a)	GSALES923 (b)	GSALES934 (c)	GLABOUR (d)	GLABOUR923 (e)	GLABOUR934 (f)	PPS (g)	CAPACITY (h)	INVEST (i)	DEBTR (j)	EXP (k)
CONSTANT	0.15 (2.72)	-0.05 (-0.15)	0.19 (1.19)	-0.34 (-4.43)	-0.29 (-2.10)	-0.19 (-3.86)	0.02 (0.17)	6.20 (0.05)	-5.69 (-1.94)	-0.61 (-2.66)	-32.40 (-0.05)
ENT1	0.06** (3.64)										
ENT2	-0.10** (-2.83)		-0.11* (-1.89)	-0.05* (-1.85)	-0.10 (-1.24)	-0.07** (-2.27)		93.42** (2.18)	-0.84 (-1.53)	0.12 (1.58)	
ENT3		0.04 (0.77)	0.04 (0.77)	-0.03 (-0.96)				103.64** (2.84)			
ENT4	0.05 (1.60)	-0.02 (-0.35)			-0.10** (-2.81)				-0.71 (-1.36)		-1.13 (-1.05)
COMP1											
COMP2							0.05** (2.54)				
COMP3									1.35** (-2.30)	-0.33** (-2.95)	
INFRA1					0.09* (1.84)						
INFRA2		-0.21** (-2.84)						93.84*** (3.08)			
REG1	0.19** (5.94)			-0.04 (-1.77)		-0.06** (-2.13)	-0.03 (-1.24)			0.11 (1.48)	
REG2				0.08** (2.64)		0.13** (4.25)					
REG3	-0.12** (-3.28)		-0.21** (-3.76)	-0.03 (-1.27)		-0.05* (-1.82)					
STRA1					-0.67** (-2.83)		-0.03 (-1.62)	-179.91* (-1.70)			-81.87** (-2.00)
STRA2	0.28** (4.24)	0.31** (2.43)	0.49** (4.21)	0.09 (1.51)			-0.06** (-2.07)		-4.94* (-1.60)		12.04 (1.10)
STRA3	0.37** (6.99)	0.33** (2.97)	0.42** (5.85)	0.18** (3.68)	0.09 (1.11)	0.11** (2.64)			-3.27 (-1.42)		-0.08 (-0.02)
STRA4								-94.70** (-2.25)	-2.93* (-1.76)		-10.17* (-1.71)
STRA5		0.09 (0.84)		0.04 (0.66)					1.44 (0.97)		22.88** (2.20)
STRA6	-0.09* (-1.86)		-0.05 (-0.71)	-0.04 (-1.13)	-0.15 (-1.86)		-0.11** (-2.39)	48.36 (1.35)	-2.12* (-1.60)	-0.63** (-3.39)	-14.28* (-1.93)
STRA7			0.09* (1.77)	0.08** (2.03)			-0.03* (-1.82)			0.26** (3.06)	
CAMER		0.07 (0.38)	0.18 (1.24)			-0.11* (-1.74)		-150.17 (-1.48)	-0.60 (-0.49)	0.59** (3.07)	17.72 (0.03)
PUBLIC		0.50** (2.88)	0.03 (0.17)					-610.81** (-4.31)		0.85** (4.95)	
FOOD	0.20** (2.15)	0.16 (0.63)	0.18 (1.20)	0.14* (1.75)		0.12 (1.51)	0.04 (0.69)	86.15 (0.87)	0.77 (0.53)	0.37* (1.90)	2.79 (1.13)
TEXTILE		-0.04 (-0.27)	0.15 (1.11)	0.11* (1.70)			0.03 (0.78)	101.35 (1.26)	-1.28 (-1.02)	0.36 (1.59)	2.31 (0.99)
WOOD	-0.15** (-2.22)	-0.34** (-2.58)	-0.21 (-1.50)	0.41** (3.42)		0.23** (2.34)	-0.03 (-0.39)	-7.61 (-0.10)	-2.70* (-1.74)	0.39** (2.30)	-0.14 (-0.02)
MICRO		0.04 (0.13)	0.09 (0.41)			0.26** (3.70)	-0.03 (-0.20)	586.71** (3.25)	3.02* (1.81)		
SMALL		0.29 (0.96)	-0.18 (-1.49)	0.33** (3.98)	0.16 (1.05)	0.12* (1.93)	-0.01 (-0.11)	285.23** (2.27)	3.87* (1.78)		
MEDIUM	-0.20** (-2.63)	0.11 (0.36)	-0.42** (-2.67)	0.23** (2.86)	0.58 (3.08)		-0.04 (-0.36)	213.62* (1.90)			-2.22 (-1.33)
Adjusted R2	0.67	0.31	0.47	0.47	0.25	0.31	0.26	0.19	0.41	0.31	0.68
#OBS	47	42	42	49	43	48	78	54	58	48	64

markets, which clearly makes sense in an environment such as Cameroon's. In addition, growth appears to be higher in food products and lower in wood products. Also, medium-sized firms appear to have lower growth, which is confirmed by a look at the descriptive data gathered.[10] As an example, from Table 10.6, and using only the factors that are significant, the growth of sales equation can be written as follows:

$$Gsales = 0.15 + 0.06*Ent1 - 0.10*Ent2 + 0.19*Reg2 - 0.12*Reg3$$
$$+ 0.28*Stra2 + 0.37*Stra3 - 0.09*Stra6 + 0.20*Food$$
$$- 0.15*Wood - 0.20*Medium$$

The overall growth of labour is affected by a set of factors similar to that of the overall growth of sales.

In comparison, *profit/sales ratio* is quite poorly explained. It is possible that profit is not a realistic variable to measure in such settings, given the frequent tendency to evade taxation.

The so-called *quasi-performance variables level of explanation* is rather weak.

All these findings lead to the following general proposition, which confirms our expectations at the outset and general findings in the strategic management literature (Schendel and Hofer, 1978; Andrews, 1987).

Proposition: Leadership characteristics, environmental conditions and strategic choices explain the performance of Cameroonian firms.

Discussion and implications for research and practice

This research shows a clear relationship between the proposed dimensions of leadership, environment and strategy, and firm performance. This relationship is probably not limited to the Cameroonian setting; similar findings have been reported in other countries. In particular, research has abundantly shown the importance of environment on performance (see Hafsi and Farashahi, 2005; or Kiggundu *et al.*, 1983 for syntheses). As an example, Tsang's research (1998) on nineteen Singaporean firms in China concludes that "[m]any of the problems arise because a foreign investor has not fully prepared to deal with local characteristics." Similarly, Neelankavil *et al.*'s (2000) survey of Chinese, Indian, Filipino and US middle-level managers "support[s] the notion that culture has a significant impact on managerial practices." Also, on the topic of leadership influences, Msimangira (1994) studied the role of senior and middle-level managers in public manufacturing firms in Tanzania, arguing that "[m]iddle managers do not have as much influence to effect changes as do senior managers." Fall and O'Sullivan (1982), in a study of program success in Senegal, conclude further that successful implementation requires that local administrators be involved. Finally, Goldsmith (1996) argued the importance of strategy in performing firms of developing countries, while Sim and Teoh (1997), studying the relationships between strategy, environment and control in three different settings, find that "there are significant relationships between strategy types (using the Miles and Snow typology) and environmental characteristics and control system attributes." All this makes us comfortable with the findings.

As the results suggest important institutional undercurrents, it may be useful to check the institutional framework effects (Scott, 2001). For example, it is increasingly argued that theory developed in Western settings is applicable to developing country situations (Hafsi and Farashahi, 2005). Even though powerful institutions come to bear on such a trend, it would be useful, though not easy, to design research that allowed meaningful comparisons. One step would be to use the same conceptual framework. Second, it is necessary to reduce confounding factors to a minimum. Therefore, one could sample firms in the same industry and countries with similar characteristics of size and economic development.

In general, research in developing countries suffers from many difficulties. It is hard enough to collect data in settings that do not have the political stability of the Western world. In addition, the quality of data is often questionable, first because of the inevitable gap that exists between the language used by researchers and local mores and vernacular. This is compounded when the researcher does not speak the local language. Second, business behavior is not always seen as legitimate. Firms are pressured by governments to be socially responsible and politically pliable in return for economic rent favors. This leads to dissimulation and a generalized lack of transparency. Third, institutional instability makes for unstable business behavior. What is collected and observed by researchers is often opportunistic, at best valid here and now, and may have no link with any sought-after stable pattern of behavior. Creative procedures have yet to be invented to provide meaningful research findings in developing countries.

Nevertheless, practitioners could take note that leadership, environmental and strategy characteristics are real determinants of performance. The fit among these factors is a must for better performance. In particular, older, better-trained and more experienced, urban and well-to-do managers have better chances of success. This shows also that developing countries are not lands of opportunities where every Horatio Alger can succeed. Strategic choices that appear to succeed are generally related to good relationship with government, which may accentuate the previous discriminatory factors if government officials belong to the same socioeconomic group as firm managers. Young managers of lower socioeconomic origins may take comfort in the idea that entrepreneurial activities are still important in transition economies, but may be warned that government is a key factor. Entrepreneurs learn soon enough that entrepreneurial activities should also cover government action, thus should generate the relationships that are needed to gain access to critical resources in a less than perfect market. Close attention to the Cameroonian case shows also that there is a lot of efficiency to be gained, especially in capacity utilization. A competitive structure appears to be effective in improving profitability, but reduces the slack available for further development. Finally, small and medium-sized firms, though less profitable, seem to be doing better in terms of growth (including capacity to invest and to borrow) and general efficiency (in particular, capacity utilization) than large firms, so it may be that, in transition economies, small is beautiful.

Notes

1 The period 1992–1995 is a period of significant change in Cameroon, as important structural adjustment programs were being implemented.
2 For example, commitment to the status quo, a psychological orientation, has been shown to be associated with (1) tenure in the industry, (2) present performance, and (3) the belief that successor will have the same characteristics.
3 Of the 202 firms in the sample, 142 were located in Douala, the economic center of the country, fifty-seven in the capital, Yaoundé, and three in the provincial cities of Edea (2) and Limbe (1).
4 For informal and micro firms, in the absence of an official census of enterprises in Cameroon, private sources were used, and were complemented through field identification, with the help of local associations and cooperatives. Forty such firms were included. The quality of the sample of informal and micro firms is hard to assess, and should be considered indicative if not necessarily representative of the population of these firms.
5 For the formal firm sample, all the 1,500 business enterprises of the "Répertoire d'entreprises camerounaises"of ESSEC were examined in search of firms belonging to the four sectors and to the main cities, selected for study. Only 162 were identified. Therefore, the sample of formal firms may be considered to be, if not the total population, highly representative.
6 The questionnaire is too long to be included in this chapter but it is available upon request from the authors.
7 Training sessions were conducted with each team of interviewers prior to the six-week survey in order to reconcile potentially different interpretations of the questions and to reduce interviewer bias.
8 How to define the strategy variables is debatable. One could argue that all strategy variables are performance variables as well, because strategy is intended to become behavior, and thus performance. What is strategy or performance is simply a matter of focus of attention for managers. For example, market share or relative market share, as well as product quality and the various marketing expenditures (important cost factors), are in most research used almost indifferently as strategy or as performance variables. Managers on the other hand use any of these as a performance variable to emphasize the point of application of the corporate energies. The same ambiguity applies to the variables used here. We have used them as performance variables simply because managers in Cameroon appeared, at the time of the field research, to measure their performance relative to that of competitors on the basis of these variables.
9 All these estimations were run using the Stata 4 software.
10 Growth of sales in the two periods considered in the data, 1992–1993 and 1993–1994, show similar results, but the significant factors are sometimes slightly different. The differences may be explained by the dramatic 50 percent devaluation of the currency that took place in 1993, which probably changed the dynamics between the two years under study.

References

Allen, P. M. (1988) "Evolution, innovation and economics," in G. Dosi, C. Freeman, R. Nelson, G. Silverberg and L. Soete (eds.) *Technical Change and Economic Theory*, London: Pinter.

Andrews, K. R. (1987) *The Concept of Corporate Strategy*, 3rd edn., Homewood, IL: Irwin.

Ansoff, I. (1965) *Corporate Strategy*, New York: McGraw-Hill.

Arellano, R. (1994) "Informal-underground retailers in less-developed countries: An explora-tory research from a marketing point of view," *Journal of Macromarketing*, 14 (2) 21–36.

Barney, J. B. (1986) "Types of competition and the theory of strategy: Toward an integ-rative framework," *Academy of Management Review*, 11 (4): 791–800.

—— (1990) "Strategic groups: Untested assertions and research proposals," *Managerial and Decision Economics*, 11 (3): 187–199.

Boeker, W. (1997) "Strategic change: The influence of managerial characteristics and organizational growth," *Academy of Management Journal*, 40 (1): 152–171.

Brautigam, D. (1997) "Substituting for the state: Institutions and industrial development in eastern Nigeria," *World Development*, 25 (7): 1063–1080.

Butler, R. J. and Carney, M. (1986) "Strategy and strategic choice: The case of telecom-munications," *Strategic Management Journal*, 7 (2): 161–178.

Chakravarthy, B. S. (1986) "Measuring strategic performance," *Strategic Management Journal*, 7 (5): 437–458.

Chamberlin, E. H. (1933) *The Theory of Monopolistic Competition*, Cambridge, MA: Harvard University Press.

Chandler, A. D. (1962) *Strategy and Structure*, Cambridge, MA: MIT Press.

Daily, C. M. and Dalton, D. R. (1992) "The relationship between governance structure and corporate performance in entrepreneurial firms," *Journal of Business Venturing*, 7 (5): 375–387.

De Soto, O. (1990) *The Other Path: The Invisible Revolution in the Third World*, New York: Harper & Row.

DiMaggio, P. J. and Powell, W. W. (1983) "The iron cage revisited: Institutional isomor-phism and collective rationality in organizational fields," *American Sociological Review*, 48: 147–160.

Fall, M. and O'Sullivan, E. (1982) "Importing program evaluation by developing nations: A view from Senegal," *International Journal of Public Administration*, 4 (1): 39–64.

Finkelstein, S. and Hambrick, D. C. (1995) "The effects of ownership structure on con-ditions at the top: The case of CEO pay raises," *Strategic Management Journal*, 16 (3): 175–194.

Gauthier, B. (1995) *La dynamique des entreprises manufacturières au Cameroun*, Mon-ographie du Cétai, Ecole des HEC, Montréal.

—— (1996) "Small-scale enterprise development during structural adjustment in Cam-eroon," *Small Enterprise Development*, 7 (2): 42–48.

Geletkanycz, M. A. and Hambrick, D. C. (1997) "The external ties of top executives: Implications for strategic choice and performance," *Administrative Science Quarterly*, 42 (4): 654–681.

Glueck, F. W., Kaufman, S. P. and Walleck, A. S. (1980) "Strategic management for competitive advantage," *Harvard Business Review*, 58 (4): 154–161.

Golden, B. R. and Zajac, E. J. (2001) "When will boards influence strategy? Inclination times power equals strategic change," *Strategic Management Journal*, 22 (12): 1087–1111.

Goldsmith, A. A. (1996) "Strategic thinking in international development: Using manage-ment tools to see the big picture," *World Development*, 24 (9): 1431–1439.

Gomez-Mejia, L. R. and Balkin, D. B. (1987) "Pay compression in business schools: Causes and consequences," *Compensation and Benefits Review*, 19 (5): 43–55.

Hadjimanolis, A. and Dickson, K. (2000) "Innovation strategies of SMEs in Cyprus, a small developing country," *International Small Business Journal*, 18 (4): 62–79.

Hafsi, T. and Fabi, B. (1996) *Le changement stratégique: fondements*, Montreal: Éditions Transcontinental.

Hafsi, T. and Farashahi, M. (2005) "The applicability of management theories to developing countries: A synthesis," *Management International Review*, 45 (4): 483–511.

Hafsi, T. and Faucher, P. (1996) "Investissement direct étranger et développement. Concilier compétitivité et gouvernabilité," *Politique et Management Public*, 14 (4).

Hafsi, T., M'basségué P. and Gauthier, B. (1997) "Caractéristiques des dirigeants et performance. Le cas des entreprises camerounaises," St.-Jean, Terreneuve: Congrès de l'ASAC.

Hambrick, D. C. and Mason, P. (1984) "Upper echelons: The organization as a reflection of its top managers," *Academy of Management Review*, 9: 193–206.

Hambrick, D. C., Geletkanycz, M. A. and Frederickson, J. W. (1993) "Top executive commitment to the status quo: Some tests of its determinants," *Strategic Management Journal*, 14 (6): 401–418.

Hoskisson, R. E., Eden, L., Ming Lau, C. and Wright, M. (2000) "Strategy in emerging economies," *Academy of Management Journal*, 43 (3): 249–267.

Hrebeniak, L. G. and Joyce, W. F. (1985) "Organizational adaptation: Strategic choice and environmental determinism," *Administrative Science Quarterly*, 30: 336–349.

—— (1986) "The strategic importance of managing myopia," *Sloan Management Review*, 28 (1): 5–15.

Ibghy, R. and Hafsi, T. (1992) *Determinants of National Development: Some Propositions*, Montreal: École des hautes études commerciales.

Jacobson, R. (1992) "The Austrian school of strategy," *Academy of Management Review*, 17 (4): 782–807.

Khota, S. and Orne, D. (1989) "Generic manufacturing strategies: A conceptual synthesis," *Strategic Management Journal*, 10 (3): 211–232.

Kiggundu, M. N., Jorgensen, J. J. and Hafsi, T. (1983) "Administrative theory and practice: A synthesis," *Administrative Science Quarterly*, 28: 65–84.

Kim, L. and Lim, Y. (1988) "Environment, generic strategies, and performance in a rapidly developing country: A taxonomic approach," *Academy of Management Journal*, 31 (4): 802–827.

Kirzner, I. M. (1979) *Perception, Opportunity, and Profit*, Chicago: University of Chicago Press.

—— (1981) "The 'Austrian' perspective," in D. Bell and I. Kristol (eds.) *The Crisis Economic Theory*, New York: Basic Books.

Klingner, D. E. (1996) "Public personnel management and democratization: A view from three Central American republics," *Public Administration Review*, 56 (4): 390–399.

Knight, D., Pearce, C. L., Smith, K. G. and Olian, J. D. (1999) "Top management team diversity, group process, and strategic consensus," *Strategic Management Journal*, 20 (5): 445–465.

Learned, E. P., Christensen, C. R., Andrews, K. R. and Guth, W. D. (1965) *Business Policy: Text and Cases*, Homewood, IL: Irwin.

Martinez-Vasquez, J. and McNab, R. M. (2000) "The tax reform experiment in transitional countries," *National Tax Journal*, 53 (2): 273–298.

Mathews, V. E. (2000) "Management in a developing nation: and we thought American managers had it tough," *Multinational Business Review*, 8 (2): 10–16.

Michel, J. G. and Hambrick, D. C. (1992) "Diversification posture and top management team characteristics," *Academy of Management Journal*, 35 (1): 9–38.

Miller, D. (1981) "Toward a new contingency approach: The search for organizational gestalts," *Journal of Management Studies*, 18: 1–26.

—— (1982) "Top executive locus of control and its relationship to strategy-making, structure, and environment," *Academy of Management Journal*, 25 (2): 237–254.

—— (1996) "Configurations revisited," *Strategic Management Journal*, 17 (7): 505–513.

Miller, D. and Friesen, P. (1984) *Organizations: A Quantum View*, Englewood Cliffs, NJ: Prentice Hall.

Mintzberg, H. (1978) *The Structuring of Organizations: A Synthesis of the Research*, Englewood Cliffs, NJ: Prentice Hall.

Mises, L. (1949) *Human Action: A Treatise on Economics*, New Haven, CT: Yale University Press.

Msimangira, K. A. B. (1994) "The role of senior and middle management in developing countries: A case study of public manufacturing firms in Tanzania," *International Journal of Public Sector Management*, 7 (1): 25–37.

Neelankavil, J. P., Mathur, A. and Zhang, Y. (2000) "Determinants of managerial performance: A cross-cultural comparison of the perceptions of middle-level managers in four countries," *Journal of International Business Studies*, 31 (1): 121–140.

Negandhi, A. R. (1971) "American management abroad: A comparative study of management practices of American subsidiaries and local firms in developing countries," *Management International Review*, 11 (4–5): 97–107.

Oliver, C. (1997) "Sustainable competitive advantage: Combining institutional and resource-based views," *Strategic Management Journal*, 18 (9): 697–713.

Ouedraogo, A. (2003) "Alliances stratégiques dans les pays en développement, spécificités, management et conditions de performance," PhD thesis, Université de Montréal: HEC.

Pegels, C. C., Song, Y. I. and Yang, B. (2000) "Management heterogeneity, competitive interaction groups, and firm performance," *Strategic Management Journal*, 21 (9): 911–923.

Peng, M. W. and Heath, P. S. (1996) "The growth of the firm in planned economies in transition: Institutions, organizations, and strategic choice," *Academy of Management Review*, 21 (2): 492–528.

Penrose, E. (1959) *The Theory of the Growth of the Firm*, Oxford: Basil Blackwell.

Porter, M. E. (1980) *Competitive Strategy*, New York: Free Press.

—— (1994) "Competitive strategy revisited: A view from the 1990s," in P. Barker Duffy (ed.) *The Relevance of a Decade*, Boston: Harvard Business School Press.

Prescott, P. S. and Venkatraman, N. (1990) "The market share–profitability relationship: Testing temporal stability across business cycles," *Journal of Management*, 16 (4): 783–806.

Reuber, A., Dyke, L. S. and Fischer, E. M. (1992) "An inter-industry examination of the impact of owner experience on firm performance," *Journal of Small Business Management*, 30 (3): 72–88.

Robinson, J. (1933) *The Economics of Imperfect Competition*, London: Macmillan.

Rumelt, R. P. (1991) "How much does industry matter?" *Strategic Management Journal*, 12: 5–29.

Schendel, D. E. and Hofer, C. (1978) *Strategic Management: A New View of Business Policy and Planning*, Boston: Little, Brown.

Schumpeter, J. (1950) *Capitalism, Socialism and Democracy*, 3rd edn., New York: Harper.

Scott, W. R. (2001) *Institutions and Organizations*, 2nd edn., Thousand Oaks, CA: Sage.

Selznick, P. (1957) *Leadership in Administration*, New York: Harper & Row.

Shaker, Z. A. and Covin, T. J. (1993) "Business strategy, technology policy and firm performance," *Strategic Management Journal*, 14 (6): 451–478.

Shoemaker, P. J. H. and Amit, R. (1994) "Strategic assets and organizational rent," *Strategic Management Journal*, 14 (1): 33–46.

Sim, A. B. and Teoh, H. Y. (1997) "Relationships between business strategy, environment and controls: A three country study," *Journal of Applied Business Research*, 13 (4): 57–73.

Stiglitz, J. (1998) "Towards a new paradigm for development: Strategies, policies and processes," Prebisch Lecture at UNCTAD, 19 October, Geneva.

Tsang, E. W. K. (1998) "Foreign direct investment in China: A consideration of some strategic options," *Journal of General Management*, 24 (1): 15–34.

Uskiden, B. and Pasadeos, Y. (1995) "Organizational analysis in North America and Europe: A comparison of co-citation networks," *Organization Studies*, 16 (3): 503–527.

Venkatraman, N. and Grant, J. H. (1986) "Construct measurement in organizational strategy research: A critique and proposal," *Academy of Management Review*, 11 (1): 71–87.

Venkatraman, N. and Prescott, P. S. (1990) "Environment-strategy coalignment: An empirical test of its performance implications," *Strategic Management Journal*, 11 (1): 1–24.

Venkatraman, N. and Ramanujam, V. (1986) "Measurement of business performance in strategy research: A comparison of approaches," *Academy of Management Review*, 11 (4): 801–814.

Wallis, J. and Dollery, B. (2001) "Government failure, social capital, and the appropriateness of the New Zealand model for public sector reform in developing countries," *World Development*, 29 (2): 245–263.

Wernerfelt, B. (1984) "A resource-based view of the firm," *Strategic Management Journal*, 5 (2): 171–181.

—— (1995) "The resource-based view of the firm: Ten years after," *Strategic Management Journal*, 16: 171–174.

Westphal, J. D. and Zajac, E. J. (1995) "Defections from the inner circle: Social exchange, reciprocity and the diffusion of board independence in U.S. corporations," *Academy of Management Journal*, 42 (1): 161–183.

Woodworth, W. P. (2000) "Third World economic empowerment in the new millennium: Microenterprise, microentrepreneurship, and microfinance," *SAM Advanced Management Journal*, 65 (4): 19–27.

Zajac, E. J. and Shortell, S. M. (1989) "Changing generic strategies: Likelihood, direction, and performance implications," *Strategic Management Journal*, 10: 413–430.

Part IV

Emerging global roles of local firms

11 Multinationals and corporate environmental strategies

Fostering subsidiary initiative

Cătălin Raţiu and Rick Molz

Introduction

Research on international environmental management shows that most multinational corporations (MNCs) employ reactive global environmental strategies. Reactive firms rarely manage to develop valuable environmental capabilities and stand to gain little more than cost reductions and efficiencies, which are not sources of competitive advantage for them. In contrast, the corporate sustainability literature shows that organizations stand to gain a lot more if they adopt a proactive approach to their corporate environmental strategies. These are essentially two different paths firms choose, and they lead to radically different outcomes.

In this chapter we construct an argument that MNCs can use proactive environmental strategies as a source of competitive advantage if they build valuable capabilities, transferable throughout the organization. This argument is founded on the natural-resource-based view of the firm. Drawing from the corporate entrepreneurship literature, we additionally propose that valuable capabilities at the level of the MNC are built through effective fostering of subsidiary initiatives. The chapter contributes by showing that subsidiary initiatives act as a moderating variable improving the environmental and financial performance of the MNC. We illustrate our points through a comparative look at two subsidiaries of Royal Dutch Shell, with radically different experiences.

The international sustainability literature has not typically focused on the role of subsidiaries as potential reinforcers of the MNC's commitment to proactive environmental strategy. But in a global climate where, increasingly, firms invest in their fringe resources for competitive advantage, the subsidiary can play an important part in improving environmental and social performance, both locally and globally.

The general topic of this chapter is the moderating role of subsidiaries regarding corporate environmental strategies. This topic fits within the broader theme of the book in several ways. First, we discuss how MNCs approach an important aspect of their operations, with ramifications beyond the host developing country. Second, we challenge the notion that constraints in the local environment should be associated by MNCs with threats. Third, and consistent with most contributors to this volume, we propose a solution to the uneasy local–global interaction by showing a process from which both local actors and MNC agents have much to gain, simply by recognizing a broader role for subsidiaries in developing countries.

Challenges of global strategic sustainability

The work presented here develops at the intersection of several bodies of literature. First, we draw on research on corporate environmental strategy, with an interest in the international and global aspects. Second, we borrow the notion of subsidiary initiative, which has been developed as part of scholarship on corporate entrepreneurship. Third, we join insights from both streams under the local and global dynamics presented in this volume.

This chapter complements other chapters in this book because in it we focus our attention on a very specific context of the local–global interaction: the MNC's approach to environmental strategies. With that comes a terminology specific to the literature that deals with issues of organizations and the natural environment. We will define those terms, as a basis for subsequent discussion.

Corporate environmental strategy: the domain

The issue of corporate environmental strategy is being widely discussed in the management literature at the moment. In short, corporate environmental strategy refers to the coordinated actions taken by firms to improve their environmental performance. Environmental performance refers to measurable results of an organization's environmental management as they pertain to the control of environmental policy, objectives and targets. This literature differs from the corporate social responsibility stream in that environmental concerns are treated not as ethical issues, outside the core of the organizations, but as strategic opportunities, inside the organization.

When we discuss environmental strategies we refer to the organization's approach to its role within the natural ecosystem, where it extracts, uses and releases (natural) resources. Organizations, whether reactively or proactively, are now under increasing pressure to create comprehensive strategies that improve their use of resources. Similarly, when we discuss sustainability we refer to the set of comprehensive strategies formulated and implemented by organizations to deal with environmental concerns regarding their activities. In summary, this chapter discusses sustainability and the environment from the perspective of the organizational interaction with the natural environment. These terms are not used in their broader meaning typically employed by strategic management scholarship.

Corporate environmental strategy at the level of MNCs is generally concerned with the achievement of competitive advantage by improving environmental performance. Issues of interest include scope (Bansal and Roth, 2000; Buysee and Verbeke, 2003; Levy and Newell, 2000; Rugman and Verbeke, 1998);

globalization effects and sustainability (Christmann and Taylor, 2001; Nieuwen-huys, 2006); sustainability in MNCs, and what determines their environmental policies and differences among location of subsidiaries (Christmann, 2004); the codes of conduct of MNCs (Kolk and van Tulder, 2005); reporting practices in international operations of firms (Kolk, 2008a, b); the regime of organizations' international operations in the context of multilateral agreements (Rugman and Kirton, 1999); and the distinctive role of MNCs in improving the environmental and social fortune of the emerging or developing countries they operate in (Chan, 2005; Kolk and van Tulder, 2006).

In discussion of multinationals' scope, scholars have questioned whether MNCs favor locations with less constrictive environmental regulations (Rugman and Verbeke, 1998), or examined how firms manage environmental strategies through self-regulation by employing a standardized approach across their global operations (Christmann and Taylor, 2001). Some studies are also looking at strategic responses to the emergent issue of carbon or emissions trading (Busch and Hoffman, 2007; Pinske, 2007; Pinske and Kolk, 2007). A promising, though still emerging, path is assessing how firms from emerging economies formulate environmental strategy when operating abroad (King and Shaver, 2001), showing a growing interest in studies focused on emerging multinational corporations (E-MNCs).

Formulating locally relevant strategy

What seems to be a common thread among researchers is an interest in understanding response and adaptation to environmental concerns. Intriguingly, samples collected at the level of local organizations (whether national or subsidiaries) distinguish between reactive and proactive environmental strategies, whereas studies focusing on global organizations seem to report mostly on reactive strategies. This is indeed puzzling, as many authors have already found a strong link between proactive strategies and competitive advantage, whereas such a link is either weak or non-existent for reactive approaches.

With this in mind, the natural question is: Why do MNCs overwhelmingly adopt reactive stances to environmental strategies? In a survey of corporate environmental strategy, Epstein and Roy (2007) found that most MNCs adopt global environmental standards. A combination of items may indicate why this is done, including the level of centralization in MNCs' environmental management, and the convenience of developing environmental programs that can be uniformly deployed in all subsidiaries. These programs are generally developed by parent organizations to conform to internationally accepted protocols, such as the Equator Principles and others. Furthermore, there is the problem of integration of coordination – a noteworthy concern to MNCs operating large, diversified businesses across the globe – which is more easily facilitated through a global approach. Consider that, until very recently, a business case had not been constructed to highlight the economic benefits of environmental practices; therefore, firms structured the environmental problem as a response to pending regulation. Given these challenges, it becomes evident that the natural tendency of MNCs is to consider subsidiaries from developing countries strictly as economic inputs to the corporate production process.

While we concede that a global approach is a reasonable tactic given the inherent tensions described, and that it even offers many desirable features, we assert that it also makes MNCs less responsive to the local environments of their host developing countries, which are usually not strong players in the negotiations of these protocols. It seems almost counterintuitive, then, that MNCs should consider their developing country locations and subsidiaries there as strategic assets supporting their proactive environmental strategies. But every so often, MNCs are faced with problems in developing countries. There are numerous accounts of instances when firms adopted a global standard without any consultation with local stakeholders. This resulted in unwanted disruptions and erosion of goodwill. For instance, Kaszewski and Sheate (2004) report on a situation where stakeholder groups demanded that new real estate developments be sustainable. Similarly, Neilson and Pritchard (2007) report on the case of "green coffee" and how developing countries resented and then contested the development of a common code for the coffee community because it did not address key issues of producer countries.

To summarize our review of the literature, the argument to this point stands as follows: A good deal of evidence has accrued to support claims that firms deploying proactive sustainability strategies build capabilities that set them apart from their competitors, allowing them to operate with less harm to the environment while earning superior returns (Sharma and Vredenburg, 1998; Aragon-Correa and Sharma, 2003). Yet at the international level, firms choose to adopt standardized environmental strategies, as they provide a predictable, if edgeless, routine to mitigate risk (Christmann, 2004). Moreover, when it comes to sustainability, MNCs do not appear to see their subsidiaries as sources of innovation. This approach leads MNCs to gain few if any competitive advantages from their environmental strategies globally. Our purpose is to propose a moderating role for subsidiary initiative, based on well-documented outcomes by scholars of corporate entrepreneurship, to strengthen theory and provide information on opportunities for application.

Carving a role for subsidiary initiative

The goal of our model, as illustrated in Figure 11.1, is to provide a theoretical explanation for how the moderation of subsidiary initiative affects the link between the MNC's formulated environmental strategy and its environmental performance. The model additionally delineates the processes in which this moderation is expected to occur. While the figure may display many variables, these are part of a theory- and literature-driven explanation of the processes expected to drive the development of capabilities that warrant the active and strategic encouragement of subsidiary initiatives. While the model portrays a dynamic occurrence of events, the logical beginning of these events, and the natural starting point when analyzing the figure, is found at the level of *internal triggers* and *external contingencies*.

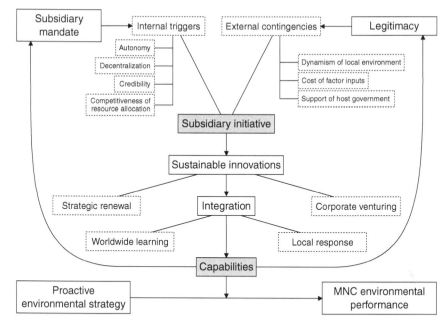

Figure 11.1 The moderating role of subsidiary initiatives.

Why subsidiaries?

The extant literature on subsidiary initiative provides a persuasive case for the positive role remote business units can accomplish within the larger structure of the organization. Subsidiaries are operational units managed by MNCs, located outside their home country and known to leverage MNCs' dispersed assets. Subsidiary initiatives typically encompass new markets or new products (Birkinshaw, 1997). Initiatives are a form of entrepreneurship characterized by proactive, risk-taking behavior, use of resources beyond subsidiary control, and the acquisition and use of power and influence (Lu *et al.*, 2007). The results of successful initiatives can include maintaining or increasing subsidiary mandates (Birkinshaw, 1996), increased visibility within the corporate system (Birkinshaw *et al.*, 1998) and increased responsibility within the MNC (Sargent and Matthews, 2006), the last two of these building on the notion that subsidiaries within a multinational corporate structure compete for resources among themselves.

It seems that the most fruitful approach to dealimg with the conundrum presented in the review of the literature is to shift the paradigm in which MNCs operate and change the perspective from which subsidiaries are viewed concerning corporate environmental strategies. In this section we develop an argument showing that MNCs may not fully capitalize on location advantages in their developing-country subsidiaries. Alternatively, by interpreting local constraints as opportunities for learning and innovation, MNCs could create the bases for a culture of active and ongoing subsidiary initiative. This, in turn, would lead to the development of valuable capabilities, transferable to other parts of the organization.

The unit of analysis is the initiative at the subsidiary level. As a result, our primary level of analysis is the developing country subsidiary. However, we are also interested in the dynamic feedback mechanisms that create measurable outcomes for the MNC – our secondary level of analysis. Note that this research is not concerned with the relationship between headquarters and subsidiaries, though we realize the central role parent companies play in the kinds of decisions discussed here. That level of refinement does not seem necessary, as the headquarters' characteristics are included in several of the variables discussed on the subsidiary side, especially the internal triggers. Thus, a separate discussion of those relationships seems superfluous.

Local constraints build global capabilities

We bring subsidiary initiative into the realm of multinational environmental strategy based on an extension of the notion of location advantages, and argue that initiatives developed at the subsidiary level can be rare and valuable, owing to contextual factors which are geographically bound. Specifically, local context provides constraints in the form of resource scarcities and limitations, which may be seen as location advantages by perceptive managers, because within those constraints firms are more likely to develop competitive coping mechanisms than they are in locations where those constraints do not exist. This notion is similar to that initiated by Bottom of Pyramid (BOP) research, which began with Prahalad's (2006) work looking at the level of innovation that those markets can churn. But the thrust of that research is poverty alleviation through poor market development, which does not change the existing view of the developing country presented earlier in this chapter – as not being part of a significant feedback mechanism that allows it to contribute to the MNC beyond revenues and low labor costs.

We insist on capability development because capabilities are transferable to other units within the MNC, and have significantly more potential for MNC growth. Similarly, coping mechanisms developed at the subsidiary level in the developing country are also transferable to other units, even if those units are not struggling with the same resource scarcities. Transferring innovations builds valuable capabilities within the organization which improve its competitiveness overall.

To illustrate this point, consider an analogy with high-altitude training. As part of their training, many athletes include a section of higher-altitude events. Training at high altitude prepares bodies to handle lower oxygen levels. Athletes do this because it was found that if they can adjust their body so that it can perform at competitive levels at low levels of oxygen, then they should benefit from greater endurance when at sea level. This strategy prevents the early buildup of lactic acid and keeps the heart rate at lower levels than average. In that sense, a higher-altitude training site, through its apparent constraints, provides the ideal training ground for the development of valuable capabilities for the athlete. The use of such a site provides a distinct location advantage.

In much the same way, organizations can use constraints in their local environment to develop capabilities that can provide value to all units of the MNC if transferred. For instance, a subsidiary located in Mexico's arid north (where many maquiladoras still operate) is most likely faced with water shortage and the need to rationalize the use of water. Whether environmental sustainability is part of the MNC's corporate strategy or not, the subsidiary will probably develop ways to optimize the use of water in the facilities, because of either external pressures, such as higher costs and regulation, or internal triggers. Innovations at that level, if fostered within the MNC, can be integrated and brought in at other units of the corporation. The optimization of water use, if integrated throughout the MNC, stands to provide sustainable and financial value for the whole organization through improved practices.

Below, we continue outlining the process, explaining the role of subsidiaries by including discussions of determinants and consequences of subsidiary initiative.

Determinants of subsidiary initiative

Corporate entrepreneurship scholars have systematically catalogued the antecedents leading to successful subsidiary initiatives, and noted that context plays an important role. Specifically, two contextual categories seem to drive this process: corporate context and local environmental context (Verbeke *et al.*, 2007). Many different factors have been studied under each category, of which we retain only a few that display a good theoretical fit with the discussion of corporate environmental strategies. For the corporate context we focus on subsidiary autonomy, decentralization of decision making, credibility of subsidiary management and competitiveness of resource allocation, and label them internal triggers leading to subsidiary initiative. For the local environmental context we focus on local resource scarcity, dynamism of local competitive environment, cost of factor inputs and support from the host government, and label them external contingencies leading to subsidiary initiative.

Variations in these variables lead to variation in the level of initiative-taking that subsidiaries of developing countries engage in. For instance, internal triggers aligned to foster initiatives would assume a high level of subsidiary autonomy in a decentralized MNC structure, where the subsidiary's management benefits from reasonable credibility, and the competition for corporate resources among business units is not high. Similarly, external contingencies would qualify as supporting subsidiary initiative when local natural resources are scarce (this assumes non-strategic resources necessary for the operation of the facility), the local business environment is dynamic, input factors are competitively priced and the host government supports the adoption of environmental strategies.

We acknowledge that the scenario presented above is an idealized picture and that subsidiaries rarely operate in situations where all the conditions are met. At the same time, we hold that the more of these distinct antecedents are favorably aligned, the more likely subsidiaries are to initiate valuable environmental innovations.

Consequences

Scholars have engaged in a complex debate regarding the possible outcomes of subsidiary initiatives. The complexity stems from the multilevel nature of this process, whose effects are themselves felt at various levels of the MNC. As is shown in Figure 11.1, subsidiary initiatives lead to sustainable innovation. Innovations can be either of strategic renewal or of corporate venturing (Verbeke *et al.*, 2007). *Strategic renewal* is an internal outcome and refers to significant changes within the organization's modus operandi. Examples of strategic renewal include product and process innovations. *Corporate venturing* refers to the creation of new business opportunities, which is a disruptive outcome. Examples from the corporate sustainability literature include business model innovations, where firms, having pursued proactive sustainability strategies, discover ways to diversify their portfolio by venturing into green business areas. Hart and Milstein (1999) advocate creative destruction as the primary source of competitive advantage for organizations pursuing green strategies.

Birkinshaw (1997) inquired about the consequences of subsidiary initiative, and found that, conditioned by the development of important innovations, initiatives from the subsidiaries can provide further benefits both locally and globally. Positive outcomes include local responsiveness, worldwide learning and global integration. We show this relationship in Figure 11.1, where integration follows sustainable innovations. Nevertheless, we see the integration of subsidiary initiatives as a central outcome, one that guides both local responses and worldwide learning.

We also hypothesize a set of previously unobserved relationships between innovation outcomes (renewal and venturing) and integration outcomes (learning and responsiveness). We see a link between strategic renewal and worldwide learning, where process and product innovations at the subsidiary level are likely to be adopted by other business units within the MNC. On the other side, corporate venturing is linked with local responsiveness, as new ventures initiated at the subsidiary level are likely to be driven by stimuli from the local environment (such as external contingencies), and thus are more likely to fulfill the needs of local stakeholders, thereby rendering the MNC more locally responsive.

We have so far presented the process that connects subsidiary initiatives with capability development. The final step is to look at the feedback loop, which shows how capabilities influence the determinants of subsidiary initiative, both internal and external, and feed this dynamic process.

The dynamic character of initiative taking

First, we look at internal aspects of this dynamic process, which influence variation in the internal triggers that determine initiatives. At the MNC level, innovations developed by subsidiaries to deal with environmental concerns are expected to improve environmental and financial performance. The ways in which this occurs are well documented in the corporate sustainability literature.

At the subsidiary level the development of distinctive capabilities has been previously shown to have mandate-related consequences (Birkinshaw, 1996). Subsidiaries often operate in an environment of competitive corporate resource allocation, where mandates can be gained or lost, developed or diminished, sustained or phased out. Birkinshaw (1996) has empirically tested the link between subsidiary capability development and subsidiary mandates and shown that if capabilities are proven, add value and are country specific, they are more likely to lead to enhanced subsidiary mandates. Delany (2000) gives a glimpse into the evolution of subsidiaries' role over several iterations of initiative taking, and shows that over time, subsidiaries can move from basic or start-up mandates to advanced mandates, where they become a strategic pivot for the MNC. On the other hand, if subsidiaries do not build distinctive, value-adding, strategically related capabilities, they risk mandate loss (Birkinshaw, 1996).

These findings support the claim that the burden of subsidiary initiative does not rest with the headquarters only – though this may be a counterintuitive solution, as the relationship between many subsidiaries and their headquarters is often governed by an agency relationship. Nevertheless, there seem to be strong incentives for subsidiaries themselves to engage in initiative taking, as doing so seems to pay off.

Second, we turn to the external aspects of this dynamic process, which may influence variation in some of the external contingencies, determining further initiatives. At the MNC level we expect that environmental innovations integrated by the organization will lead to worldwide legitimacy for the MNC, and will further build momentum for more innovation. Specifically, the multinational is better equipped to tackle resource scarcity in other local environments, compete in dynamic markets and gain the goodwill of host governments. At the subsidiary level, environmental innovations are expected to improve legitimacy in the host country, along with the relationship with local actors through higher levels of responsiveness.

Thus, we have presented a model that explains how subsidiary initiative moderates the relationship between the MNC's environmental strategy and performance. This model presented a dynamic process complete with antecedents and outcomes developed around subsidiary initiatives. We now look at two published examples of subsidiaries' experiences. The MNC in question is Royal Dutch Shell and the respective subsidiaries are Shell Canada (Maharaj and Herremans, 2008) and Shell's Sapref oil refinery in South Africa (Van Alstine, 2009).

Two subsidiaries, one initiative

Consider the examples of two subsidiaries of Royal Dutch Shell, one located in a developed country (Canada) and one located in a developing country (South Africa). The two case studies have been published elsewhere in theoretically distinct contexts (Maharaj and Herremans, 2008; Van Alstine, 2009). However, they are both stimulating and fitting illustrations of the points we developed earlier.

Shell Canada

The context of this study is corporate governance, and the authors look at Shell's environmental reporting practices. At the outset, they "ask what motivated Shell Canada, a subsidiary of Royal Dutch Shell, to be one of the first companies in the world to report its environmental initiatives in 1991" (Maharaj and Herremans, 2008: 235). They trace the evolution of Shell Canada's environmental reports and observe a number of important landmarks.

First, Shell Canada started reporting initiatives at a time when few organizations were concerned about these issues. Its parent, Royal Dutch Shell, was not even considering adopting such practices.

Second, having adopted a proactive approach to reporting, Shell Canada executives realized that there were few benchmarks in the industry to go by. As a result, Shell Canada had to develop its own reporting format. During many iterations over several periods, the company learned what mattered in a report, how it was to be measured and how to communicate it.

Third, Shell Canada used reporting as a tool to build important and valuable capabilities. While improving its environmental reporting, the company built important bridges with local stakeholders who were engaged in the process. Shell Canada also built a strong reputation for transparency in reporting and action. Finally, these capabilities presented a valuable proposition to its parent, when the time came to develop environmental reports at the MNC level. In the words of the authors:

> Now that Shell Canada's parent company also publishes an environmental report, both parent and subsidiary learn from each other. Royal Dutch Shell for example, was identified as one of a few companies to disclose data on exploration and production activities not covered by the Environmental Protection Agency's (EPA) Toxic Release Inventory.
>
> (Maharaj and Herremans, 2008: 241)

The case study makes several important points, which can be plotted on our theoretical framework. Shell Canada initiated reporting practices without a mandate from its parent. It was an initiative started at the subsidiary level, motivated by core values and principles. Shell Canada had high autonomy and benefited from a decentralized corporate structure. Because it had been established for a long time, its management had credibility with the corporate parent. At the same time, this initiative did not require corporate resources, therefore there was no competition with other subsidiaries.

External factors had less weight in the development of this initiative, as reporting is not a resource-intensive activity. Nevertheless, the development and measurement of relevant environmental indicators required a significant resource commitment, which at the time may not have been easily available. The article does not report on any governmental support given to firms willing to undertake environmental reporting activities in the 1980s and 1990s, though we are now aware that governments incentivize proactive approaches to environmental management.

Shell South Africa

Van Alstine (2009) reports on a subsidiary of Shell operating in a developing country: the Sapref oil refinery in Durban, South Africa. The context of this study is also corporate environmental strategy. In terms of methodology, Van Alstine too employs a case-study format, looking at evolution over time. These important similarities between the two cases make for pertinent comparisons.

The case explores changes in Sapref's environmental performance over time. The unit of analysis that allows for this exploration is the contestation of industrial pollution at the South African refinery, starting in 1994, which corresponds to the beginning of South Africa's new democracy, and ends in 2006. The beginning year has important political implications for the case as it marks the end of Sapref's reliance on social capital with members of the government to obtain its operating license. It was forced to reach out to a broader set of stakeholders and proactively engage with them. This important shift is indicative of the firm's approach to environmental strategy: its strategy before 1994 was to negotiate environmental flexibility with the government. For this strategy to work, the role of the subsidiary was minimal. After 1994, Sapref started to struggle, as it was not equipped to engage with other stakeholders. The subsidiary had essentially no capabilities to enact proactive environmental strategy. Meanwhile, there was no shortage of activism against the firm's environmental practices, from bodies ranging from post-apartheid groups to international NGOs. Contestations were made regarding Sapref's industrial pollution, and the reputation loss was felt at the MNC level. The main concern was that Shell's solution to environmental problems in the region was through a global governance structure. This was thought highly unresponsive to the local situation. In the author's words:

> Increasingly, legitimacy was contested on moral grounds, seeking normative institutional change. [Another oil refinery in the region] was the first to publicly engage in this new space of legitimate environmental performance through its voluntary environmental improvement program, but interestingly, even though Shell was revising its business principles and repairing public relations damage due to the Brent Spar and Nigerian crises, little public engagement with stakeholders appeared proactively from Sapref.
>
> (Van Alstine, 2009: 114)

Along with escalating dynamics among refineries, regulation also began to evolve. In 2000 the government launched a multipoint plan setting up new environmental standards for businesses operating in the region. It was the convergence of these factors that provoked change at Sapref and forced it to take action, action that within a few years led to significant improvements in its public image.

This case too contains elements that can be mapped on our theoretical framework. First, we see a subsidiary that is not autonomous as regards the formulation of environmental strategy. Strategic decision making is centralized, making the organization very slow to respond. This explains how contestations by stakeholder groups mounted for several years before Sapref took action. It also explains why Sapref was not a first mover in the region to enact proactive environmental strategy. External factors seemed to carry significant weight in pushing the subsidiary to react and change its approach. The local environment became more dynamic concerning pollution prevention, and the host government enacted regulation to support the country's commitment to greenhouse gas reduction.

While Sapref's reputation improved, the case illustrates an example where the lack of subsidiary initiative created a significant delay in corporate response to changes in the environment. There were also negative spillovers at higher levels, with the MNC's reputation suffering in the process as well. What is more important, the organization both at local and global levels failed to build valuable capabilities that would enable it to compete globally. Van Alstine fittingly points out that "[t]he analysis highlights mechanisms of institutional change and how MNC environmental performance can be contested and constructed from the bottom up, thus calling into question the effectiveness of the global environmental governance processes" (2009: 109).

Discussion and conclusion

The illustrations of an MNC's experiences with subsidiaries abroad is compelling evidence of how a seemingly intuitive construct – subsidiary initiative – is not easily applied in practice. The two cases display a satisfactory fit with our model and support a number of interesting inferences about MNCs' environmental strategies in developing countries. Using the cases of the two Shell subsidiaries, we illustrated the theoretical model presented in this chapter. Although we were interested in a similar research context – the environmental strategies of MNCs – our framework is essentially different from those used by the authors of the case studies. Maharaj and Herremans (2008) used a corporate governance approach, focusing on reporting mechanisms. We used reporting as the proxy for subsidiary initiative, and built our interpretive scheme from there, showing how reporting led to the development of capabilities that contributed to both subsidiary and MNC levels. Van Alstine (2009) used an institutional and networks approach to understand the evolution of institutional processes. Building on the case study's rich data on the internal and external environments, we again used our framework to examine an instance that proved the moderating role of subsidiary initiative, albeit in the opposite direction, where internal and external triggers predictably did not foster subsidiary initiative, which in turn created a delayed response by the MNC. We agree with the author of the article that both subsidiary and MNC were at a disadvantage. At the MNC level this disadvantage may have been absorbed by positive operations in other locations. At the subsidiary level it could lead to a loss of mandate.

We started this chapter by proposing a moderating role for developing-country subsidiaries. We built this argument on the basis of existing literature, which contains sufficient evidence for the positive outcomes when MNCs foster corporate entrepreneurship. At the same time, the international corporate sustainability literature provides overwhelming evidence that most MNCs have an ethnocentric approach, formulating global environmental strategies which they expect to work locally. The comparative analysis of the two Shell subsidiaries showed how in one case subsidiary initiative provided significant value to the MNC, whereas in the other the lack of initiative had negative repercussions.

The need to advocate for a positive role for developing country subsidiaries is that much more critical now, as even our comparative analysis suggests that perhaps MNCs may use different standards with developed- and developing-country subsidiaries; developed-country subsidiaries may be granted more autonomy and credibility to develop new initiatives than developing-country subsidiaries. Further research could use the mandate typology developed by Delany (2000) and see whether subsidiaries of developed and developing countries consistently differ in the types of mandates they are granted.

This research also has implications concerning location choices. Firms may consider the constraints of certain locations as strategic opportunities for the development of valuable capabilities. This suggests that firms can use the factors presented here to make location choices which support subsidiary initiative.

References

Aragon-Correa, J. A. and Sharma, S. (2003) "A contingent resource-based view of proactive corporate environment strategy," *Academy of Management Review*, 28 (1): 71–88.

Bansal, P. and Roth, K. (2000) "Why companies go green: A model of ecological responsiveness," *Academy of Management Journal*, 43 (4): 717–736.

Bartlett, C. A. and Ghoshal, S. (1989) *Managing across Borders: The Transnational Solution*, Boston: Harvard Business School Press.

—— (1998) *Managing across Borders: The Transnational Solution*, 2nd edn., Boston: Harvard Business School Press.

Birkinshaw, J. (1996) "How multinational subsidiary mandates are gained and lost," *Journal of International Business Studies*, 27 (3): 467–495.

—— (1997) "Entrepreneurship in multinational corporations: The characteristics of subsidiary initiatives," *Strategic Management Journal*, 18 (3): 207–229.

Birkinshaw, J., Hood, N. and Jonsson, S. (1998) "Building firm-specific advantages in multinational corporations: The role of subsidiary initiative," *Strategic Management Journal*, 19 (3): 221–241.

Busch, T. and Hoffman, V. H. (2007) "Emerging carbon constraints for corporate risk management," *Ecological Economics*, 62 (3–4): 518–528.

Buysee, K. and Verbeke, A. (2003) "Proactive environmental strategies: A stakeholder management perspective," *Strategic Management Journal*, 24 (5): 453–470.

Chan, R. Y. K. (2005) "Does the natural-resource-based view of the firm apply in an emerging economy? A survey of foreign invested enterprises in China," *Journal of Management Studies*, 42 (3): 625–672.

Christmann, P. (2004) "Multinational companies and the natural environment: Determinants of global environmental policy standardization," *Academy of Management Journal*, 47 (5): 747–760.

Christmann, P. and Taylor, G. (2001) "Globalization and the environment: Determinants of firm self-regulation in China," *Journal of International Business Studies*, 32 (3): 439–458.

Delany, E. (2000) "Strategic development of the multinational subsidiary through subsidiary initiative-taking," *Long Range Planning*, 33: 220–244.

Epstein, M. J. and Roy, M.-J. (2007) "Implementing a corporate environmental strategy: Establishing coordination and control within multinational companies," *Business Strategy and the Environment*, 16: 389–403.

Gupta, A. K. and Westney, D. E. (2003) *Smart Globalization: Designing Global Strategies, Creating Global Networks*, San Francisco: Jossey-Bass.

Hart, S. L. and Milstein, M. B. (1999) "Global sustainability and the creative destruction of industries," *Sloan Management Review*, 41 (1): 23–33.

Jones, C. A. and Levy, D. L. (2007) "North American business strategies towards climate change," *European Management Journal*, 25 (6): 428–440.

Kaszewski, A. L. and Sheate, W. R. (2004) "Enhancing sustainability of airport developments," *Sustainable Development*, 12 (4): 183–199.

King, A. and Shaver, M. (2001) "Are aliens green? Assessing foreign establishments' environmental conduct in the U.S.," *Strategic Management Journal*, 22 (11): 244–256.

Kolk, A. (2008a) "A decade of sustainability reporting: Developments and significance," *International Journal of Environmental and Sustainable Development*, 3 (1): 51–64.

—— (2008b) "Sustainability, accountability and corporate governance: Exploring multinationals' reporting practices," *Business Strategy and the Environment*, 17 (1): 1–15.

Kolk, A. and van Tulder, R. (2005) "Setting new global rules? Multinationals and codes of conduct," *Transnational Corporations*, 14 (3): 1–27.

—— (2006) "Poverty alleviation as business strategy? Evaluating commitments of frontrunner multinational corporations," *World Development*, 34 (5): 789–801.

Kostova, T. (1996) "Success of the transnational transfer of organizational practices within multinational companies," unpublished doctoral dissertation, University of Minnesota, Minneapolis.

Levy, D. L. and Newell, P. (2000) "Oceans apart? Business responses to the environment in Europe and North America," *Environment*, 42 (9): 8–20.

Lu, T.-E., Chen, L.-J. and Lee, W.-R. (2007) "Subsidiary initiatives in subsidiary role changing – in the case of the Bartlett and Ghoshal typology," *Journal of American Academy of Business, Cambridge*, 11 (1): 280–284.

Maharaj, R. and Herremans, I. M. (2008) "Shell Canada: Over a decade of sustainable development reporting experience," *Corporate Governance*, 8 (3): 235–247.

Neilson, J. and Pritchard, B. (2007) "Green coffee? The contradictions of global sustainability initiatives from an Indian perspective," *Development Policy Review*, 25 (3): 311–331.

Nieuwenhuys, E. C. (2006) *Neo-liberal Globalism and Social Sustainable Globalisation*, Leiden, Netherlands: Brill.

Pinske, J. (2007) "Corporate intentions to participate in emission trading," *Business Strategy and the Environment*, 16 (1): 12–25.

Pinske, J. and Kolk, A. (2007) "Multinational corporations and emissions trading: Strategic responses to new institutional constraints," *European Management Journal*, 26 (5): 441–452.

Prahalad, C. K. (2006) *The Fortune at the Bottom of the Pyramid*, Upper Saddle River, NJ: Wharton School Publishing.

Rugman, A. M. and Kirton, J. (1999) "Multinational enterprise strategy and the NAFTA Trade and Environment Regime," *Journal of World Business*, 33 (40): 438–454.

Rugman, A. M. and Verbeke, A. (1998) "Corporate strategies and environmental regulations: An organizing framework," *Strategic Management Journal*, 19: 363–375.

Sargent, J. and Matthews, L. (2006) "The drivers of evolution/upgrading in Mexico's maquiladoras: How important is subsidiary initiative?" *Journal of World Business*, 41: 233–246.

Sharma, S. and Vredenburg, H. (1998) "Proactive corporate environmental strategy and the development of competitively valuable organizational capabilities," *Strategic Management Journal*, 19: 729–753.

Van Alstine, J. (2009) "Governance from below: Contesting corporate environmentalism in Durban, South Africa," *Business Strategy and the Environment*, 18: 108–121.

Verbeke, A., Chrisman, J. J. and Yuan, W. (2007) "A note on strategic renewal and corporate venturing in the subsidiaries of multinational enterprises," *Entrepreneurship Theory and Practice*, 31 (4): 585–600.

12 Emerging multinationals from developing countries

Would their exposure to eclectic institutional conditions grant them unique comparative advantages?

Ali Taleb

Introduction

This chapter is rather exploratory in nature and focuses on emerging multinationals from developing markets. The ultimate objective is to foster a growing debate on the characteristics and possible uniqueness of such firms. Accordingly, the reader is presented with some thought provoking ideas on potential sources of their comparative advantages.

In recent years, scholars and practitioners alike have shown mounting interest in the behavior and performance of MNEs from emerging markets (EM-MNEs). These are defined as multinationals that were initially created as local firms to serve their home markets in emerging countries and then became international players. Developing markets along with transitional markets – that is, former socialist countries – constitute what are generally referred to as emerging markets. These are defined as "low-income, rapid growth countries using economic liberalization as their primary engine of growth" (Hoskisson *et al.*, 2000: 249). This trend is essentially driven by the growing conviction that emerging markets are redrawing the picture of international trade (Inkpen and Ramaswamy, 2007) as their home-grown EM-MNEs outperform their competitors from more economically developed economies (DM-MNEs), both at home (Bhattacharya and Michael, 2008) and abroad (Cuervo-Cazurra and Genc, 2008). In fact, a quick look at the recent evolution of the Global Fortune 500 or Financial Times 500 lists of the most powerful global companies suffices to make clear that EM-MNEs are steadily gaining a strong and unprecedented foothold in the global economy. The central inquiry of this chapter is to discuss whether the recent success of an increasing number of EM-MNEs is sustainable over time and whether it is scalable to a larger population of comparable firms.

While some scholars suggest that EM-MNEs may not represent a homogeneous population (Ramamurti, 2009), we contend that they do share comparable experiences, as they developed in institutional environments that exhibit a number of similarities, from poor physical infrastructure and regulatory apparatus (Khanna and Palepu, 2006) to unpredictable "moods" of government officials (Wells, 1983) to highly informal institutions (Jütting *et al.*, 2007). Accordingly, the understanding of EM-MNEs' behavior lies, at least partially, in the characteristics of their institutional environments (Peng *et al.*, 2008), which may clarify why they seem to act differently from DM-MNEs, since they "respond to the threats and opportunities arising from globalization with their own distinctive competitive advantages" (UNCTAD, 2006: xxv). Given the nature of the phenomenon at hand, the explicit separation of institutional effects from other influences may be fruitful (Dunning and Lundan, 2008b), especially because institutional diversity calls for both strategic adaptability and managerial versatility.

In the subsequent sections of this chapter we first discuss the distinctive nature of EM-MNEs in relation to the advantages and disadvantages that are generally associated with their context in developing markets. Subsequently, we propose an analytical framework that contrasts four ideal-types of institutional environments so as to identify the specific features of emerging markets that shape the behavior of locally grown firms. Then we use this typology to discuss the possible implications and opportunities for EM-MNEs as they leverage their contextual learning experience and exposure to multiple institutional logics.

Contextualizing emerging multinationals' behavior

The institutional environments of emerging countries are unique in comparison to those of more developed economies. While the majority of comparative international studies focused on the liability such a situation may represent for EM-MNEs, some recent findings argue the opposite. A key assumption of our argument is that the institutional environments of emerging markets represent sources of both competitive disadvantages and comparative advantages for local firms.

Disadvantages of being from emerging markets

EM-MNEs have long been portrayed as easy targets for DM-MNEs, which, it seemed, could do away with them as they pleased, essentially because of the EM-MNEs' relatively smaller size (Wells, 1983) in addition to their weak competitive assets when it comes to advanced technology, brand recognition (Lall, 1983), sophisticated resources and superior knowledge (Bartlett and Ghoshal, 2000). By contrast, their competitors from developed markets "not only possess well-known brand names, efficient innovation processes and management systems, and sophisticated technologies but also have access to vast reservoirs of finance and talent" (Khanna and Palepu, 2006: 62).

In the past, this situation helped DM-MNEs dominate knowledge-based and brand-intensive industries, while EM-MNEs held an advantage in industries where production efficiency and proximity with local consumers are critical (Ghemawat and Hout, 2008). More recently, a growing number of EM-MNEs have managed to compensate for their limited international experience by partnering with DM-MNEs or by investing in the human capital required to operate in such global environment (Ghemawat and Hout, 2008). Others have overcome their latecomer disadvantage by adopting a "springboard approach" (Luo and Tung, 2007), which consists in buying critical strategic assets from DM-MNEs, allowing them to mitigate the competitive and institutional challenges they face in their home markets.

Besides these ownership disadvantages (Dunning, 2001), which, for that matter, we contend are equally applicable to any late-mover DM-MNE with limited resources, EM-MNEs suffer from the generally gloomy perception of their home countries as suppliers of low-quality products (Bilkey and Nes, 1982). In addition, and perhaps more importantly, developing countries lack well-developed institutional infrastructures, which hinders market efficiency (Khanna and Palepu, 1997, 2006) and thus impedes the sustainable growth and performance of local firms.

Advantages of being from emerging markets

Nonetheless, what appears to be a liability under certain conditions may be an asset under other circumstances, and disadvantages may turn into advantages over time. That is why "emerging giants" (Khanna and Palepu, 2006), "homegrown champions" (Bhattacharya and Michael, 2008; Ghemawat and Hout, 2008) and "global challengers" that grew up in developing markets (Aulakh, 2007) are not your usual suspects (Ghemawat and Hout, 2008; Wells, 1983). Their successes are not limited to protecting their local markets anymore; they also venture and gain market shares in other developing, developed and least-developed economies.

First, many EM-MNEs are found to outperform their rivals at home, thanks essentially to their familiarity with local market dynamics, which allows them to take advantage of local institutional structures (Dawar and Frost, 1999). They often exploit the unique expectations of local customers (Khanna and Palepu, 2006) to create differential competitive advantages in comparison with foreign competitors. Their proximity with their local markets makes up for product-related weaknesses, especially when local customers have special consumption habits (Ghemawat and Hout, 2008). They also know how to deal with weak institutions in developing countries (Aulakh, 2007) and leverage local institutional gaps to their advantage. Consequently, we contend that EM-MNEs have a double advantage in their home countries. On the one hand, they are able to turn some of the weaknesses of their home countries into advantages. On the other hand, DM-MNEs may find it difficult to deal with – let alone to exploit – the unfamiliar institutional conditions of emerging markets.

Second, the capability of dealing with weak institutional environments that EM-MNEs developed while growing in their home country may also be handy in markets with similar institutional conditions. Not only are they familiar with the specific economic, political and institutional conditions, which are relatively comparable across developing countries in general, but also they have production and distribution systems that are tailored to suit these markets (Lall, 1983). Their lower overhead costs, combined with cultural similarities with other developing countries, allow them to coordinate their foreign operations more cost-effectively than DM-MNEs can (Cuervo-Cazurra and Genc, 2008), as they operate in markets with equivalent institutional infrastructures.

Third, the corollary is that EM-MNEs are more inclined to venture in least-developed markets than are DM-MNEs (Cuervo-Cazurra and Genc, 2008). Since developing and least-developed economies have relatively similar institutional structures, EM-MNEs know how to operate effectively under such conditions. Their familiarity with the peculiar institutional conditions of emerging markets allows them not only to come up with well-informed responses to market contingencies but also to identify opportunities to bundle ancillary services and products (Ghemawat and Hout, 2008) so as to mitigate the potential threats from incoming DM-MNEs.

Finally, EM-MNEs are no longer fulfilled by making the most of niche markets that have been abandoned by conventional multinationals (Chudnovsky, 1993; Wells, 1983). They also dare to engage in large (Aulakh, 2007) and aggressive (Luo and Tung, 2007) foreign direct investment operations. In fact, the success of EM-MNEs in developing and least-developed economies brings about opportunities for further success in developed markets as well (Khanna and Palepu, 2006). Indeed, EM-MNEs not only circumvent local institutional weaknesses and tailor their strategies to local markets, but also innovate and deliver high-quality products and services in their home markets. Subsequently, their products are becoming more and more competitive in developed countries as they respond to the growing pressures of increasingly demanding customers in developing markets, especially pressures for superior quality.

In short, EM-MNEs seem to differ from DM-MNEs in at least two ways. Firstl, they develop unique abilities to operate in diverse institutional environments. Second, they implement different strategies than DM-MNEs when they approach both local and foreign markets. For instance, Luo and Tung (2007) found that they are neither path-dependent nor evolutionary in selecting their entry modes and project location. Such distinctiveness presents DM-MNEs with a dual challenge: they must emulate some of EM-MNEs' strategies while developing others that are hard for competitors to replicate (ibid.). However, they need first to revisit their preconceptions about the institutional environment of developing countries (Prahalad and Hammond, 2002) and recognize that they seem to follow a different development path rather than lagging behind developed economies in a predefined "best way" trail (Bhattacharya and Michael, 2008). Indeed, DM-MNEs tend to assume that all countries must adopt the same institutional systems in order to prosper, yet it is not clear whether any set of institutions is superior to others (Khanna and Palepu, 1997). While one may argue that developing countries may not form a homogeneous population, their institutional environments do exhibit relatively similar characteristics, especially in comparison to developed markets (Jütting *et al.*, 2007; Khanna and Palepu, 2006; Wells, 1983).

Consistent with the contingency view of strategic management, strategies are expected to vary in order to fit their environment requirements. Consequently, the identification of the distinctive institutional characteristics of emerging markets may shed some light on the behavior, capabilities and performance of MNEs in general and of EM-MNEs in particular.

Positioning emerging multinationals in the global institutional context

The remarkable development of the institution-based view of business strategy (Peng, 2002) in recent years has been driven essentially by the need for a better understanding of the pluralistic context of MNEs. International comparative studies identify and contrast the characteristics of multiple institutional settings in order to understand the underlying rules of the game that shape economic activity (North, 1990). Since institutions are also meant to ensure the stability and meaning of social life (Scott, 2008), their forces have both economic (Coase, 1998; North, 1990) and sociological (DiMaggio and Powell, 1983; Scott, 2008) dimensions. Therefore, the power of institutions derives not only from the discipline mechanisms of economic markets and political arenas (Dunning and Lundan, 2008a) but also from their social norms, cultural codes and kinship structures (Jütting *et al.*, 2007), which have direct influence over decision makers (Peng, 2002). Institutional systems are composed of both economic and social institutions, and their study may not be complete unless both their formal and their informal dimensions are analyzed. Indeed, differences among organizations "reflect not only an attempt by firms to upgrade their organizational effectiveness, but also mirror wider societal norms" (Dunning and Lundan, 2008a: 12).

Institutional formality

The degree of a country's institutional formality reflects the extent to which its institutions and rules of the game are formalized in writing and made known to all interested parties. Formal institutions include laws, regulations, legally enforced property rights, contracts, conventions, discipline of economic markets, and political mechanisms (Dunning and Lundan, 2008a; Jütting *et al.*, 2007). The degree of formality is posited to be of particular importance to MNEs entering a new country because it determines how tacit or explicit the rules of the game are in the targeted market. In this regard the dilemma of public policy makers is essentially to arbitrate and strike a balance between too much and not enough formalization, so as to allay and retain investors. On the other hand, there are many social norms that represent taken-for-granted rules or informal institutions which shape the decisions, actions and behaviors of decision makers. Informal institutions are either generally accepted social norms such as customs and traditions, or deliberate deviations from existing formal rules (Jütting *et al.*, 2007) which may lead to unethical conduct such as corruption and nepotism. Relevant to this distinction is Scott's (2008) delineation of three types of institutions: regulative, normative and cognitive. We suggest that these pillars of institutional environments reflect, in this specific order, decreasing levels of formality: regulations are more formal than norms, which are in turn more formal than culture. In fact, informal institutions prevail when formal rules are lacking, irrelevant or simply ignored by influential actors who feel their interests are threatened by formalization. Indeed, informal institutions may substitute for, compete with or complement formal institutions (Jütting *et al.*, 2007). Accordingly, formal institutions may not be understood apart from informal ones because the latter carry the real motivations and belief systems that explain the former (Dunning and Lundan, 2008a).

While formal institutional rules are essentially sanctioned through coercive and legal mechanisms, non-compliance with the expectations of informal institutions is sanctioned socially (DiMaggio and Powell, 1983; Scott, 2008), as they heighten or lessen the social capital of involved actors (Dunning and Lundan, 2008a). Therefore, overlooking informal institutions may be as costly as disregarding formal rules (Jütting *et al.*, 2007), but in different ways. That is because institutions may be differently designed yet functionally equivalent (Dunning and Lundan, 2008a). However, the effectiveness of institutions in fulfilling their intended functions will essentially depend on their ability to mature and sustain themselves over time.

Institutional maturity

The very existence of institutions implies their persistence and stability (Scott, 2008). The degree of maturity of both formal and informal institutions depends on the extent to which actors comply with the underlying requirements and expectations. A low degree of compliance with a particular institutional rule makes it unstable, immature and vulnerable to possible substitutions. While institutional stability is the ultimate objective of institutionalization processes, there are two intrinsic side effects of maturity that are relevant to the understanding of the phenomenon at hand. First, institutions may be so entrenched in the habits of actors that any attempt to adjust them will face inertia and resistance from stakeholders. Second, the institutionalization of a new set of rules often requires the deinstitutionalization of another, competing set of conventions that are already in place. Such situations may lead to institutional instability during the transition because institutional change and institutional stability are utterly interdependent (Lindner, 2003).

In summary, institutional formality and institutional maturity are two complementary dimensions of the same phenomenon. The former is concerned with the sources of institutional pressures, whereas the latter deals with their enforcement. For foreign firms that are entering a country, both formality and maturity are critical to their success. Firms should be more comfortable entering and operating in new markets with levels of institutional formality and maturity that are comparable to the ones they are accustomed to in their home countries. Therefore, we combine the two concepts to develop an analytical framework in order to highlight the unique characteristics of emerging markets in general and understand the behavior of EM-MNEs in particular.

Toward a typology of country institutional environments

The characteristics of the institutional context in which decision makers are embedded influence their decisions and actions (Peng, 2002). Accordingly, the examination of the distinctive characteristics of the institutional environment in which EM-MNEs have been growing up may shed some light on their comparative advantages and behavior.

First, *developing and least-developed economies face relatively similar institutional challenges*. Both suffer from poor physical infrastructures and inadequate market mechanisms, as well as lacking sophisticated market research, reliable supply chain partners and appropriate regulatory apparatus (Cuervo-Cazurra and Genc, 2008; Khanna and Palepu, 2006). Essentially, their markets exhibit three key failures: information problems, misguided regulations and inefficient judicial systems (Khanna and Palepu, 1997). Accordingly, informal institutions prevail in both environments because most of their formal institutions are either deficient or ignored. However, while informal institutions continue to prevail in least-developed economies, developing markets drift progressively toward more formality as they upgrade their market infrastructure. One of their challenges is to deal with the struggle between outgoing informal logics and incoming formal rules, because informal norms and values of a society condition the institutional evolution that will occur in it (Dunning and Lundan, 2008a). While developing and least-developed countries have relatively similar institutional infrastructure (formality), they do face different challenges from an institutionalization process (maturity) standpoint. On the one hand, least-developed countries are captives of their institutional deficiency and the persistence of informal institutions that hinder economic efficiency. On the other hand, developing countries have initiated institutional change programs to break the institutional paradigms that least-developed economies are faced with. Institutional change implies that well-grounded informal institutions should be dismantled while new formal institutions are being developed. Managing such transition is a risky task and may lead to institutional decoupling where two systems – one formal and the other informal – coexist and compete against each other, and thus lead to confusion and ambiguity for market actors. A good example of persistent informal institutions in least-developed countries is the endemic corruption that hinders transparency and undermines efficiency in their markets. Several developing countries (e.g. India, South Africa) appear to truly seek to fight the phenomenon by reinforcing their regulatory institutions and initiating communication campaigns. However, breaking such a strong paradigm is not easy to undertake because corruption, once established in a particular socio-economic setting, becomes sheltered not only by economic imperatives but also by social norms.

Second, among the four ideal-types of institutional environments, *developed countries maintain the most formal and mature market institutions*. This is not to say that informal institutions do not exist in the most advanced economies. Quite the contrary: one of the reasons why these countries' formal institutions persist over time is that they coexist with strong informal institutions that complement and support them. As the levels of maturity of both social and economic institutions increase, formal and informal logics become so entangled that they lead to institutionalized bureaucracy as the two types of institutions prevent each other from evolving. A good illustration of such a dilemma is found in some developed countries (e.g., France, Germany) that have strong labor regulations, powerful organizations of employers and historically influential unions of employees. Institutional reforms in such settings are often tricky to resolve because change of both formal and informal institutions is a prerequisite (Dunning and Lundan, 2008a; Meyer and Estrin, 2001; Meyer and Peng, 2005) to unlocking their institutional systems. As pointed out by Hurst (2003), the regulatory systems of least-developed countries are highly influenced by their colonial heritage, and these countries are found to regulate business the most. Therefore, both least-developed and developed economies may potentially suffer from over-regulation, although for different reasons. Heavy regulations in some developed countries may lead to bad outcomes because of the burden they represent for businesses when they are enforced. Conversely, over-regulation in least-developed economies often leads to corruption and nepotism, which are just as bad, if not worse, for local businesses.

Finally, while developing countries take an incremental approach to the upgrading of their institutions and thus drift slowly from informal to formal dominant logics, *transitional economies are faced with a singular dilemma.* Since they are shifting from highly formal socialist institutions to a new set of formal but market-driven institutions, their main institutional challenge is to build a whole new institutional system while dismantling the existing one which they spent decades engineering and promoting to their populations. Indeed, the process of institutional evolution is path dependent (Dunning and Lundan, 2008a), and the social norms inherited from incumbent systems may constitute a serious impediment to a successful transition to another system that mobilizes different economic and social rationalities. In Russia, for instance, part of the institutional heritage of transitional markets is the state's own elites, who redirect the power and resources available to them to safeguard – instead of changing – existing institutions because they draw an advantage from preserving them (de Soysa and Jütting, 2007). As a result, transitional countries run the risk of ending up with two decoupled and competing systems where informal institutions will play a major arbitration role.

The above discussion allowed us to briefly expose the dynamics and challenges that are specific to each of the four ideal-types of country institutional environments. Depending on its ideal-type, a market may suffer from institutional inefficiency as a result of institutional persistence in the face of need for change, and/or institutional decoupling in the face of ambiguity of operating rules. The ability to internalize and mobilize multiple institutional logics necessary to operate efficiently in a variety of institutional contexts would be an instrumental competitive advantage which an MNE that is expanding globally must nurture. We contend that EM-MNEs have a unique positioning within the

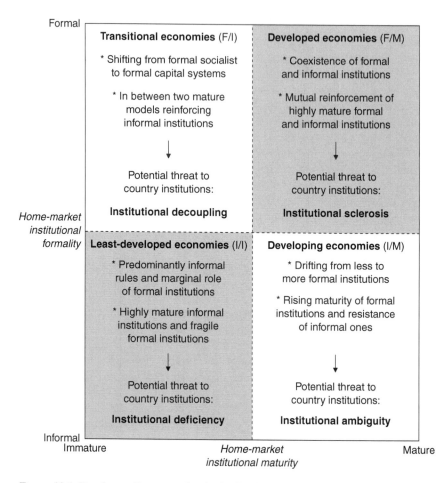

Figure 12.1 Typology of home-market institutional environments.

above-described institutional eco-system. To support this claim we now discuss how the unique institutional experience of EM-MNEs may grant them a competitive edge over their competitors, especially those coming from more developed markets.

Likely sources of comparative advantages for emerging multinationals

EM-MNEs operate in a globally integrated environment and thus face the potential consequences of their liability of foreignness as they venture in unfamiliar markets (Zaheer, 1995). While foreignness is often associated with liability, and even more so for EM-MNEs, it may also be a source of competitive advantages (Bilkey and

Nes, 1982; Eden and Miller, 2004). For instance, it has been argued that some EM-MNEs become successful players on the international stage by turning market imperfections in their home countries into global competitive advantages (Cuervo-Cazurra and Genc, 2008). In the same vein, and in line with the learning perspective of international expansion (Johanson and Vahlne, 1977), EM-MNEs may take advantage of their exposure to different operating logics to develop the necessary comparative advantages to dealing with global institutional diversity. This institutional exposure is associated with three complementary learning mechanisms: institutional incubation, institutional heritage and institutional observation. They all constitute potential sources of competitive advantages.

Institutional incubation as a potential source of comparative advantages

Country institutions act as incubators for local firms and shape their market and organizational behaviors though complex mechanisms. EM-MNEs are embedded in the economic and social contexts of emerging markets, and their managers develop the skills necessary to deal with local institutional conventions (Cuervo-Cazurra and Genc, 2008; Khanna and Palepu, 2006). Such contextualized learning experience confers on them the ability to operate in any market with institutional characteristics similar to those of their home countries. Institutional conditions are functionally equivalent (Dunning and Lundan, 2008a) across emerging economies, which is the reason why EM-MNEs manage to keep DM-MNEs at bay in their home markets (Bhattacharya and Michael, 2008), and even outperform them in other emerging markets (Ghemawat and Hout, 2008).

Institutional heritage as a potential source of comparative advantages

The institutions of emerging markets are relatively more formalized than those that prevail in least-developed markets, essentially because of the need for adapted structures to respond to exceptional economic growth. However, the capabilities that EM-MNEs develop to operate in emerging economies are transferable to least-developed markets (Cuervo-Cazurra and Genc, 2008) because their institutional contexts are still comparable. Indeed, institutions are path dependent (Dunning and Lundan, 2008a), and those of emerging markets are constrained by their institutional heritage, just as firms are inhibited by their administrative heritage (Zaheer, 1995). The bias of policy makers and business managers alike is shaped by this heritage (Bartlett and Ghoshal, 1987) and thus makes them embrace institutional reconfiguration and upgrading with great caution (Dunning and Lundan, 2008a). Given the recent history of emerging economies as least-developed countries, they share the same administrative heritage and institutional "genes" (Kostova, 1999), and it requires tremendous efforts to dilute these over time. This is the main reason why EM-MNEs understand the unwritten rules of the informal institutions in force in least-developed markets better than DM-MNEs do.

Institutional exposure as a potential source of comparative advantages

While developed markets are relatively saturated or growing at a slower rate than those of emerging countries, developing markets are fast-growing and represent an untapped market potential for both local and foreign firms (Bhattacharya and Michael, 2008). However, resistance from home-grown companies is increasing rapidly as DM-MNEs become aware of the growth prospects. Indeed, EM-MNEs succeed in outperforming DM-MNEs in these markets not only because of their ability to develop hard-to-copy competitive advantages but also because DM-MNEs make wrong assumptions about the institutional environment of emerging countries (Ghemawat and Hout, 2008; Prahalad and Hammond, 2002). Moreover, the unprecedented increase in foreign investments inflows to emerging markets contributes to the learning experience of local firms (Luo and Tung, 2007) as they scrutinize the behavior of DM-MNEs operating locally. From their successes and failures they learn about their strengths and weaknesses, and subsequently design strategies to mitigate the former and exploit the latter. Levering the benefits of their unique experience, EM-MNEs design distinctive policies and experiment with innovative management mechanisms (Ghemawat and Hout, 2008) that are hard for DM-MNEs to copy, rather than confronting them head-on with similar strategies. Consequently, EM-MNEs manage to develop sustainable competitive advantages that are more adapted to developing and least-developed markets, thanks to their exposure to the ways DM-MNEs operate in these markets.

In short, it is suggested that EM-MNEs have a unique opportunity to develop the institutional flexibility they need to deal with institutional diversity as they expand internationally. Developing markets may help them learn and develop an eclectic repertoire of "multistrategic postures" (Zaheer, 1995) and operating logics that can be enacted selectively, depending on contexts, in order to overcome the "unidimensional bias" of their heritage (ibid.).

Conclusions

In this chapter we propose an analytical framework that clusters institutional environments into four ideal-types – developed, developing, transitional and least-developed – in relation to the country level of economic development. While ideal-types may be decried for oversimplifying reality, they are particularly handy tools for the comparative study of concrete cases (Blau, 1963). In this instance, they are useful instruments that simplify the complexity and heterogeneity of country institutional environments. The conceptualization of institutional contexts is important because their conditions act as contingencies upon local decision makers and thus determine the identity and behavior of organizations. Consequently, an understanding of the relative positioning of EM-MNEs helps shed some light on their competitiveness as local as well as global players.

Global institutional diversity calls for managerial versatility, and the ability to operate in diverse and multiple contexts is instrumental to organizational performance. This requires MNEs to develop dynamic capabilities (Helfat, 2007) and hybrid structures (Hoskisson *et al.*, 2000) in order to effectively bridge business units operating in eclectic institutional contexts. By discussing the comparative characteristics of the four categories, we argue that developing markets represent a fertile context for EM-MNEs to learn and develop a rich repertoire of strategies they could mobilize in order to operate in multiple and diverse institutional environments. Indeed, developing markets represent an open laboratory where EM-MNEs are exposed not only to local institutional conditions but also to the behavior of DM-MNEs as they struggle with the peculiar contingencies of developing countries. The resulting institutional versatility is contended to be the main reason why some EM-MNEs outperform DM-MNEs not only at home but also in foreign markets, particularly in developed and least-developed countries. This is even more plausible as EM-MNEs start to have access to superior resources and benefit from the first-mover advantage in least-developed markets. In addition to their location and ownership advantages (Dunning, 2001), we also argue that EM-MNEs benefit from the misconceptions of DM-MNEs about emerging markets as being behind – rather than being different from – developed economies (Bhattacharya and Michael, 2008).

However, the opportunity to develop such strategic and operational versatility does not necessarily mean that EM-MNEs will take advantage of it or that competing DM-MNEs will not try to mitigate the effects of such threats. For instance, DM-MNEs may try to compensate by hiring away key personnel from EM-MNEs (Ghemawat and Hout, 2008), or give ample autonomy to their subsidiaries, especially those operating in dissimilar institutional environments. Likewise, the time dimension and the internationalization path of EM-MNEs must be taken into account in relation to their ability to sustain their unique identity and competitive advantages. As their level of multinationality increases, EM-MNEs develop cross-border teams, standardize their capabilities and ultimately become assimilated in developing markets. Therefore, the ability of EM-MNEs to sustain the comparative advantages they have acquired through their experience in developing markets may diminish either because of the evolution of the institutional and economic heritages of their home country or because of their own internationalization experience and global integration.

Reflecting back on our initial inquiry on whether the exposure of EM-MNEs to eclectic institutional conditions would grant them unique comparative advantages, we suggest that they may well lead the next wave of market globalization. This is because they are in a relatively better position than DM-MNEs to rethink their business metrics, especially the traditional focus on high gross margins (Prahalad and Hammond, 2002), and adopt strategies that are particularly fit for emerging countries. Given the tremendous growth potential that is credited to emerging and least-developed markets (ibid.), EM-MNEs are well equipped to challenge DM-MNEs in a decisive way. For this to happen, however, they must develop and sustain a dual identity that combines the competitive skills they learned at home, on the one hand, and the unique institutional sensitivity they developed while growing up in developing markets, on the other hand.

References

Aulakh, P. S. (2007) "Emerging multinationals from developing economies: Motivations, paths and performance" (editorial), *Journal of International Management*, 13: 235–240.

Bartlett, C. A. and Ghoshal, S. (1987) "Managing across borders: New strategic requirements (Part 1)," *Sloan Management Review*, 28 (4): 7–17.

—— (2000) "Going global: Lessons from late movers," *Harvard Business Review*, 78 (2): 132–142.

Bhattacharya, A. K. and Michael, D. C. (2008) "How local companies keep multinationals at bay," *Harvard Business Review*, 86 (3): 84–95.

Bilkey, W. J. and Nes, E. (1982) "Country-of-origin effects on product evaluations," *Journal of International Business Studies*, 13 (1): 89–99.

Blau, P. M. (1963) "Critical remarks on Weber's theory of authority," *American Political Science Review*, 57 (2): 305–316.

Chudnovsky, D. (1993) *Transnational Corporations and Industrialization*, London: Routledge.

Coase, R. (1998) "The new institutional economics," *American Economic Review*, 88: 72–74.

Cuervo-Cazurra, A. and Genc, M. (2008) "Transforming disadvantages into advantages: Developing-country MNEs in the least developed countries," *Journal of International Business Studies*, 39 (6): 957–979.

Dawar, N. and Frost, T. (1999) "Competing with giants: Survival strategies for local companies in emerging markets," *Harvard Business Review*, 77 (2): 119–129.

de Soysa, I. and Jütting, J. (2007) "Informal institutions and development: How they matter and what makes them change," in J. Jütting, D. Drechsler, S. Bartsch and I. de Soysa (eds.) *Informal Institutions: How Social Norms Help or Hinder Development*, OECD Development Centre Studies, Paris: Organisation for Economic Co-operation and Development.

DiMaggio, P. J. and Powell, W. W. (1983) "The iron cage revisited: Institutional isomorphism and collective rationality in organizational fields," *American Sociological Review*, 48 (2): 147–160.

Dunning, J. H. (2001) "The eclectic (OLI) paradigm of international production: Past, present and future," *International Journal of the Economics of Business*, 8 (2): 173–190.

Dunning, J. H. and Lundan, S. M. (2008a) "Institutions and the OLI paradigm of the multinational enterprise," *Asia Pacific Journal of Management*, 25 (4): 573–593.

—— (2008b) *Multinational Enterprises and the Global Economy*, Cheltenham, UK: Edward Elgar.

Eden, L. and Miller, S. R. (2004) "Distance matters: Liability of foreignness, institutional distance and ownership strategy," in M. A. Hitt and J. L. C. Cheng (eds.) *Theories of the Multinational Enterprise: Diversity, Complexity and Relevance*, Amsterdam: Elsevier JAI.

Ghemawat, P. and Hout, T. (2008) "Tomorrow's global giants: Not the usual suspects," *Harvard Business Review*, 86 (11): 80–88.

Helfat, C. E. (2007) *Dynamic Capabilities: Understanding Strategic Change in Organizations*, Malden, MA: Blackwell.

Hoskisson, R. E., Eden, L., Lau, C. M. and Wright, M. (2000) "Strategy in emerging economies," *Academy of Management Journal*, 43 (3): 249–267.

Hurst, S. (2003) *Doing Business in 2004: Understanding Regulation*, Washington, DC: World Bank.

Inkpen, A. and Ramaswamy, K. (2007) "End of the multinational: Emerging markets redraw the picture," *Journal of Business Strategy*, 28 (5): 4–12.

Johanson, J. and Vahlne, J.-E. (1977) "The internationalization process of the firm – A model of knowledge development and increasing foreign market commitments," *Journal of International Business Studies*, 8: 23–32.

Jütting, J., Drechsler, D., Bartsch, S. and de Soysa, I. (2007) *Informal Institutions: How Social Norms Help or Hinder Development*, OECD Development Centre Studies, Paris: Organisation for Economic Co-operation and Development.

Khanna, T. and Palepu, K. (1997) "Why focused strategies may be wrong for emerging markets," *Harvard Business Review*, 75 (4): 41–51.

—— (2006) "Emerging giants: Building world-class companies in developing countries," *Harvard Business Review*, 84 (10): 60–69.

Kostova, T. (1999) "Transnational transfer of strategic organizational practices: A contextual perspective," *Academy of Management Review*, 24 (2): 308–324.

Lall, S. (1983) *The New Multinationals: The Spread of Third World Enterprises*, New York: Wiley.

Lindner, J. (2003) "Institutional stability and change: Two sides of the same coin?" *Journal of European Public Policy*, 10 (6): 912–935.

Luo, Y. and Tung, R. L. (2007) "International expansion of emerging market enterprises: A springboard perspective," *Journal of International Business Studies*, 38 (4): 481–498.

Meyer, K. E. and Estrin, S. (2001) "Brownfield entry in emerging markets," *Journal of International Business Studies*, 32 (3), 575–584.

Meyer, K. E. and Peng, M. W. (2005) "Probing theoretically into Central and Eastern Europe: Transactions, resources, and institutions," *Journal of International Business Studies*, 36 (6): 600–621.

North, D. C. (1990) *Institutions, Institutional Change, and Economic Performance*, Cambridge: Cambridge University Press.

Peng, M. W. (2002) "Towards an institution-based view of business strategy," *Asia Pacific Journal of Management*, 19 (2/3), 251–267.

Peng, M. W., Wang, D. Y. L. and Jiang, Y. (2008) "An institution-based view of international business strategy: A focus on emerging economies," *Journal of International Business Studies*, 39 (5): 920–936.

Prahalad, C. K. and Hammond, A. (2002) "Serving the world's poor, profitably," *Harvard Business Review*, 80 (9): 48–57.

Ramamurti, R. (2009) "What have we learned about emerging-market MNEs?" in R. Ramamurti and J. V. Singh (eds.) *Emerging Multinationals in Emerging Markets*, Cambridge: Cambridge University Press.

Scott, W. R. (2008) *Institutions and Organizations: Ideas and Interests*, 3rd edn., Thousand Oaks, CA: Sage.

UNCTAD (2006) *FDI from Developing and Transition Economies: Implications for Development*. New York: United Nations.

Wells, L. T. (1983) *Third World Multinationals: The Rise of Foreign Investment from Developing Countries*, Cambridge, MA: MIT Press.

Zaheer, S. (1995) "Overcoming the liability of foreignness," *Academy of Management Journal*, 38 (2): 341–363.

13 Conclusion

The challenges of developing competitive advantage from local and differential logics

Rick Molz, Cătălin Raţiu and Ali Taleb

Introduction

The chronically misunderstood and uneasy nature of interactions between global agents and local actors is arguably the root cause of many political, social and administrative disharmonies across the globe. Existing theories rarely take into account the stakes of both local and global constituencies, making for difficult advancement of knowledge, along with displeased managers scrambling to equip themselves with operable tools for decision making. Understanding the dynamics between local and global offers not only the chance for more munificent relationships between multinational enterprises and their host countries, but also important business opportunities beyond market growth.

We began our journey in this book with the genuine wish to deepen our understanding of the dynamics between the local and the global. We asked contributing authors to consider this issue from the vantage point of their own area of interest, understanding that their approach would also display sensitivity to multidisciplinary integration. As a result, the work presented in this volume looks at this topic from a broad array of perspectives and contributes to a number of important fields, such as business strategy, international management, organizational behavior, sociology, corporate sustainability and more.

What is the picture that is gradually revealed from this celebration of multidisciplinary research work? Is there a homogeneous storyline that is being told by the authors of these chapters? Are there strong themes that appear throughout? Notwithstanding the significant similarities and overlaps, the book has been successful in achieving high diversity of opinions and voices. This is in keeping with our wish to be open in our exploration of this subject. For instance, while some chapters, through broader brushstrokes, consider emerging theories and models needed to understand current realities, and thereby complement existing knowledge on multinationals operating in emerging markets, other chapters have looked at more specific issues and presented evidence to substantiate theory or simply to expose existing practices.

The diversity of perspectives is also apparent from the different types of chapters presented, based on approaches to theory development and methodologies.

For instance, of the theoretical chapters, most aim to *extend* existing theoretical models that have proved incomplete in shaping our understanding of local–global dynamics. In fact, five of the book's chapters aim to extend theories, be they on political strategy (Ul-Haq and Farashahi, Chapter 5), goal setting (Lirio, Chapter 3), institutional (Soussi, Chapter 1, and Taleb, Chapter 12) or corporate governance (Totskaya, Chapter 6).

Other chapters aim to *reconcile* theories. This is certainly the case for the chapter by Edwards (Chapter 4), who proposes an emergent global institutional logic as a solution to the inadequate explanation provided by both institutional and multinational theories. Meanwhile, in other chapters organizational theories are *contrasted*, with the aim of assessing their resilience and applicability to the phenomena of interest (Marcotte *et al.*, Chapter 2).

To complement theoretical development, some of the authors chose to build on existing theories and attempt to endorse them with evidence from *cases*. This is certainly true of Bosquetti *et al.* (Chapter 8), who validate an existing theoretical model through evidence from electrical utilities in Brazil. A case-based approach is also used in the chapters by Hafsi and Gauthier (Chapter 10) and Naguib (Chapter 9). Finally, two chapters use comparative case evidence to advance theory (Marcotte, Chapter 7, and Raţiu and Molz, Chapter 11).

These different approaches allow for a mixed bag of ideas and insights to be developed and contribute to the topic of interest. As a result, these chapters provide a number of really interesting and important contributions to both support further academic inquiry and enrich the toolbox of practicing managers. The specific theoretical and practical contributions are outlined in the next section.

Developing sustainable strategies building on competitive and comparative advantages

A number of key ingredients emerge in the local–global puzzle, all of which have one theme in common: the importance of local knowledge as a solution to relaxing local–global tensions. Through possessing such knowledge, firms are able to improve their competitiveness and make location choices that grant them the full benefits of comparative advantages. This theme is paramount in the theoretical program set forth by Marcotte *et al.* (Chapter 2), where the authors identify the interactionist approach as an emerging and superior model of MNEs relating to their host countries. A similar theme is supported by the analytical model proposed by Soussi (Chapter 1).

Furthermore, Bosquetti and colleagues (Chapter 8) reinforce the importance of culture and traditions as key elements of dominant logics, and at the same time show that key success factors include internalized knowledge of these local referents. In fact, their empirical evidence shows that successful adaptation by, and sustainable advantage for, the firm are directly correlated with the level of knowledge of and embeddedness in the local market. This theme is echoed in the theoretical model developed by Taleb (Chapter 12), who stresses the emergence of EM-MNEs as powerful global players. Similarly, Raţiu and Molz (Chapter 11) discuss local knowledge as a source of competitive advantage in firms where autonomy and license to act are encouraged at the subsidiary level.

Further discussions of the importance of local knowledge come from Chapter 3 by Lirio, who explores adaptation of Western models to workforce patterns in the emerging environment in the Philippines. She makes a powerful argument for the necessity of adapting known theories to the significant particularities of emerging markets around the world as a way to integrate competitive and comparative advantage opportunities. This is not unlike the approach taken by Naguib in Chapter 9, who notices that successful multinationals that have operated in Malaysia for many decades have been able to survive difficult economic and political periods chiefly because of their ability to form "smart partnerships" with local players. These partnerships were possible as a result of the firms' desire to learn from the local in their quest to serve these markets. The chapter rightly suggests that firms that did not survive in these markets have been forced out by a lack of interest or ability to learn.

Institutional theorists will take note of the solid grounding provided by the work of Edwards (Chapter 4), who proposes a model of adaptation through deinstitutionalization and the creation of an adapted institutional logic. Her model strongly suggests that MNCs should be able to move beyond the constraints of dominant institutional logics. Another contribution to institutional theory research which highlights the importance of knowledge in the emergent local–global paradigm is that of Marcotte (Chapter 7), who reconciles institutional arguments and entrepreneurial arguments regarding knowledge transfer.

Environmental factors regarding the formulation of strategies are considered in Chapter 10 by Hafsi and Gauthier, who validate leadership, strategy and general environment as antecedents to firm performance, but also show that local factors such as entrepreneurial propensity and government are critical. Ul-Haq and Farashahi build on this notion in Chapter 5, showing that political strategies for the local environment are increasingly important to multinationals, which should be reflected in international business and strategy research. Still looking at the external environment of the firm, Totskaya (Chapter 6) brings to focus characteristics of corporate governance specific to emerging markets on a firm and country level, and proposes that both ownership and state are inputs to how MNEs govern their activities.

To summarize, notice how all the chapters contribute to various organizational theories by stressing the importance of local knowledge as a way to balance the local–global debate. While this issue is not new, some of the perspectives developed here are. Contributions either validate emerging theoretical models or propose extensions and reconciliations of existing theories to update, adjust or adapt these to the current reality of multinationals operating in emerging economies. These amendments are necessary, as the world has changed significantly since many of these theories were conceived, and emerging markets are now more powerful and more significant players in the global economy (as evidenced by Taleb in Chapter 12).

Success in the face of adversity: navigating local and global logics

All the authors who have contributed to this volume are motivated in their intellectual pursuit by the need to equip managers with updated and relevant tools for decision making. In fact, much of this research is, at its roots, based on a desire to reconcile reality as observed by the contributors (many of whom are multicultural individuals born or partly educated in developing or emerging countries) with existing theory (much of which was generated in the bastions of academic thought of developed countries). The result is a compelling and convincing set of accounts that help managers understand the complex reality of working in developing or emerging markets, or the reality of competing with firms that originate in any of these countries.

Implications for practice can be categorized in three subthemes. First, several of the chapters discuss issues of internal and external governance relevant to practical decision making. Second, entrepreneurship emerges as a critical theme. Third, relationships between parent corporations and their subsidiaries are insightfully approached.

On the issue of governance, Bosquetti and colleagues warn that the composition of the board of directors is a key practical issue that can be tackled by firms in their quest to improve the performance of their subsidiaries, whereby a larger number of local directors will ensure that strategy formulation is more appropriate to the local environment. This theme is carried forward by subsequent chapters which suggest that performance improvements depend on the firm's ability to engage with the local environment and representative stakeholders (Hafsi and Gauthier, Chapter 10) or that multinational firms need to increase their awareness of national business practices (Totskaya, Chapter 6). Finally, governance is explored at the national level by Ul-Haq and Farashahi (Chapter 5), who argue that MNEs need to develop political strategies to deal with the legal and political dynamics of host countries.

Meanwhile, on the topic of entrepreneurship, Marcotte in Chapter 7 enthusiastically hails the rise of micro-multinationals, suggesting that there are increasing opportunities for small and medium-sized firms to benefit from a flattening world and technological advances. Moreover, Hafsi and Gauthier in Chapter 10 provide evidence for the claim that local entrepreneurial activities are tied to firm performance. Finally, Taleb in Chapter 12 farsightedly shows that developing countries represent unique opportunities for local firms and argues for the need to develop an eclectic repertoire of strategies for developed countries as well.

Concurrently, the parent–subsidiary relationship is discussed in several of the chapters. This topic is common in the international management literature, but the take of the authors here is novel. For instance, Raţiu and Molz discuss subsidiary initiative and argue for the need to create an environment where developing or emerging country subsidiaries have the autonomy to initiate action. They base this argument on the fact that location choices could be made to take into account the possibility that constraints have a strategic role in encouraging local managers to innovate. Further on this topic, Bosquetti *et al.* show that the relationship between parent and subsidiary directly determines success of the MNE.

The future of local–global dynamics

Contributors to this volume converge on a number of issues regarding the need to continue research in this domain. Most of the theoretical work calls for evidence of the validity of the propositions through empirical research. Some authors, whose work was primarily theoretical, are eager to see it tested (Lirio, Chapter 3; Ul-Haq and Farashahi, Chapter 5). Others outline ways in which theories could be empirically tested to add value, such as looking at other developing countries apart from the ones already explored, or designing comparative studies in various transitional settings (Hafsi and Gauthier, Chapter 10).

Apart from the need to test theory empirically, the authors also discuss limitations of their models and ways in which they could be further refined. For instance, Ul-Haq and Farashahi point to the importance of looking at ethical dilemmas resulting from political strategies; Totskaya would like to incorporate more social context; Edwards would like to explore moderating effects of institutional change processes; Hafsi and Gauthier would like to test institutional framework effects.

Most of the chapters contribute thoughts to important questions asked by students of international management. Significant advances are proposed here, and, as noted earlier, both managers and academics can find gems in this book. Yet there are still lingering questions that have not been exhausted here, and will likely guide future efforts in this field. For instance, scholars will continue to examine the extent to which existing theories apply to emerging markets. This volume has proposed different answers to this question, but, as theories develop and as emerging markets continue to grow, this question will benefit from further examination. Another question that will continue to fascinate researchers is: Are EM-MNEs that different from MNEs? In answering this question the volume makes some strides, but the next few years will probably see increasing interest in the topic.

A philosophical inquiry: can dominant logics change?

As we bring closure to our research work of more than five years, our ever-expanding group is left with just as many intriguing questions about local and global dynamics. Some of the theories we built on to advance knowledge are more than two decades old, and we are deeply indebted to their authors for their longevity. Further, the case studies used to illustrate arguments in this book sweep through a similar span of time. Through these years we have observed significant economic and political changes. More importantly, however, changes continue to occur at a very rapid pace as we write these concluding remarks. As a result, we are eager to leave the reader with some engaging questions that will carry this research forward into the next decade.

Unquestionably, dominant logics play a critical role in understanding the relationships between global agents and local actors. A core underlying assumption of this dialectic relationship is the fact that these dominant logics are highly disparate. Still, what if, given the increasing globalization, regionalization or flattening of the world, logics become less heterogeneous and the fine line between agents and actors becomes indistinguishable? Assuming that local actors provide a certain degree of resistance to global agents, in part because of their lack of awareness of the latter's logic, how will things change if more individuals from emerging countries are educated in Western universities? Will an MBA from North America or Europe provide the emerging-country graduate with grounding in the global logic, which will prevent her from opposing it if she confronts it in her home country? Alternatively, in the long run will there be a convergence of logics?

Globalization adepts might argue that convergence of logics will naturally occur in the long run. Yet is that the case? For instance, we know that MNEs have a natural tendency to standardize operations, products and processes. However, this natural tendency has not translated into realized strategy for most global industries; firms are forced to implement competitive transnational strategies that take into account both a need to achieve scale and scope economies, and the necessity for local adaptation. This example shows how natural tendencies are not immune to environmental pressures; therefore, a convergence of logics becomes a theoretically possible, but practically debatable, topic.

Nonetheless, balanced against the possibility of convergence, is there any indication that the meeting of logics will lead to the disappearance of tension between the local and the global? It seems highly unlikely that even complete awareness of the two logics will take away the core values associated with each. Specifically, a complete eradication of tradition and culture from the local is not a practical assumption, while a radical turnaround of the global economic logic is also inconceivable. These facts lead us to conclude that the stream of research carried out by our group and featured in this volume should continue to provide interesting research avenues in the future.

Index

For Product Safety Concerns and Information please contact our EU
representative GPSR@taylorandfrancis.com Taylor & Francis Verlag GmbH,
Kaufingerstraße 24, 80331 München, Germany

Printed and bound by CPI Group (UK) Ltd, Croydon, CR0 4YY
11/04/2025
01844009-0020